Life LESSONS

INSPIRING
TRUE STORIES OF
FAITH & GROWTH

Other Books by Dr. Trina Boice

Via Dolorosa: Christ's Path to the Cross

Making Our Money Stretch: The Ultimate Guide to Earning & Saving Money

Ancestry: How to Research Your Family History and Climb Your Family Tree

Baby Announcement Ideas and Gender Reveals: 200 Creative Ways to Share your Great News

The Ultimate Mystery Shopping Guide: How to Get Paid to Eat, Shop, & Play

How to Stay Up in a Down Economy

Gift of Love: For Every Kind of Love in Your Life

Primarily for Cub Scouts

Bright Ideas for Young Women Leaders

Dad's Night: Fantastic Family Nights in 5 Minutes or Less

Sabbath Solutions: More than 350 Ways You Can Worship on the Lord's Day

Great Ideas for Primary Activity Days

Easy Enrichment Ideas: Thinking Outside the Green Gelatin Box

Parties with a Purpose: Exciting Ideas for Ward Activities

The Ready Resource for Relief Society and Melchizedek Priesthood (Multiple Volumes)

The Ready Resource for Relief Society (Multiple Volumes)

Valiant Primary Children: Gospel Games & Activities for the Lord's Youngest Disciples

Visit **www.TrinaBoice.com** to learn more.

Praise for *Life Lessons*

"As I began to read *Life Lessons*, I immediately became engrossed by the power internalized in this book! Dr. Trina Boice has incorporated so many interactive and life-changing steps to improve oneself and become a better person. The stories are true and of real people. She weaves scriptures and great quotes into her narrative. You need to read this book."

—Mark T. Saunders, MD, author of *Learning to Trust in the Lord*

"Much of Trina's literary work is focused on creating effective tools for her readers. This book is just one great example. It provides all you need for an impactful family night or church lesson on a great variety of foundational subjects."

—Sharla Goettl, author of *Spiritual Resilience: Leading Our Youth to Go and Do*

"My favorite way to learn is through stories. Trina Boice has them in spades. Gems!"

—Karl Beckstrand, author of *Anna's Prayer*

"This was so fun to read! The stories were engaging and memorable, sometimes even making me laugh out loud, and the commentary was insightful and encouraging. While reading, I was constantly reminded of the thirteenth article of faith, and that's exactly how I'd describe this book: virtuous, lovely, of good report, and praiseworthy. After finishing this, I feel inspired to be a better person, a better wife and mother, and a better disciple of Christ."

—Liz Kazandzhy, author of *The Holy Ghost from A to Z*

"I thoroughly enjoyed this treasure of a book. It is full of engaging, motivating stories that teach valuable lessons. Trina recalls and writes about her life experiences with wit, wisdom, and such perspective. This book will be a great tool to use in preparing a talk, lesson, or an activity since it's also full of quotes, scriptures, and challenges for growth."

—Emily Alexander

"Dr. Trina Boice's Life Lessons of the Heart: Inspiring True Stories of Faith and Growth is a work of art that speaks straight to the soul. It is most thoughtful and enlightening. I recommend this book to everyone!."

—Sarah Hinze , author of *The Announcing Dream*

"Life's Lessons of the Heart is just that. Dr. Boice masterfully illustrates through simple, often personal, stories how we can live enriched, abundant lives. Studying this book and participating honestly in the challenges will improve your life!"

—Gale Sears, author of *Brilliant*

Life LESSONS

INSPIRING TRUE STORIES OF FAITH & GROWTH

DR. TRINA BOICE

CFI
An imprint of Cedar Fort, Inc.
Springville, Utah

Paperback ISBN 13: 978-1-4621-4973-5
eBook ISBN 13: 978-1-4621-4974-2

Published by CFI, an imprint of Cedar Fort, Inc.
2373 W. 700 S., Suite 100, Springville, UT 84663
Distributed by Cedar Fort, Inc., www.cedarfort.com

Library of Congress Cataloging Number: 2025939296

Cover design by Shawnda Craig
Cover design © 2025 Cedar Fort, Inc.
Edited and Typeset by Liz Kazandzhy

Printed in the United States of America

10 9 8 7 6 5 4 3 2 1

Printed on acid-free paper

Dedication

To Cedar Fort Publishing & Media and everyone on the publishing team: Thank you for believing in this book and in the power of these true stories. A special thanks goes to Emily Clark for your guidance, support, and vision, which helped bring this project to life. I am deeply grateful for your dedication to sharing words that uplift, inspire, and encourage others on their journey of faith and growth.

To my wonderful family and friends: Thank you for generously sharing your stories, your wisdom, and your love. Your willingness to open your hearts has helped make this book what it is. Each story shared is a light that will continue to shine, guiding others through this life of lessons and transformation. A special thanks goes to my sweet friend, Marci Tanner, who has read and offered helpful counsel on every single one of my books over the years!

This book is evidence that we touch one another's lives in ways that leave lasting marks in our hearts and souls every day. In the words of Luciano De Crescenzo, "We are each of us angels with only one wing, and we can only fly by embracing one another."[1]

Every lesson learned, every moment shared, and every encouragement spoken has been a blessing to me beyond measure.

Contents

Introduction

I've spent years reflecting on the journey that each of us undertakes throughout our lives. I've realized something significant: Life's most important lessons often come not from grand, sweeping moments but from the small, meaningful experiences that shape us daily. As I've navigated my own challenges, triumphs, failures, and lessons learned along the way, I've been struck by the truth that there is so much wisdom to be gained if we pause long enough to reflect on what is happening around us and within us.

All the stories in this book are true. Some are from my own life experiences, some from my amazing friends and family, and a few from people whose names might be familiar to you. They are a blend of timeless principles and gospel truths that can help you grow and transform into the best person you can be. You'll find principles woven throughout the pages that can ground your faith, relationships, and life's pursuits.

But I want this book to be more than just a collection of inspirational stories; I want it to be a tool that empowers you to take action in your own life. In each chapter, you'll find a challenge that offers tips on how to incorporate a specific principle into your character each day to help you build a life filled with meaning, purpose, and joy.

Whether it's a journaling exercise to help you process your thoughts and feelings, a step-by-step guide to building new skills, or a list of simple actions that can help you cultivate certain behaviors in your daily life, this book is designed to be a hands-on resource that you can use to move forward in your own journey of growth.

One of the most important aspects of this book is that it's meant to be interactive. I want you to engage with these stories and principles in a way that feels personal and relevant to you. In each chapter, I encourage you to pause and reflect on the lessons you're learning. Take the time to write down your thoughts and feelings. Don't just read for the sake of reading; instead, engage with what you're reading. Write about your own experiences and how they relate to the stories and principles shared in this book. By doing so, you'll begin to see patterns emerge, and you'll find that the answers you seek are often already within you, waiting to be uncovered.

As you read, I also encourage you to share what you're learning with others. Whether it's by sharing a story or insight with a friend or family member or even in a Sunday School lesson, revealing what you're learning creates opportunities for connection, growth, and mutual support. The lessons we learn are not just for ourselves; they are meant to be offered to others, to help lift them and encourage them along their own journey.

This book is not about perfection; it's about progress. I want you to know that it's okay to take small steps, to stumble along the way, and to learn as you go. The goal is to become more aware, more intentional, and more connected to what truly matters. Each day is an opportunity to be better, to love more deeply, and to grow in ways that will ultimately lead us to more joy, more peace, and a stronger connection to the divine.

My hope is that the stories within the pages of this book will inspire you and serve as a guide and companion on your journey. May it provide you with the encouragement, wisdom, and tools you need to create a life that is filled with meaning, purpose, and faith. May you be empowered to reflect on the lessons in your own life, to embrace the transformation that is waiting for you, and to share your story with others. May you find peace, joy, and growth in every step you take.

Agency

Story

I served a full-time mission in Spain, where the legendary painter Pablo Picasso is revered as an artistic genius. The story is often told there about a woman who had the incredible opportunity to meet Picasso. She was so captivated by his fame and talent that she immediately asked him to draw her portrait. Picasso, however, wasn't initially interested. He was a busy artist, well-versed in the demands of his time and fame, and simply didn't feel like doing a portrait at that moment. But the woman was persistent. She wouldn't take no for an answer. She offered to pay him whatever he asked. No amount of money was considered too high. Impressed by her determination, Picasso finally agreed.

Without wasting any time, Picasso took up his brush and began to sketch. In less than fifteen minutes, he had completed a portrait of the woman—one that captured her essence perfectly, with the flair and precision that only someone with his immense talent could achieve. The woman was overjoyed by the result. She marveled at how quickly he had worked and how effortlessly he had brought her image to life.

She asked, "How much do I owe you?"

Without hesitation, Picasso replied, "$10,000."

Shocked, the woman was taken aback. "$10,000? But how can you ask for such a large sum when it only took you fifteen minutes to complete the portrait?" The amount seemed far too high for something that had taken so little time.

Picasso, with a calm demeanor, looked at her and responded, "It took me thirty years to be able to draw that in fifteen minutes."

His answer, though simple, carried profound weight. In those thirty years, Picasso had honed his craft, faced failures, learned, experimented, made sacrifices, and dedicated himself to his art. Those thirty years were essential to his ability to produce a masterpiece in such a short period. The time and effort he had invested in developing his skills couldn't be measured by the minutes it took to complete the portrait—it was the culmination of decades of hard work, study, and experience.

Our life is filled with choices. The quality of our lives is determined by those choices. Our divine right is to use our agency to choose how we will spend our life. Our divine obligation is to choose the right.

Quote

"I am not the product of my circumstances. I am a product of my decisions." —Stephen R. Covey (American and Latter-day Saint businessman and author)[2]

Scripture

"Wherefore, men are free according to the flesh; and all things are given them which are expedient unto man. And they are free to choose liberty and eternal life, through the great Mediator of all men, or to choose captivity and death, according to the captivity and power of the devil; for he seeketh that all men might be miserable like unto himself." (2 Nephi 2:27)

Lesson Learned

This story serves as a powerful reminder of the truth that every choice we make today shapes the future we will have tomorrow. Just as Picasso's talent and expertise were built over decades of dedication, the decisions we make today lay the foundation for the life we'll live in the coming years. Whether we realize it or not, the small choices we make today—the way we spend our time, the habits we form, the people we surround ourselves with—have a long-lasting impact on the course of our lives.

It's easy to feel frustrated with where we are in life and think that our current circumstances are beyond our control. But the truth is that every moment is an opportunity to choose differently, to create new habits, and to make decisions that will ultimately shape a better future. You may not see the results of your choices immediately, but over time, your efforts will pay off.

Heavenly Father has given us agency for us to choose in this life. That's what the War in Heaven was all about before we came here! (See Revelation 12:7–9.) Agency is that important to Him. We can't control everything that happens in this life, but there are definitely things we can and should control through our wise decisions. If you're not happy with your life now, it's not too late to start making better decisions. Small, positive changes add up, and the impact they have in five or ten years will be profound. Like Picasso, you may find that what seems like an effortless achievement in the future is really the result of years of hard work, focus, and growth. The key is to start today—because the future starts with the choices you make now.

Using our agency to make good choices is one of the greatest gifts we have. Every day, we're presented with opportunities to choose paths that lead to growth, happiness, and fulfillment, or to make choices that can steer us off course. Our agency allows us to decide how we will respond to challenges, what we will prioritize, and how we will treat others.

Challenge

Imagine how you would like your life to be in five years and start making choices that will get you there. A mental exercise that can help you make better choices is to practice the "10-10-10" rule. Whenever you have a big decision to make, ask yourself:

- How will I feel about this decision in ten minutes?
- How will I feel about it in ten months?
- How will I feel about it in ten years?

This simple strategy helps shift your perspective beyond immediate emotions and consider the long-term consequences of your choices.

It encourages thoughtful decision-making and helps avoid impulsive mistakes. Over time, this habit strengthens your ability to weigh options wisely and choose what aligns best with your values and goals.

What energizes you and fills you with joy? Do more of that!

Atonement

Story

When I was young, I used to think that the Atonement was really meant for people who committed terrible sins so that they could repent and try again. I wasn't planning on robbing any banks or killing anyone, so I didn't fully grasp the depth of what the Savior had done for me personally. It wasn't until I was a young mother that I finally appreciated the part of the Atonement that applied directly to me.

I had just lost a baby and my heart was broken. Both my spirit and body grieved for the loss of my little one. I could hardly function and spent weeks in a dark depression. One afternoon, while I was listening to a church talk to try to calm my tormented soul, I felt the Savior's loving arms embrace me. No, I didn't feel His actual arms, but I *knew* He was right there next to me. I felt an overwhelming sense of love and peace. I knew that everything would be okay and that the Savior knew me, loved me, and was sad with me. The cleansing tears began to flow down my cheeks. It changed everything for me.

I suddenly remembered that part of the Atonement included the pains of the world that Jesus experienced in the Garden of Gethsemane, which were so great that He bled from every pore. He suffered for all our sins, but He also felt the weight of our troubles and sorrow from mortality . . . even those *not* connected with sin. He understood fully what it feels like to be mortal. I realized that Jesus knew exactly how I was feeling, because He had felt it already before me. His Atonement washes over sins *and* the tears of mortal living. For the first time, the Atonement became very real to me.

I love it when Nephi refers to the Savior as "my Jesus" (2 Nephi 33:6). His atoning sacrifice really was for *me*. I knew He could heal my heart and make my burden light. He was the only one who could do it.

I had greater empathy and understanding for others who had lost their babies. I loved the children I did have even more. I wanted to be better. My trial seemed to shorten the distance between me and my Heavenly Father. I became instantly focused on what truly mattered in life. Would I wish that pain on anyone? Absolutely not. But I recognize the importance of the trial in teaching me some important lessons in life. Whatever your cross is in life (there will be many!), bear it well. Learn from it. Be thankful for the opportunity to learn and grow.

I knew a dear woman who committed adultery. She stopped going to church because she thought she wasn't worthy to go anymore. One day, she surprised me when she asked if she could ever be forgiven for what she had done. It had been a long time since she had been to church, and she had simply forgotten about the power of repentance and the Atonement. When I explained that was the exact reason why Jesus Christ was born into this world, she cried with joy. There is power through Christ's Atonement to heal, comfort, and redeem.

The Atonement is real and works in our lives every day. The gift of the Atonement is evidence of how much the Lord loves us.

Quote

"Our salvation depends on believing in and accepting the Atonement. Such acceptance requires a continual effort to understand it more fully." —President James E. Faust (Second Counselor in the First Presidency)[3]

Scripture

"For it is expedient that an atonement should be made; for according to the great plan of the Eternal God there must be an atonement made, or else all mankind must unavoidably perish; yea, all are hardened; yea, all are fallen and are lost, and must perish except it be through the atonement which it is expedient should be made." (Alma 34:9)

LESSON LEARNED

The Atonement of Jesus Christ is the central act of love and mercy in the Christian faith. Through His suffering, death, and resurrection, Jesus took upon Himself the sins, pains, and burdens of the world, offering a way for all to be healed, forgiven, and reconciled with God. His Atonement allows us to repent, receive forgiveness, and be cleansed from our mistakes while also providing comfort and strength during times of sorrow, pain, or trial.

The Atonement makes it possible for us to return to the presence of God and live with Him forever if we choose to follow Him. It is not only a gift of redemption but a demonstration of Christ's boundless love for each of us—love that transcends all understanding and offers hope in every circumstance. Through His Atonement, Jesus invites us to find peace, healing, and joy, knowing that He has already overcome the world on our behalf.

CHALLENGE

Here are a few challenges that could help individuals better understand and connect with the Atonement of Jesus Christ:

- **Reflection Challenge:** Write in a journal about moments when you have felt the Savior's healing power or how His grace has helped you in times of struggle.
- **Scripture Study Challenge:** Commit to studying a specific set of scriptures that focus on the Atonement, such as Isaiah 53, Matthew 26–28, or Alma 7.
- **Acts of Service Challenge:** Serve others in a way that mirrors Christ's love.
- **Prayer Challenge:** Thank Heavenly Father for the sacrifice of His Son and ask for the strength to better appreciate and apply the Atonement in your life.
- **Forgiveness Challenge:** Take time to forgive yourself or someone else.

- **Gratitude Challenge:** Each day for a week, write down one thing you are grateful for that you believe is made possible by the Atonement of Jesus Christ.

Attitude

Story

My dad had this magical ability to wake up every morning as if it were the best day ever in the history of the world. The first thing we'd hear as he was getting out of bed was the song "Oh, What a Beautiful Morning!" from the stage musical *Oklahoma*. He didn't just sing it; he belted it with all the flair of a Broadway star, even though he might have missed a note or two (or three). But none of that mattered. His enthusiasm was so infectious that we would immediately smile under our covers and laugh when he walked in our rooms to wake us up. It didn't matter that Daddy wasn't going to be the next big thing on the West End—his positivity was a show all its own.

It wasn't just the singing though. No matter what time of day, no matter what was going on, Daddy had this attitude that could only be described as "ridiculously optimistic." I honestly don't think I ever saw him wake up in a bad mood. He was like a walking, talking piece of sunshine. No storm was ever too big for him to weather, and it was almost like he had this secret stash of happiness that he'd dole out generously to everyone around him.

That positivity wasn't just for show. It was genuine. He found the good in absolutely everything. Stuck in traffic? "Well, at least we're not walking!" Rained out of a picnic? "Perfect time for a nap inside!" It was relentless optimism and one of his superpowers.

At his funeral, one of his granddaughters stood up and sang "Oh, What a Beautiful Morning!" just as he had done for us countless times before. And let me tell you, when she hit that first note, you could feel the room holding its breath, everyone knowing what was coming. The tears started flowing almost immediately. Not just because the song was beautiful, but because at that moment, it felt like Daddy was still there, singing right alongside her, his voice echoing in every heart. There wasn't a dry eye in the room. It wasn't just the song that made us cry; it was the reminder of how his joy, his attitude, and his love had touched every single person in that room.

So, yes, Daddy's singing might not have won any awards, but it was the soundtrack to our lives, filled with laughter, love, and endless optimism. In a world that seems to be growing darker, we need more people like Daddy who not only see the sunshine but reflect that light to others.

Quote

"Attitude is a little thing that makes a big difference." —Winston Churchill (British statesman, military leader, writer, and Prime Minister of the United Kingdom during World War II)[4]

Scripture

"Weeping may endure for a night, but joy cometh in the morning." (Psalm 30:5)

Lesson Learned

Life is hard. Having a positive attitude is essential for navigating life's challenges with resilience and grace. The question isn't whether or not we will be faced with hard times but how we will face them. When we approach situations with optimism and hope, we are better equipped to handle obstacles and setbacks.

A positive attitude helps us stay focused on solutions rather than problems, enabling us to find opportunities even in difficult circumstances. It not only influences our own physical and emotional well-being but also impacts those around us. People are naturally drawn to positive individuals, as optimism creates an uplifting atmosphere.

Developing a positive mindset fosters better health, improves relationships, and helps us to grow and learn from our experiences.

Challenge

- So today, look for the silver lining in your current situation
- Find a task that you think is menial or unpleasant and see if you can turn it into a more enjoyable game (You have to do it anyway, so you might as well enjoy yourself! Otherwise, you're just robbing yourself of joy)
- Give one sincere compliment to someone each day (It improves your attitude because focusing on the good in others changes how you view the world)
- Each time you catch yourself complaining, reframe it with a positive angle (It improves your attitude because it builds mental resilience and trains your mind to find solutions instead of dwelling on problems)
- Be of good cheer (Be sunshine!)

Being a Good Example of Living the Gospel with Joy

Story

My parents were party animals, so when we moved into a new house and school when I was in eighth grade, they wanted my twin sister and me to throw a big party at our home to get to know people. We were excited and invited as many people as we knew. Twins are noticeable, so word got out that "the twins" were throwing a party, and a ton of people showed up. We were thrilled to fill the house with new friends.

One of the guys who came to the house had a reputation of being a "real" partier . . . as in "Party hard, dude!" He was cool and popular, so we wanted him to stay, you know, to increase the "coolness factor" of the event.

"Where's the kegger, man?" he asked as he took one look around and realized it wasn't going to be one of "those" parties. We joked about the snacks on the table, which were included in our innocent spread, and somehow we convinced him to stay. It was a fun night, and we became buds.

Jump ahead a few years to our high school graduation. He and I had stayed friends during all those gloriously awkward teen years, even though he kept up his serious party-boy rep. After the graduation ceremony, he came up to me and asked, "You know what the best party I ever went to was?" I shrugged and replied, "I don't know, dude . . . you went to a *lot* of parties!" He laughed and then suddenly got serious. He said, "Remember that sweet party you hosted at your house when we were just kids in eighth grade?" I was surprised he even remembered. In fact, I joked and told him that it was probably his favorite because he was usually so drunk at all the other parties that ours was probably the only one he *did* remember! He agreed but said, "Nah, yours was just really fun." It may have been the only party he ever attended where people weren't getting drunk or stoned. Instead, we played games, danced, laughed, and had good, clean fun. That really made an impression on him. I had no idea how much of an impact that made on him.

You want to know what's funny? He owns a bar now! We still keep in touch. No, he never joined the Church, but he knows what it looks like when someone is living the gospel with joy.

Quote

"Example is not the main thing in influencing others. It is the only thing." —Albert Schweitzer (German theologian, philosopher, physician, and humanitarian)[5]

Scripture

"Let your light so shine before this people, that they may see your good works and glorify your Father who is in heaven." (3 Nephi 12:16)

Lesson Learned

If the "gospel" means "good news," then Christians should be the happiest people around! Being a good example of living the gospel of Jesus Christ with joy is essential not only for our own spiritual growth but also for influencing others. When we live with joy, we reflect the Light of Christ, showing others the peace and happiness that come from following His teachings. This joy isn't merely a surface-level emotion but stems from a deep sense of purpose, knowing that we are striving to live in alignment with God's will and that we have purpose here on earth. The way we carry ourselves—whether through acts of kindness, maintaining a positive attitude, or sharing the gospel—serves as a witness to the power of Jesus Christ in our lives.

Living the gospel with joy makes us more approachable and helps others see the true beauty of discipleship. In a world where many struggle with fear, anxiety, or uncertainty, joy becomes a beacon of hope. When we approach life's challenges with faith and optimism, we demonstrate that living the gospel doesn't mean avoiding difficulties or living by strict commandments but facing them with the assurance that God will provide strength. This mindset can inspire others to seek the same peace and joy that we have found in Christ.

Challenge

One of the first steps to living joyfully is to develop a personal relationship with Jesus Christ through prayer, scripture study, and worship. Living the gospel with joy involves living in harmony with the commandments and the teachings of Christ. By striving to follow His guidance, we find greater peace and happiness. If you're not currently living the way you know you should, it's time to level up. You will *feel* a difference in your life.

Do you want to feel more peace in your life? The principles of obedience, honesty, integrity, kindness, and charity are not just commandments; they are keys to living a life that is fulfilling and joyful. When we live in alignment with God's will, we feel the Spirit more abundantly, and that connection brings happiness. Though living the gospel can sometimes require sacrifice or self-discipline, these efforts lead to blessings that bring lasting joy, including inner peace, stronger relationships, and a deeper sense of purpose.

Do you want to feel happier? Gratitude helps us see God's hand in our daily lives, filling our hearts with joy and appreciation for all He provides. When we look for the positive in our experiences and in others, we begin to see the world through a lens of joy, which can transform even the most challenging circumstances. When we put our trust in Him, we're able to maintain a joyful heart, even when life doesn't go as expected.

Help others recognize the Savior in your example. The most powerful lessons aren't always taught with words but with the quiet, consistent example of a life well lived.

Being Nice vs. Being Important

Story

Many years ago, I had the privilege of working as a legislative assistant for a congressman in his Washington, DC, office. It was an exciting job, and one of the perks was that the congressman trusted me to represent him at numerous receptions, banquets, and political gatherings almost every night. I loved the energy of our nation's capital, the conversations, the networking, and the opportunity to meet influential people shaping the country's policies.

One evening, I had two events to attend. The first was a small, intimate gathering to honor a few senators. As I made my way into the venue, I walked over to the bar to get some water, casually chatting with the bartender while taking in the room. Although I don't drink alcohol, I've always found bartenders to be great conversationalists.

As we were talking, a well-dressed man and woman approached the bar and sat down on the stools next to the counter. The man turned to the bartender and said, "The congresswoman would like to order a cocktail."

Excited, I immediately turned to the woman and said, "Wow! You're a congresswoman? How wonderful!" I was genuinely impressed—it wasn't every day that I met a female member of Congress, and I respected the position she held.

However, the moment she realized I was no one important—just some young staffer without political influence—her demeanor instantly changed. She sneered at me, gave a curt "yes," and then turned her back without another word. The conversation was over before it had even begun.

In that moment, my admiration for her vanished. A title alone wasn't enough to impress me anymore—it was how people treated others that truly mattered. I also thought it was foolish of her to treat me with such disinterest because, for all she knew, I could have been one of her constituents. I suddenly felt no desire to linger at the event and decided to head to my next stop, a large reception just around the corner.

This second event was the complete opposite of the first. It was packed with high-profile political figures, including some of the most powerful lawmakers in the country. As I made my way through the crowd, I spotted the Speaker of the House. He was a towering political figure, one of the most influential people in Washington at the time. I wasn't sure what to expect or even what to say to him, but I decided to stand in line to meet him.

When it was my turn, I introduced myself, fully expecting a quick handshake and a polite but dismissive nod. After all, I held no real political clout. But to my surprise, the Speaker greeted me with a warm smile and a big hug, as if I were an old friend. He didn't rush the conversation and was excited to hear who I worked for. He didn't look over my shoulder for someone more important to talk to. In that brief moment, he made me feel like I actually mattered.

Here's the interesting part: I didn't even agree with his political party's beliefs. But that didn't matter. What mattered was the way he treated people—*all* people—regardless of their status, political persuasion, or influence.

That night, I learned a powerful lesson about leadership. Titles don't make someone a great leader—character does. The ability to treat everyone with kindness and respect, whether they hold power or not, is what truly sets people apart.

Quote

"It's nice to be important, but it's more important to be nice." —John Templeton (American-born British investor, banker, philanthropist)[6]

Scripture

"And be ye kind one to another, tenderhearted, forgiving one another, even as God for Christ's sake hath forgiven you." (Ephesians 4:32)

Lesson Learned

In a world that often values status, power, and recognition, it's easy to believe that being important is the ultimate goal. However, true greatness isn't measured by titles or achievements—it's measured by how we treat others. If you want to see someone's true character, watch how they treat waiters, cashiers, or behave when they think no one is watching. Being kind and compassionate leaves a lasting impact far beyond any position of authority. People may forget what you accomplished, but they will never forget how you made them feel.

A kind word, a helping hand, or a moment of genuine care can change someone's day, how they view themselves, or even their life. While importance is fickle and can be fleeting, kindness creates a ripple effect that continues long after we're gone. At the end of the day, the world doesn't need more important people; it needs more people who choose to be kind and make others feel important. Kindness leaves a legacy that titles and achievements never can.

Challenge

Be kind to everyone. Everyone is struggling with their own challenges and could use a smile. Remind yourself that everyone you meet is carrying something unseen—worries, wounds, dreams. When you look beyond their behavior and into their humanity, kindness becomes your default. It's easy to judge or compete, but kindness thrives when we replace comparison with compassion. Celebrate others' successes. Be gentle with their failures. Extend that same grace to yourself. Another tip is to pause before reacting. A moment of silence can prevent a moment of regret. In that pause, you create space to choose empathy instead of anger, patience instead of pride. At the end of each day, ask yourself:

Did I lift someone today?

Did I listen with love?

Did I make someone feel seen?

If you want to become a nicer person in a week, follow this seven-day challenge:

Seven-Day Kindness Challenge:

- **Day 1:** Give someone a genuine compliment.
- **Day 2:** Do a small, unexpected favor (hold the door, help carry something, etc.).
- **Day 3:** Write a kind message (text, note, or social media comment).
- **Day 4:** Listen more—ask someone about their day and really focus on them.
- **Day 5:** Express gratitude—thank someone sincerely.
- **Day 6:** Give without expecting anything in return (donate, tip generously, etc.).
- **Day 7:** Reflect—write down how being kind made you feel.

Body and Spirit Connection

Story

Tracey was a vibrant BYU student who had been called to serve as the Relief Society president in her singles ward at school. Known for her empathy and intuition, she had built strong connections with the other sisters, offering encouragement and wisdom during their challenging academic journeys.

One snowy evening, the bishop invited Tracey into his office. His warm but concerned expression set the tone. "Tracey," he began, "I've noticed a troubling pattern. Many of the young women in the ward have been coming to see me, overwhelmed by depression and anxiety. I'm worried about their well-being, but I need your help to understand what's truly going on. Will you be my sleuth?"

Tracey nodded, determined to uncover the cause of the struggles plaguing the sisters she cared so much about. She spent the following week checking in with the sisters during casual conversations, group gatherings, and late-night chats. She listened carefully, piecing together their stories. A clear pattern emerged:

- **Sleepless Nights:** Mid-term exams were looming, and the young women were sacrificing sleep to cram for big tests. Late-night study marathons had left them exhausted and irritable.
- **Nutritional Neglect:** Tight budgets meant many were surviving on instant ramen, with little thought to fresh fruits,

vegetables, or protein that they couldn't afford on their small student budgets. Their bodies were yearning for nourishment.

- **Seasonal Struggles:** Winter's long, dark nights and frigid temperatures left them cooped up indoors, feeling isolated and drained.

The picture was clear: These young women were physically depleted, and it was taking a toll on their mental and emotional health.

Tracey reported her findings to the bishop, who listened thoughtfully. That Sunday, he addressed the ward with a talk that resonated deeply. "My dear brothers and sisters," he began. "Our bodies and spirits are deeply connected. When we neglect the needs of our bodies, our spirits feel the strain. The late nights, poor nutrition, and lack of sunlight may seem like small sacrifices for your academic success, but they are costing you some physical, emotional, and spiritual health."

He quoted from the book *The Body Keeps the Score: Brain, Mind, and Body in the Healing of Trauma* by Bessel van der Kolk, explaining how the physical toll on our bodies often manifests in emotional and spiritual struggles. For many of these young men and women, this was the first time they realized that how they treated their bodies absolutely affected the health and wellness of their spirits!

The kind bishop urged everyone to prioritize self-care, reminding them that God cared deeply about their well-being. "Sleep is sacred," he said. "Nourishment is a gift. Moving our bodies and feeling sunlight are acts of worship in their own right. Let's honor the miracle of our bodies and, in doing so, strengthen our spirits."

Inspired by the talk, Tracey rallied the young women in the ward. She organized a "Self-Care Saturday," complete with cooking classes, a yoga session, and a workshop on time management. She encouraged them to share quick, healthy recipes and to take study breaks for short walks.

Gradually, the mood began to shift. The women found small ways to prioritize their well-being—an earlier bedtime here, a fresh apple there. With Tracey's loving leadership and the bishop's inspired counsel, they learned that caring for their bodies was an essential step in nurturing their spirits.

As winter gave way to spring, the women felt renewed, not just in their studies but in their sense of purpose, joy, and respect for their bodies, recognizing that their physical well-being and spiritual well-being were directly connected.

Quote

"The body is the servant of the mind. It obeys the operations of the mind, whether they be deliberately chosen or automatically expressed." —James Allen (British philosopher and author of *As a Man Thinketh*)[7]

Scripture

"Know ye not that your body is the temple of the Holy Ghost which is in you, which ye have of God, and ye are not your own? For ye are bought with a price: therefore glorify God in your body, and in your spirit, which are God's." (1 Corinthians 6:19–20)

Lesson Learned

They say happiness is having your health. If that's true, then what are you *doing* about it? There is a very close relationship between your physical health and your spiritual development. We all know that when you drink alcohol, smoke any substance, or do drugs, you're handing over your agency to things that control your mind. They will dull your conscience and your mind so that you can't make wise choices. What is less known is that when you eat a lot of junk food, don't exercise, or don't get enough sleep, your spiritual senses can be dulled.

Exercise is the most underused antidepressant. Food is the most abused anxiety drug. Sunlight is the most overlooked happy pill. Sleep is the most underappreciated healer. Mindset is the most underrated life tool.

When I was first trained to teach water aerobics at a fitness center, my instructor would always say, "Movement is the celebration of life!" I thought that was such an empowering thought that it made me want to move! Then he would quietly add with a wink, "Pain is the reminder that we're alive." The health of our physical bodies and spiritual strength are connected.

Challenge

Being mindful of the body-spirit connection involves nurturing both aspects of ourselves with intention. Here are a few ways to strengthen that awareness:

- **Practice Daily Prayer and Meditation:** Taking time to communicate with God or reflect in stillness can bring peace and align your spirit with your physical self.
- **Listen to Your Body:** Pay attention to how your body responds to different situations. Fatigue, stress, or unease may be signals that your spirit needs rest, prayer, or a shift in focus.
- **Engage in Meaningful Movement:** Exercise, stretching, or even mindful walking can help connect your body to your spirit. Activities like being in nature can be especially grounding.
- **Fuel Your Body with Intention:** Eating nourishing foods and drinking enough water can help you feel more spiritually alert and physically energized.
- **Serve Others:** Acts of kindness and service not only uplift the soul but also bring a sense of purpose and fulfillment that resonates in both body and spirit.
- **Express Gratitude:** A thankful heart enhances spiritual well-being and positively impacts physical health by reducing stress and promoting joy.

Brain Health

Story

Let me share an embarrassing experience that taught me a simple principle. When I was a teenager, I accepted a contract to work for a company for one week during the Christmas break. Like most teenagers, I had hunted around for opportunities to earn money, and I was excited to find a short-term gig in a nearby factory.

My heart sank when I saw that my job consisted of standing next to a conveyor belt and waiting thirty seconds to put four discs that popped out of the machine into a box. After only a few minutes, I felt like I was going to die of boredom. I finally understood the phrase "brain-dead work." I survived the first day but complained to my family that I just couldn't return the next day. My sister reminded me that I had a secret weapon: her! We're identical twins, so she volunteered to do the work for me the next day since she also wanted to earn money over the Christmas break and they probably wouldn't even notice it wasn't me.

When she returned home, I couldn't wait to hear her complain so we could wallow in misery together. Instead, she said it was really fun! I was completely shocked and assumed she must have been given a different job than what I had the day before. Nope. She had the same boring job that I had been given, but she figured out a way to challenge her brain while she waited those thirty seconds in between tasks.

She challenged herself to see how much content she could memorize before those discs emerged on the conveyor belt. She had taken flashcards to work to memorize some of the vocabulary and formulas she was supposed to be learning in school. Why hadn't I thought of that? I was supposed to memorize all that stuff too! She wanted to go back the next day, but this time, I *wanted* to go! I followed her great example and had a productive and even fun rest of the week at that job.

Quote

"The brain is like a muscle. When it is in use, we feel very good. Understanding is joyous." —Carl Sagan (American astronomer, astrophysicist, and cosmologist)[8]

Scripture

"Be ye transformed by the renewing of your mind." (Romans 12:2)

Lesson Learned

Keeping your mind active and engaged is essential for brain health, much like exercise is for the body. The brain thrives on learning, problem-solving, and meaningful conversations, all of which strengthen neural connections and improve cognitive function. Just as muscles weaken when not used, the mind can also decline if not regularly challenged. Reading, writing, learning new skills, and even engaging in deep thinking and spiritual reflection can keep your brain sharp and resilient.

Positive thoughts and mindfulness can reduce stress, which is crucial for mental well-being. Experts in dementia and Alzheimer's disease have discovered that by intentionally using your mind for growth, creativity, and wisdom, you not only protect your brain from decline but also enhance your ability to navigate life with clarity, purpose, and joy.

Challenge

Mindlessly scrolling social media doesn't build your brain's power. Instead, look for ways that actually help you develop critical thinking skills. When you find yourself sitting in the car at a stoplight, waiting in a dentist's office, or washing the dishes, challenge your brain. Consider these ideas:

- Memorize a church hymn
- Memorize scriptures
- Listen to a podcast or audiobook
- Learn vocabulary words in a foreign language
- Solve a problem by mentally debating its pros and cons
- Write a poem
- Memorize your Social Security number, birth dates and anniversaries, or phone numbers
- Play Sudoku, Chess, word searches or other brain games
- Learn how to play a musical instrument
- Eat foods rich in omega-3s, antioxidants, and healthy fats, like salmon, blueberries, walnuts, spinach, and olive oil
- Meditate
- Write your full name slowly with your non-dominant hand to snap your brain out of autopilot and into the present
- Stand on one foot while thinking something through to force your brain to focus by clearing out background noise and thoughts

Bringing Souls to Christ

Story

Would you like eternal and delicious joy? I'll use the analogy of ice cream since that's something that brings me joy in this life. When I was in high school, my boyfriend, Dale, joined the Church. What a wonderful scoop of ice cream! It was awesome! It was an amazing experience to go through the missionary discussions with him, sit next to him in seminary and church, discover answers to both of our questions, and grow spiritually together. Delicious ice cream. Incomprehensible joy. I highly recommend it!

When Dale turned nineteen, he was called to serve a mission. I was so excited for him and couldn't wait to write to "my" missionary. I was so proud of him and discovered an increasing amount of joy in reading about his experiences and watching him deepen his understanding of the gospel and love for the Savior. Pass the double scoop of ice cream. I felt more than happiness—I felt an abiding joy that I knew was eternal.

Now here comes the really delicious part . . . When Dale was almost finished with his mission, I received a very special letter in the mail. It was from a teenager who had been baptized by Dale. He submitted his own mission papers and had just received a call to serve. In the letter, he thanked me for being brave and teaching Dale about the gospel of Jesus Christ. I can't even describe the depth of joy I felt to know that my meager missionary efforts with my boyfriend had rippled out to include this stranger who would then go on to teach others. My heart almost burst. That, my dear friend, is a hot fudge sundae.

Quote

"Wherever you are on this earth, there are plenty of opportunities to share the good news of the gospel of Jesus Christ." —Elder Dieter F. Uchtdorf (member of the Quorum of the Twelve Apostles)[9]

Scripture

"This is my glory, that perhaps I may be an instrument in the hands of God to bring some soul to repentance; and this is my joy." (Alma 29:9)

Lesson Learned

There is no joy equal to that of bringing others to Christ. As you share the gospel with others, you learn to love them as the Savior does. Remember when Alma and the sons of Mosiah went on missions? You can tell they were great missionaries because of the pure love they felt for the people, even the rotten Lamanites. In Mosiah 28:3, it says, "Now they were desirous that salvation should be declared to every creature, for they could not bear that any human soul should perish; yea, even the very thoughts that any soul should endure endless torment did cause them to quake and tremble."

Do you feel that way about people? Even toward the mean people you see every day? (There sure are a lot of them out there, right?) That's the kind of pure love the Savior has and wants us to develop while we're here on earth. In fact, that's one of the big lessons we're supposed to learn while we're here. Just keep serving others, and your capacity to love will grow.

Bringing souls to Christ is one of the most meaningful and rewarding acts we can do in this life. It isn't just about preaching—it's about living in a way that reflects His love, kindness, and truth. When we serve others, uplift them in their struggles, and share our testimony, we create opportunities for them to feel the Savior's influence. Christ's invitation is for all, and we can help extend that invitation through our words and actions. Whether through missionary work, teaching, or simply being a light in someone's life, we can play a role in guiding others to Him. As Alma said in the Book of Mormon, bringing even one soul to Christ is a source of great joy. The beauty of this work is that as we help others come unto Him, our own faith deepens and we draw closer to Him as well.

Challenge

The first challenge is to simply work into conversations with others that you're a member of The Church of Jesus Christ of Latter-day Saints. That can open doors for you because people with questions about the Church or the Book of Mormon will know they can come to you!

- Be brave and share your testimony of Jesus Christ with someone
- Serve others and be an example of Christ's love (That alone speaks volumes to others)
- Invite friends or neighbors to activities at church, so they can experience being in our buildings in a non-threatening (non-preachy) way (They might say no, but now they'll be used to your invitations, so it won't seem as scary the next time!)
- Invite someone over to dinner with the missionaries
- Do splits with the missionaries
- Start a YouTube channel to share your beliefs in Jesus Christ
- Be bold and open your mouth!
- Post a scripture, uplifting thought, or short story of faith (Share things that feel genuine to you; you never know who is quietly watching and searching)
- A book, card, or simple gift that includes a scripture or gospel insight can plant seeds of faith (Personalize it with a short note about why it matters to you)
- Often, the best way to share Christ is simply to listen when someone is struggling; gently offer hope from the gospel when the Spirit prompts you
- If someone opens up to you, offer to pray with them right then; it's a powerful way to invite the Spirit and show them how faith works in real life
- Pray for opportunities each day to be a light and to recognize who needs to feel God's love through you (The Holy Ghost will guide your words, timing, and approach)

Building Connections

Story

There was something special about the way he walked into that bank, like he was bringing with him a burst of sunshine. It wasn't his suit or his smile, though both were always present; it was the flowers. Every time my grandpa visited a bank, whether it was for a quick transaction or a longer chat, he would walk up to the tellers with a fresh bouquet, as if the blooms were as essential to his visit as the money he was there to handle.

The tellers, busy with the usual tasks, never saw it coming. But the moment they laid eyes on him, a quiet wave of warmth spread across their faces. "Ah, it's Mr. Bates," one of them would whisper, already knowing what was about to happen. And sure enough, there he stood, with flowers in hand and a big smile on his face.

It wasn't about the grand gestures, not really. The flowers were a simple mix of daisies, lilies, and roses, the kind that anyone could find in the flower department of a grocery store. But it was the thought behind them that made them special. Grandpa wasn't just a customer. He was someone who noticed, who appreciated. He didn't need anything but a smile, and in return, he received something even greater: the genuine affection of the tellers.

"Thank you," one of them would say, eyes sparkling, holding the flowers like they were the most precious gift. "You always know how to make our day brighter." The other tellers would nod in agreement, and it was always the same: laughter, good conversation, and a few moments of lightness amid their busy routine.

Over time, Grandpa became a sort of legend at that bank. Whenever a new teller started, they were always told about the man who brought flowers. And when he walked in, no matter how busy the bank was, it seemed as if the entire atmosphere shifted. There was always a buzz of excitement, a sense of anticipation. His simple act of kindness had the power to turn an ordinary day into something worth remembering.

The connection he made with the tellers was genuine. He loved people, but he also understood that building connections with others was good for business. It was no surprise that the tellers always gave this man their best care. Grandpa's transactions were often complicated, but he knew he'd get the help he needed with patience and attention to detail. He taught his children and grandchildren to always be kind to tellers, waiters, the postman, and really . . . everyone.

The tellers didn't just know his name. They knew his heart. And because of those flowers, they always greeted him with an extra bit of cheer. It was as if they had been reminded, in the most unexpected way, of the good things in life—the small acts of kindness that can change an entire day, even an entire mood.

Quote

"Kindness is a language which the deaf can hear and the blind can see." —Mark Twain (American writer, humorist, and lecturer)[10]

Scripture

"By love serve one another." (Galatians 5:13)

Lesson Learned

Simple acts of love and attention can create lasting impressions and build connections. It's easy to forget that how we treat others says more about us than it does about them. We might be quick to judge or even dismiss those who are serving us, whether it's a waiter at a restaurant, a cashier at a store, or a receptionist at an office. But the truth is, how we interact with people in these roles reflects our character and the values we hold. When we choose kindness, patience, and respect, we show that we understand the inherent dignity in everyone, no matter what their position or status.

Unfortunately, many people fail to recognize this. Some individuals treat waiters, cashiers, or other low-level employees with a disregard that is shocking. They might raise their voice when their order isn't right, make rude comments about the service, or even ignore the person entirely. These actions can stem from a belief that those in service roles are somehow "less than," but nothing could be further from the truth.

Everyone deserves to be treated with the same level of respect, regardless of their job or title. It's easy to be kind to those in positions of power or influence, but it takes true character to show respect to those who may not be able to do anything for us in return.

Everyone, no matter their background or job, deserves to be treated with kindness, patience, and dignity. Building a connection is simply letting someone know you value them.

Challenge

The way we treat others not only brightens their day but also strengthens the connections we share with them. In a world that can often feel rushed or disconnected, acts of kindness offer a much-needed reminder of our shared humanity. Below are several simple ways we can show kindness to others that build connections.

- Smile at people
- Make eye contact with others
- Give a simple compliment
- Say thank you
- Offer to help
- Show patience
- Hold the door open
- Offer your seat
- Offer words of encouragement like "You're doing great!"

Bullying

Story

My twin sister and I have always loved being twins. We used to dress alike for many years until we finally figured out that we could have twice the wardrobe if we bought separate outfits. By the time we got to high school, we would dress alike only on rare occasions. Everyone got a kick out of it, and we would really play it up for fun. Except . . . there was this one girl who would mock us and yell, "Ooh! Look at the little twinsies!" She would laugh at us and make us feel dumb for celebrating our "twinness."

On our more confident days, we could easily blow her off, but there were other days when she really made us feel stupid and insecure. Wait, let me rephrase that: We *allowed* her to make us feel stupid and insecure.

Remember, your attitude is your choice. I had to work hard at not allowing her words to bother me. The truth is that there will always be someone who makes you feel like a loser. They obviously don't know you and your great potential, so just ignore them and move on. Your best comeback line is to completely ignore what was said and walk away.

But wait! There's more to the story, and you're going to love this. Many years later, we heard that she had gotten married and had given birth to twins! Yes! There *is* justice in this world! The story gets even better. Wait for it . . . she then gave birth to another set of twins! You can't make this stuff up! Needless to say, we're sure her attitude has changed about twins . . . and also about making fun of people. We wonder if she dresses up her twins in matching clothes . . .

By the way, if you're a twin, you *have* to go to the annual "Twins Days" festival in Twinsburg, Ohio! It's held the first weekend of every August, and even though it's a bit cheesy, it's super fun! One year, we went to the festival to celebrate our birthday. And guess what? My twin sister married a twin! He has a fraternal twin sister, so all four of us went to the festival and had a blast together!

Quote

"No one can make you feel inferior without your consent." —Eleanor Roosevelt (First Lady of the United States from 1933 to 1945)[11]

Scripture

"Let no corrupt communication proceed out of your mouth, but that which is good to the use of edifying, that it may minister grace unto the hearers." (Ephesians 4:29)

Lesson Learned

Don't ever let anyone make you feel bad for being uniquely you.

Bullying is a destructive behavior that can leave deep emotional, psychological, and even physical scars on its victims. It often stems from insecurity, a need for control, or a lack of empathy, but no matter the cause, it should never be tolerated. Whether it happens in schools, workplaces, online, or within communities, bullying thrives in silence. That's why it's essential to stand up for those who are mistreated, speak out against injustice, and foster a culture of kindness and inclusion.

True strength lies not in tearing others down but in lifting them up. If we all commit to treating others with respect and compassion, we can create environments where everyone feels safe, valued, and empowered. Jesus Christ died on the cross for everyone, showing us that every individual on this planet has value.

Bullies often do what they do because they've been hurt in some way and want to feel better about themselves. Don't let their mocking, cruel words bother you because it's about them, really, not you.

Challenge

One powerful thing someone can do about bullying is to be an upstander, not a bystander. If you witness someone being bullied, don't stay silent. Step in and offer support. This could mean speaking up to tell the bully that their behavior is wrong, comforting the victim so they know they're not alone, or reporting the situation to a teacher, manager, or authority figure who can take action.

Even small acts, like including someone who has been excluded or showing kindness, can make a huge difference. Bullies thrive on silence, but when people stand together, their power disappears.

Now, let's think about bullying in another way that might hit close to home . . . literally. Do you bully your kids? Do you bully your spouse? When you get angry that they're not doing what you want them to, it's often because you want to control them. But remember, you're not their boss. They have their own agency and the right to use it.

Celebrating Birthdays

Story

Never were there luckier kids than the three Bates girls, blessed with our very own personal clown who performed exclusively for us and our friends every year at our birthday parties. Our friends would gather wide-eyed, equal parts awestruck and jealous, secretly wishing their dads were half as cool (or as ridiculous) as ours.

We'd bask in smug pride as the first guest caught sight of Dad perched on the roof of our house, doing some sort of interpretive jig before carefully climbing down to officially kick off the party. Parties didn't really start until Dad arrived in full clown glory.

That red-and-white clown costume, which lived in our closet like a sacred relic, was a year-round reminder of just how hard Dad worked to make our birthdays unforgettable. And they *were* unforgettable—because how many kids can say their dad risked life, limb, and dignity just to make them laugh?

He also owned a Santa Claus costume for parties, and he loved wearing goofy hats and glasses for any occasion. That's probably where I got my love for costumes, passed on to my kids, and now my own grandkids!

Quote

"The more you praise and celebrate your life, the more there is in life to celebrate." —Oprah Winfrey (media mogul, talk show host, actress, author, and philanthropist)[12]

Scripture

"Blessed be the name of God, for . . . in this life I shall have joy." (Moses 5:10)

Lesson Learned

Birthdays are significant milestones that offer an opportunity to celebrate life, growth, and relationships. They mark not just the passage of another year but also the unique journey and achievements of an individual. Celebrating birthdays is an act of gratitude for life itself, a moment to reflect on past experiences, and a chance to set intentions for the future.

I've heard people say they don't want to celebrate their birthday because it makes them feel old, but that's the wrong way to think about it. Birthdays are a reminder of one's value and importance to others, as they bring loved ones together in recognition of a person's impact on their lives. Deep down, everyone wants to know they matter.

Making birthdays special goes beyond the superficial trappings of gifts and parties; it's about showing care and appreciation for someone in meaningful ways. These moments of celebration also provide a much-needed pause from the routines of daily life, allowing people to feel seen, loved, and celebrated.

Challenge

Begin by making a list of birthdays on your calendar or digital reminders to keep track of the special dates of your loved ones. Don't forget them! Those are sacred dates and an opportunity to let someone know they're valued in this world.

One challenge in making birthdays special for others is understanding and accommodating their preferences. Not everyone enjoys the same kind of celebration. While some may love big parties with friends and family, others might prefer quiet, intimate moments or even time spent alone. It can be difficult to strike the right balance between planning something meaningful and ensuring the celebration aligns with the individual's personality and comfort level. Misjudging these preferences might lead to stress for both the planner and the celebrant, potentially detracting from the joy of the occasion. Don't celebrate the birthday the way *you* want to but the way *they* want to.

A birthday doesn't need to be elaborate or expensive. A cupcake with a candle could be all that the birthday person even wants. Just do something. Everyone deserves to be celebrated!

Each birthday is a reminder that life itself is a sacred gift from God (see Jeremiah 1:5). We are His children, created with divine purpose. Just as we celebrate our birth, we can also celebrate our spiritual rebirth through Christ (see John 3:3).

Call to thank your mother for going through nine months of pregnancy and all of that pain during the delivery to bring you here. In Spanish, when a woman gives birth, they use the expression "to give light." Isn't that a sweet way to describe it? Your birth brought light into this world!

Celebrating the Gift of Everyday Accomplishments

Story

In our family, every day was a celebration thanks to my father, who believed that life's small victories deserved grand recognition. His unwavering conviction that every moment was special transformed our household into a place where joy was abundant, and no achievement was too minor to be celebrated.

Dad had a unique way of turning ordinary events into extraordinary occasions. Whether it was a successful school project, a well-cooked meal, or even a well-timed joke, he found reasons to gather us together for a good round of applause. He would don a costume or speak in a funny accent, adding a touch of humor and surprise to the ceremony. His speeches were heartfelt and often included humorous anecdotes, making each award presentation feel like a special event.

One of the most memorable ceremonies was when I managed to keep a plant alive for an entire month. Dad declared it the "Green Thumb Achievement Award" and presented me with a certificate adorned with colorful drawings. He wore a gardener's hat and spoke in a mock British accent, praising my "exceptional horticultural skills." The entire family gathered, clapping and cheering, making me feel like a true champion.

When my sisters and I were old enough to learn how to cook, my dad put us on a rotating calendar to take turns being in charge of dinner. Every night, the chef du jour received applause for her efforts. If the meal turned out especially good, we would get a standing ovation. In addition to being hungry, my dad was smart because he knew the positive reinforcement would spur us on to become better cooks. Our husbands have thanked him many times over the years!

These ceremonies were more than just fun; they instilled in us the importance of acknowledging and celebrating our efforts, no matter how small. Dad taught us that waiting for holidays or special occasions wasn't necessary to appreciate life's moments. Every day held the potential for a celebration, and every achievement, big or small, was worth recognizing.

As we grew older, these traditions continued. Even as adults, we looked forward to Dad's impromptu ceremonies, now extending to the grandchildren. They served as a reminder to pause and appreciate our accomplishments, fostering a sense of gratitude and joy in our daily lives.

Dad's approach to life was a testament to his belief in the power of positivity and recognition. He showed us that celebrating life's small wins could lead to a more fulfilling and joyful existence. His legacy of daily celebrations and heartfelt speeches continues to inspire us, reminding us to find joy in the little things and to always celebrate our achievements.

Quote

"Enjoy the little things, for one day you may look back and realize they were the big things." —Robert Brault (author and quote enthusiast)[13]

Scripture

"By small and simple things are great things brought to pass; and small means in many instances doth confound the wise." (Alma 37:6)

Lesson Learned

Celebrating life's small wins is more than just a feel-good practice; it's a vital component of personal growth, motivation, and overall well-being. Recognizing and appreciating minor achievements can lead to significant positive changes in our lives. Every day in this mortal experience deserves to be celebrated! Don't wait because you never know how many more days you get to be here.

Acknowledging small victories provides a sense of accomplishment, which can significantly boost motivation. When we celebrate these moments, we reinforce our belief in our abilities, making us more resilient and prepared to tackle larger challenges. This practice fosters a positive feedback loop, where each small win propels us toward greater success.

Celebrating small wins can elevate mood and offer relief from depressive episodes. By focusing on positive outcomes, we shift our attention away from setbacks, promoting a healthier mental state. Small wins are the building blocks of larger achievements. By setting and achieving smaller goals, we create momentum that propels us toward bigger successes.

Challenge

A "celebration" doesn't mean it has to cost money or even take a lot of time. Here are some simple ways to celebrate:

- Acknowledge the accomplishment with applause or a hug
- Take a picture to commemorate the accomplishment
- Brag on social media about your loved one's feat and tag them
- Pick a flower from your yard to present to the person
- Text them how proud of them you are for what they did, using lots of fireworks and happy-face emojis
- Cook a special dinner for them
- Serve their meal on a special plate
- Designate a "Family Achievement Night" where everyone shares their small wins from the week to a room full of applause and hugs

Challenging Yourself

Story

Tracey had always dreamed of hiking in the Grand Canyon, but the thought of preparing for such a challenging trek felt overwhelming. That's when her friends in the new ward she moved into stepped in with a plan. "Every Monday morning, we'll walk ten miles together," they declared, their enthusiasm contagious. "No excuses!"

At first, Tracey was hesitant. Ten miles sounded daunting and time-consuming, especially on chilly mornings when staying in bed seemed far more appealing. But she didn't want to let her friends down, so she laced up her shoes and joined them, even when frost and snow clung to the branches of the leafless trees outside.

Week after week, the walks became a ritual. As they strode through neighborhoods and trails, their conversations flowed effortlessly. They laughed, shared stories, vented about life, and supported one another. "This is our free mental health counseling session," they joked, savoring the camaraderie as much as the exercise.

The consistent effort paid off. Tracey not only became fitter but also felt more connected to her friends and energized by their mutual encouragement. When the day finally came to hike one of the Grand Canyon's major trails, she was ready. She marveled at the breathtaking views, her legs strong and steady as she descended into the canyon and climbed back up again, accomplishing something she once thought was impossible. She said it was one of the hardest things she had ever done.

Later, she reflected on those Monday mornings and realized they had been about more than just preparation. They had been about building friendships, boosting mental health, and proving that with a little accountability, the toughest goals were achievable. Those weeks of snowy morning walks had even prepared her for the unexpected cold and rainy weather the group of women endured on their Grand Canyon adventure.

Quote

"It is not the mountain we conquer but ourselves." —Sir Edmund Hillary (New Zealand mountaineer, explorer, and philanthropist best known for being one of the first two people to reach the summit of Mount Everest)[14]

Scripture

"I give unto men weakness that they may be humble; and my grace is sufficient for all men that humble themselves before me; for if they humble themselves before me, and have faith in me, then will I make weak things become strong unto them." (Ether 12:27)

Lesson Learned

Challenging yourself begins with understanding the power of consistency and small, incremental changes. Often, people try to overhaul their entire routine at once, only to become overwhelmed and give up. Instead, it's more effective to focus on one habit at a time and commit to it until it becomes part of your daily life. Start with something manageable and easy to incorporate, like drinking more water or dedicating five minutes to meditation each morning. Once this habit feels natural, you can build on it and gradually add more positive habits. This step-by-step approach helps avoid burnout and creates a sustainable foundation for long-term growth.

It's also important to be patient with yourself and avoid the trap of perfectionism when you challenge yourself. Building good habits and reaching your goals takes time, and there will be days when you slip up. Instead of being hard on yourself, approach setbacks with a growth mindset. Recognize that one misstep doesn't undo your progress, and you can get back on track the next day. It's consistency over time that creates lasting change, not the occasional mistake. By forgiving yourself and not letting temporary setbacks derail your long-term vision, you create a mindset that embraces progress over perfection.

Challenge

One great way to challenge yourself is to step outside your comfort zone daily. This could mean trying something new, like learning a skill, driving a different route to work, speaking up in a meeting, starting a conversation with someone you don't know, or tackling a fear. Growth happens when we push past what feels easy and familiar. Even small steps, like setting a personal goal and following through, can build confidence and resilience over time. The key is to embrace discomfort as a sign that you're stretching yourself in the right direction!

Choose a principle of the gospel you want to be better at living. Think of a Christlike quality you want to develop. Stretch yourself one day at a time. What's on your bucket list? Start taking items off your list and putting them on your calendar. This is your one life. Live it! Never underestimate the power of small habits.

Saving $8 per day is about $3000 per year!

Reading 15 pages per day is about 25 books per year!

Walking 10,000 steps per day is about 70 marathons per year!

Waking up 1 hour earlier per day is 365 extra hours of living per year!

Competition

Story

When I was in high school, I ran for class president. For a few days, no one stepped up to run against me. I secretly hoped no one would so that I could easily win without much effort. Finally, a really nice guy I admired threw his hat into the ring. He was popular and well-liked by everyone, and if I weren't running, I would have voted for him!

One day, I was in the office painting posters for a school rally when I realized that's where the ballot box was for the election. I was all alone in the office. I'm sad and embarrassed to admit that I actually considered cheating by writing my name on additional ballots that I could have easily slipped into the box. I instantly pushed that horrible and dishonest idea out of my mind, knowing that my integrity was worth more than that. I wanted to win fairly and recognized that if I did win, I would never know if it was real or simply because I had cheated.

I realized I was going to have to step up my game. I worked really hard on my little campaign and pushed myself further than I imagined I could. I was thrilled when I won the election. By having a competitor, I was forced to be better, and the victory was that much sweeter.

Quote

"What seems to us as bitter trials are often blessings in disguise." —Oscar Wilde (Irish playwright and poet)[15]

Scripture

"I can do all things through Christ which strengtheneth me." (Philippians 4:13)

Lesson Learned

Jim Rohn, who was an American entrepreneur, author, and motivational speaker, said a lot of brilliant things, but the quote I want to share with you about having challenges that stretch and push us is this: "Don't wish it were easier. Wish you were better."[16] Trials refine us. They can also draw us closer to God when we reach out to Him for strength.

Horace Bushnell, who was an American Congregational minister and theologian, stated, "The more difficulties one has to encounter, within and without, the more significant and the higher in inspiration his life will be."[17]

We're all inspired by the rags-to-riches stories and the accounts of brave people who have conquered unimaginable trials in life. Everyone loves a good underdog, right? So why is it that when we have our own problems or challenges, we whine and complain that it's not fair? No one *ever* said that life would be fair, so why do we even think that?

It's through the struggles and the hard lessons learned that our life becomes rich and meaningful. It's through pain and suffering that we are humbled and develop compassion for others. And it's often through competition that we learn we want to be better and that we can be!

Challenge

Think about a struggle you're currently having and what you're learning from it. Write down three ways a current challenge could bring growth. Write down a list of the personal trials you've had in your life. See if you can identify how you're a stronger or better person because of each one. An insightful meme was posted on social media during a horrible snowstorm on the East Coast. It said, "You can find joy in all the snow, or else you can be miserable in it. Either way, you still have a lot of snow." It's your attitude about trials that determines your growth during those difficult times.

When God wanted to make a king out of David, He didn't bring him a crown; He brought him Goliath! Your challenges prepare you for your purpose. Based on your past and current trials in life, what do you think God has been preparing you for?

Complimenting Others

Story

When I was twelve years old, I took a class at school where I learned how to type on a typewriter. Yes, an actual typewriter! That's how old I am!

One day, I wore a skirt and some high heels, which were the popular fad at the time. When I walked into the classroom, the cute boy I sat next to said, "Wow! Look at those legs!" I had no idea what he was talking about. I could understand if he had mentioned my new shoes, but he used the word "legs." I wondered what was wrong with my legs. I mean, they were normal legs. I actually went home that day after school and looked in the mirror to see if there was something wrong with my legs. I mentioned it to my older sister, and she laughed and explained that he liked my legs! It had never occurred to me that I had arrived at the age when boys my age would be interested in girls and actually think I was cute or even sexy!

That was over forty years ago, and yet I still remember it. That one simple compliment from a boy has echoed in my heart this entire time. I recently had two surgeries on my left foot and leg, and I'm painfully aware that my legs aren't very cute or sexy anymore. But I'll be forever grateful for that kind compliment that made me look in the mirror and see myself differently that day. Our kind words can help others see themselves better too. Open your mouth and shower people with drops of enlightening compliments!

Quote

"Kind words can be short and easy to speak, but their echoes are truly endless." —Mother Teresa (Catholic nun, missionary, and humanitarian)[18]

Scripture

"Pleasant words are as an honeycomb, sweet to the soul, and health to the bones." (Proverbs 16:24)

Lesson Learned

Complimenting others is a simple yet powerful way to uplift, encourage, and strengthen relationships. A genuine compliment can boost someone's confidence, brighten their day, and even inspire them to see their own worth in a new light. Words have energy, and when we use them to recognize someone's strengths, efforts, or kindness, we create a ripple effect of positivity.

Compliments also strengthen connections, making people feel valued and appreciated. Whether it's acknowledging a friend's hard work, praising a coworker's talent, or simply telling someone they have a great smile, taking a moment to uplift others costs nothing but can mean everything.

Challenge

So today, give someone a compliment. You truly never know the impact your words have on other people. An easy way to start is to simply compliment someone on an article of clothing or their hair. Next, work up to complimenting someone on their behavior or character.

These types of compliments are easy to give and feel genuine, helping to make someone feel valued without overthinking it. Try using these words if this challenge is scary for you:

- "You have a great sense of style."
- "Your smile is so contagious!"
- "I really admire your creativity."
- "You always know how to brighten up a room."
- "You make everything seem so easy."

- "You're such a great listener."
- "You have a really positive energy about you."
- "I love your enthusiasm."
- "You're really good at what you do!"
- "You always know the right thing to say."

Contagious Good

Story

One snowy winter day in Lake Tahoe, my dad pulled off a legendary feat, turning a ski resort blizzard evacuation into an impromptu concert. After a fun morning of winter skiing, ominous dark clouds rolled in. By early afternoon, the resort shut down, and everyone was herded toward the trams, a sea of grumpy faces huddling together as snowflakes fell relentlessly.

As the cold set in, so did the collective misery of the crowd. My sisters and I shivered alongside hundreds of strangers, the atmosphere so tense you could practically see cartoon storm clouds over everyone's heads. Then, out of nowhere, my dad—unbothered by the blizzard—opened his mouth and began to . . . yodel. Yes, yodel!

At first, there were a few chuckles, then outright laughter. Encouraged by this, he switched to singing. Imagine hundreds of people in heavy ski gear, crowded like sardines in a can to stay warm while the snow fell and the wind howled, belting out tunes together. My dad had them all—skiers, snowboarders, even the grumpy guy at the front—singing their hearts out and laughing. Suddenly, the cold didn't seem so unbearable, and the wait didn't feel so long. My dad had transformed a miserable situation into a moment none of us would ever forget. I remember feeling so proud to be the daughter of such an amazing man.

When we finally made it down the mountain, we weren't just relieved—we were joyful. I still think about that day and how my dad turned a potential disaster into a blizzard-side showstopper. He didn't just teach us how to ski; he taught us the power of joy in the face of snowflakes and setbacks. It was a truly inspiring miracle to behold.

It taught me that one person really can make a positive difference. Jesus was only one person, yet He changed the world.

QUOTE

"To get the full value of joy, you must have someone to divide it with." —Mark Twain (American writer, humorist, and lecturer)[19]

SCRIPTURE

"Be of good cheer; I have overcome the world." (John 16:33)

LESSON LEARNED

One person has the power to make a profound positive difference in the world, no matter how small their actions may seem. By embracing kindness, empathy, and a willingness to help others, an individual can ignite a ripple effect that touches countless lives.

One person's vision and dedication can bring about transformative changes on a larger scale. When someone commits to making a difference, they show others what's possible, reminding us all that change often begins with a single courageous step.

CHALLENGE

What can *you* do today to be a positive force for good in the world around you? When people around you begin to complain about something, choose to be positive and point out the good in the situation. If something needs to be changed, step up and lead the cause.

This might sound like you're expected to make a huge impact on the world for it to count, but that's not so; if there are dirty dishes in the sink, just wash them. Making a positive difference doesn't require big fanfare or even an audience. Just do something good today.

Courage

Story

On the oncology floor of the hospital, there was a special place that wasn't listed on any map or guide. Tucked away at the end of a quiet hallway, it was known simply as "The Wig Closet." It wasn't much to look at—just a small room with shelves and drawers—but to the patients who stepped inside, it was a sanctuary of hope and healing.

The closet was filled with an array of wigs in every imaginable style and color. Short, sleek bobs sat beside cascading curls; vibrant reds mingled with silvers, brunettes, and golden blonds. Some wigs were playful, with streaks of bold colors, while others radiated elegance and simplicity. To an outsider, it might have seemed like just a collection of hairpieces, but to the patients fighting breast cancer, it was so much more.

For many, the journey through chemotherapy was marked not just by physical pain and exhaustion but by the emotional toll of watching their hair fall out. Hair loss wasn't just a cosmetic change; it was a visible reminder of their illness, a loss of identity, and, for some, a source of shame. Many women avoided mirrors, unable to recognize the person staring back at them.

But then came the moment they were invited to the wig closet. A nurse, often with a warm smile and a comforting hand on the patient's shoulder, would lead them to the little room. It wasn't uncommon for tears to well up as patients stepped inside. "Take your time," the nurse would say. "Find one that feels like *you.*"

There was a quiet magic in the air as patients ran their fingers through the wigs, sometimes hesitant, sometimes hopeful. It wasn't just about choosing a hairstyle—it was about reclaiming a piece of themselves.

One woman, Maria, stood in front of the mirror holding a wig with soft brown waves that reminded her of the hair she'd lost. As she placed it on her head and adjusted it, she gasped. "I look like *me* again," she whispered, her voice breaking.

Another patient, Diane, chose a fiery red wig—a color she'd never dared to try before. When she saw her reflection, she laughed for the first time in weeks. "I look like I could take on the world," she said, a spark returning to her eyes.

The Wig Closet wasn't just about appearances; it was about helping these women feel whole again. It was about giving them the confidence to step out of their hospital rooms and into the world without feeling like their illness defined them. For many, wearing a wig meant they could go to the grocery store, attend their child's school play, or even sit with friends without enduring stares or uncomfortable questions.

The nurses who managed the wig closet often said it was one of their favorite parts of the job. They saw firsthand how a simple act of trying on a wig could transform a patient's demeanor. Shoulders that had been hunched in defeat would straighten, and eyes dulled by fatigue would suddenly shine with renewed confidence.

One patient summed it up perfectly as she adjusted her chosen wig in the mirror. "This isn't just hair. It's my armor. It's how I'm going to face the world." The Wig Closet became a symbol of the hospital's commitment to treating the whole person, not just the disease. It reminded everyone—patients and staff alike—that healing isn't just about medicine and treatments. Sometimes it's about helping someone see their beauty and worth, even during their hardest battle. For the women fighting cancer, the wig closet wasn't just a place to find a wig—it was a place where they rediscovered their strength, their identity, and their courage to keep fighting. They found their own beauty within the wig closet.

Quote

"You gain strength, courage, and confidence by every experience in which you really stop to look fear in the face. You are able to say to yourself, 'I lived through this horror. I can take the next thing that comes along.'" —Eleanor Roosevelt (First Lady of the United States from 1933 to 1945)[20]

Scripture

"Be strong and of a good courage; be not afraid, neither be thou dismayed: for the Lord thy God is with thee whithersoever thou goest." (Joshua 1:9)

Lesson Learned

Courage is one of the most essential traits for personal growth and living a fulfilling life. It is the quality that enables individuals to confront fear, uncertainty, and challenges head-on. Without courage, fear can become paralyzing, preventing progress and keeping us confined to the safety of the known. Developing courage empowers us to take risks, face adversity, and pursue our goals with determination, even when the outcome is uncertain. It is the foundation of resilience, helping us rise after failure and persevere through trials.

Life often requires stepping outside of our comfort zones to achieve our dreams or embrace new opportunities. Whether it's starting a new career, building a relationship, or standing up for our values, courage allows us to confront the discomfort and uncertainty that accompany change. By consistently choosing courage over fear, we grow stronger, more confident, and more capable of handling life's complexities.

Developing courage is crucial for achieving personal integrity. It allows us to stay true to our beliefs and values, even when it's inconvenient or unpopular. Courage helps us to resist peer pressure, overcome self-doubt, and make decisions that align with our principles.

Everyone experiences fear at some point, but those who cultivate courage learn to face it and grow from it. Developing courage is a lifelong journey that requires practice, self-awareness, and a willingness to take small steps forward, even when fear looms large. Courage, ultimately, is the catalyst for transformation and the key to facing life's many challenges.

Challenge

Developing courage in life is a process that requires intention, practice, and patience. One of the first steps in cultivating courage is to recognize and acknowledge our fears. Often, we try to avoid fear, believing it's a sign of weakness. Instead of allowing fear to paralyze us, we can approach it with curiosity, asking ourselves, "What am I truly afraid of, and why?" It's okay to feel fear, but you can be brave at the same time; that's what courage is.

Another powerful way to develop courage is by taking small, manageable risks. Courage doesn't have to come in grand gestures or monumental decisions. It often shows up in the small acts of daily life, speaking up in a meeting, offering a kind word to someone in need, or trying something new, even if it feels uncomfortable. By starting small, we build confidence in our ability to face challenges. Over time, these small acts of bravery accumulate, and we find ourselves able to tackle larger challenges with greater ease.

Another essential aspect of developing courage is learning to embrace failure as part of the process. Fear of failure is one of the biggest barriers to courage, but failure is not the end; it's an opportunity to learn and grow. We can also develop courage by surrounding ourselves with supportive people who encourage and inspire us. It's easy to be intimidated or discouraged when we're isolated, but when we're part of a community that values growth and bravery, it becomes easier to take risks.

Cultivating self-belief is vital for courage to flourish. We can start by reminding ourselves of past successes, focusing on our strengths, and affirming our worth. You've got this!

Decision-Making

Story

I can't help but smile when I think back on one of the most formative lessons my father taught me. It's a lesson that has stuck with me throughout my life and one I still rely on every day when making decisions. I was young at the time, probably no older than eight or nine. It happened during one of our rare formal family home evenings, those cherished moments when we would gather as a family for a gospel lesson and discussion. On this particular evening, my dad had something in store that would shape my approach to decision-making forever.

He came into the room with a big chalkboard in hand, and I remember being intrigued, wondering what he was about to do. My dad had this way of turning even the simplest moments into something memorable. That night, he drew a big line down the middle of the board. At the top, he wrote "Pros" on one side, and on the other side, he wrote "Cons." I had never heard those words before, so I was curious as to what they meant. He went on to explain that "pros" were the positive elements of a decision, and "cons" were the negative aspects.

Then, he went on to teach us how to apply this idea to making choices. He asked us to think of a decision we were facing at the time, something small but important enough to warrant some reflection. As kids, our decisions might have seemed trivial—whether to do our chores first or play outside, whether to snag a cookie before dinner or wait for dessert—but my dad wanted us to understand that even the smallest decisions could shape our lives in ways we couldn't always predict. And so he led us through the process of brainstorming the pros and cons of different choices.

We began by considering the positives of making one choice over another—what would it lead to, how would it make us feel, and what would we gain? On the flip side, he had us go through the same process about the negative ramifications of our choice. It was an eye-opening experience for me, realizing that sometimes the choices we make aren't always as straightforward as they seem at first glance. There are layers of impact, many of which we might overlook if we don't take a moment to think them through.

As we moved through the lesson, my dad showed us how to weigh the pros and cons. He gave us examples from his own life and encouraged us to consider the bigger picture when making decisions. He emphasized that while it's easy to get caught up in what might be immediately fun or gratifying, it's the decisions that may not be the easiest in the moment that can have the most positive long-term impact. This lesson wasn't just about making good choices; it was about understanding the ripple effects of our decisions.

It didn't take long for me to realize just how valuable this lesson was. Whether I was deciding how to handle a disagreement with a friend, figuring out how to prioritize my time, or weighing an important life decision in adulthood, I would often find myself pulling out a piece of paper to write down the pros and cons list. I learned that by simply stepping back and analyzing all the factors, both big and small, I could make more informed, thoughtful decisions.

Quote

"In the long run, we shape our lives, and we shape ourselves. The process never ends until we die. And the choices we make are ultimately our own responsibility." —Eleanor Roosevelt (First Lady of the United States from 1933 to 1945)[21]

Scripture

"If any of you lack wisdom, let him ask of God." (James 1:5)

Lesson Learned

Combining reason with prayer brings clarity to choices. It's important to slow down and think things through. We often rush into decisions without fully understanding the potential outcomes. Even small decisions can have significant consequences. My dad didn't just ask us to think about the immediate pros and cons; he encouraged us to consider the long-term impact of our choices.

The lesson of considering both the pros and cons of a situation has also taught me about balance. It's easy to focus solely on what we stand to gain, but my father showed me that it's equally important to consider the drawbacks.

In addition, the process of making a pros and cons list has taught me how to prioritize values. It's easy to get overwhelmed by emotions or external pressures when faced with a decision. But by breaking down the decision into its components, I've learned to clarify what really matters. This approach has helped me cut through the noise and focus on what's truly important. Whether it's a personal decision or a professional one, clarity allows me to make decisions that align with my values and long-term goals.

Perhaps one of the most valuable lessons I took from that night is the power of self-reflection. My dad didn't just teach us how to make decisions; he taught us how to think critically about our own desires and motivations. Why do we want something? What's driving our decision? These are the kinds of questions that help us make better choices, not just by looking at the external factors but by understanding our internal motivations.

Challenge

Create a pros and cons list for a decision you're currently facing. Consider the weight of each item on both sides, assigning a number from 1 to 10 on how it aligns with your values and what you want most. The side with the highest number is usually the best choice, but the process isn't done yet. Take your decision to the Lord and then pray for guidance and assurance that you've made the best choice.

Digging Deeper

Story

A friend of mine had an enlightening and amusing conversation with one of her daughters. She asked her daughter in college, "If you could get paid to do anything, what would you want to do with your life?" Her very talented daughter thought for a minute and then said, "Mom, I just want to watch Netflix all day." Yeah, I think we've all felt like that at times! Of course, we all need to have relaxing "downtime" in order to recharge. Even a rubber band stretched at full capacity for too long will eventually break. But at some point, that rubber band needs to get back to doing its job and living the purpose of its creation in order to feel fulfilled. (I know that rubber bands don't have feelings, but you get my point, right?)

One of my sons discovered one of the secrets to happiness when he was a teenager. He came home from school tired and ready for a nap. I was surprised to see him a few minutes later in his workout clothes, headed out the door. I said, "Oh! I thought you were going to take a nap!" He proudly shared with me, "Mom, I've learned that if I go to the gym, even when I'm super tired, I end up with way more energy than if I had taken a nap, and I also feel better because I've accomplished one of my goals." Bingo! I was super impressed for about ten minutes, and then I sat down to watch Netflix. (No, I'm just kidding, but I sure wanted to.)

Quote

"Continuous effort—not strength or intelligence—is the key to unlocking our potential." —Winston Churchill (British statesman, military leader, writer, and Prime Minister of the United Kingdom during World War II)[22]

Scripture

"Verily I say, men should be anxiously engaged in a good cause, and do many things of their own free will, and bring to pass much righteousness." (Doctrine and Covenants 58:27)

Lesson Learned

Reaching your goals isn't just about talent or luck. It's about digging deeper, pushing past obstacles, and refusing to quit when things get tough. Success rarely comes easy; it demands persistence, hard work, and a willingness to stretch beyond your comfort zone.

Think of a miner searching for gold—if they stop digging just a few feet too soon, they might miss the treasure completely. The same applies to our dreams. When challenges arise, it's easy to feel discouraged, but those who keep going despite setbacks are the ones who ultimately achieve great things. Whether it's mastering a new skill, growing spiritually, or achieving a lifelong ambition, the key is to keep digging, keep believing, and keep working—because the breakthrough often comes right after the hardest struggle.

Challenge

Decide which activities relax you or reenergize you. Make a list and refer to them when you need to do one or the other. Be aware of how you spend your time and energy. Next to that list, write down the things you truly want in life so that when you think you want to take a break, you're reminded of your priorities. You just might decide that digging deeper will get you that thing faster than taking a break.

Divine Intervention

Story

When I was newly married, I had a lot more "free time" than I do now, when every moment feels like a juggling act. One Saturday morning, I woke up with a slow, easy plan: a leisurely breakfast followed by a peaceful trip to the temple. I was feeling pretty relaxed about the whole thing, like this was going to be one of those mornings when I had all the time in the world to enjoy the long car ride and even stroll around the beautiful temple grounds when I got there.

But then, out of nowhere, I felt a sense of urgency. A voice in my head said, "You need to get there faster." It was like someone had pressed the "hurry up" button in my brain. I glanced at the clock. I had plenty of time, more than enough time. So why did I suddenly feel like I was in a race against the clock?

I shook it off as just a random feeling and headed out the door. But once I was in the car, things got even stranger. I found my foot pushing the accelerator down a little too hard, making the car go faster than I normally would. It was like I couldn't stop myself, even though I knew there was no reason to rush. My mind kept trying to catch up with my foot, asking, "Why the hurry? Slow down!" But my body wasn't listening.

I pulled into the parking lot and walked toward the temple entrance, trying to shake off the weird sensation that had been hanging over me. And then it happened. As soon as I stepped through the doors, several temple workers came straight toward me with the kind of hopeful expression you usually see when someone is about to ask for a favor. They barely let me catch my breath before one of them asked, "Do you speak Spanish?"

I had served a mission in Spain and excitedly said, "Yes! I speak Spanish!" It turns out they needed me to help a sweet woman who had traveled all the way from Mexico to do temple work for her grandmother. She was there to complete the entire process: baptism, confirmation, initiatory, endowment, and sealing. It was a big task, and she was understandably a little nervous and overwhelmed.

I spent the entire day with her, guiding her through the sacred ordinances and helping her feel comfortable and needed in the temple. It was one of those moments that felt so divinely orchestrated that I couldn't help but marvel at how Heavenly Father works. He knew I was available, and He knew exactly what this sweet woman needed. He also knew how to get us together—even if it meant speeding me up without my understanding why.

I still laugh about it, thinking about how I was trying to have a "relaxing" morning and instead got a personalized experience to a perfect example of how Heavenly Father works in ways we don't always expect. If I hadn't felt the promptings, I might have missed the opportunity to help this sweet sister and get a front-row seat to watch the Lord work in our lives. The whole experience taught me a valuable lesson: Sometimes when life doesn't make sense or we feel pushed to do something that feels out of the ordinary, it could very well mean that it's because we're needed for something far greater than we realize.

Quote

"God moves in a mysterious way, His wonders to perform." —William Cowper (poet and hymn writer)[23]

Scripture

"Trust in the Lord with all thine heart; and lean not unto thine own understanding. In all thy ways acknowledge him, and he shall direct thy paths." (Proverbs 3:5–6)

Lesson Learned

Divine intervention is the unseen hand of God guiding, protecting, and shaping our lives in ways we may not always recognize at the moment. Sometimes it comes as a miraculous event: a life saved, a problem solved just in time, or an unexpected opportunity that changes everything. Other times, it's the quiet whisper of inspiration, the right person appearing when we need them most, or a series of small moments that, in hindsight, were anything but coincidence.

When we trust in God and seek His guidance, we open ourselves to His divine influence, knowing that He sees the full picture even when we don't. Life's twists and turns can be uncertain, but with faith, we can move forward knowing that God is always working behind the scenes for our good.

Challenge

One powerful way to recognize divine intervention in your life is to keep a daily gratitude and reflection journal. At the end of each day, take a few minutes to write down moments when things worked out unexpectedly, when you felt peace in a difficult situation, or when someone showed up at just the right time. Over time, you'll start to see patterns of God's hand in your life—small miracles, guiding impressions, or blessings you may have otherwise overlooked. The more you actively look for His presence, the more you'll realize He has been there all along.

Like Nephi's smaller plates, I keep a separate journal where I only write about my spiritual experiences where I feel God's hand in my life. Divine intervention is a reminder that we were never truly alone. One of the challenges in life is to remember to extend that same mercy and grace to others when they have imperfect moments too.

Divine Mercy

Story

The following story is about my brother-in-law, who served a full-time mission in Montana. I asked him to tell his story in his own words.

Serving a mission in Montana was like living in a never-ending episode of *Survivor,* the kind where you're always trekking across miles of open fields and winding country roads, trying to spread the gospel to people who may or may not still think it's the 1800s. The days were long, the driving was endless, and the work was wonderful but hard. But hey, at least we always had the beautiful Montana landscape as a backdrop to our adventures.

One of my companions—a big guy from Georgia who looked like he could've played linebacker in the NFL—was not someone you'd want to mess with. His sheer presence made sure that no one would dare to mock or intimidate us. He was the kind of guy who could make a cow back down just by glaring at it. But despite his intimidating exterior, he was a softy at heart, always trying to do what was right and follow the rules, even when exhaustion had us both running on fumes.

One particularly grueling day, after a full stretch of traveling, knocking on doors, and walking through mud, my companion, who was at the wheel, started to nod off. Maybe it was the quiet hum of the car or the warm sun shining through the windows, but his eyes closed, and just like that—*bam*, he was out cold at a red light. I was too.

Now here's the alarming and amusing part: His foot was still resting lightly on the accelerator, and without realizing it, our car gave a gentle nudge to the vehicle in front of us. Guess who that vehicle belonged to? Yep, a State Trooper.

The officer immediately stepped out of his vehicle, waking both of us up to the world's most intense flash of blue lights, almost as if they were shining directly from heaven itself. My companion blinked a few times, trying to figure out where he was, and then realized . . . *uh oh* . . . we had just rear-ended a cop. The sound of his boots hitting the pavement startled and worried us. We were both living on a meager missionary's budget and couldn't afford to pay for a traffic ticket. What if our mission president heard about this? Would we be sent home? We both felt terrified and completely unprepared to handle an encounter with the law.

The trooper walked over to the window with a cranky yet entertained look that said, "You guys are in trouble." But as soon as he saw us—two young "Mormon" missionaries in suits, completely out of place in rural Montana—his face softened. He glanced at us, probably wondering how we could possibly cause any real trouble, and gave us the kindest, most understanding smile.

"I see you two have good work to do," he said, "so I'll let you go."

No ticket, no lecture, just a kind reminder that sometimes, even when you're clearly in the wrong, things have a way of working out. We may have been exhausted and in the wrong place at the wrong time, but the officer saw what we were really about and decided to show us a little mercy.

It was a humbling experience and a reminder that even the most tired, mistake-prone missionaries can sometimes catch a break . . . especially when they're in the presence of divine mercy (and a very understanding State Trooper).

Quote

"The mercy of God is an ocean divine, a boundless and fathomless flood." —Albert B. Simpson (Canadian preacher, theologian, and author)[24]

Scripture

"It is of the Lord's mercies that we are not consumed, because his compassions fail not. They are new every morning: great is thy faithfulness." (Lamentations 3:22–23)

Lesson Learned

Divine mercy is a reminder that no matter how far we may stray, God's love and compassion are always within reach. His mercy is not given based on our worthiness but out of His infinite grace, offering us forgiveness, hope, and a fresh start each day. Just as the sun rises anew every morning, His mercies are constantly renewed, providing strength in our weaknesses and light in our darkest moments.

When we turn to Him with a humble heart, we can experience the peace and healing that only His mercy can bring. Trusting in divine mercy allows us to extend that same grace to others, creating a ripple effect of kindness and love in the world. When we do what's right, everything will work out for good in the end.

Challenge

One way to feel divine mercy in your life is to practice daily repentance and gratitude. Take a few moments each day to reflect on your actions, sincerely ask for God's forgiveness where needed, and express gratitude for His love and mercy. This simple practice helps you recognize His hand in your life, feel His compassion, and embrace the peace that comes from knowing that no mistake is beyond His grace. Extend that grace to those around you too.

Divine grace and mercy are the unearned gifts that lift us when we fall, offering forgiveness and renewal—not because we deserve it but because we're loved beyond measure.

Education

Story

When I was growing up, my dad always emphasized the importance of education. He had four kids, and from the time we were little, he planted the seed in each of us: "Get a college education." It wasn't just a suggestion; it was a cornerstone of his guidance.

One of my earliest memories is of him graduating with an MBA. I was very young, and though I didn't fully understand what it meant, I knew it was significant. I remember feeling proud as I watched him in his cap and gown, holding his diploma. It left a mark on me. Even at that tender age, I sensed that education was important, not just for him but for all of us.

My dad had a simple but firm rule: Graduate from college before doing anything else. That included getting a degree before marriage, before serving a mission, before anything else. That might seem unreasonable, but he was adamant that a solid education would be the foundation for everything that followed. Watching him pursue his own education while juggling work, bills, and family made his advice resonate with us kids.

He was especially insistent that his daughters earn their college degrees. He explained that we would need to be able to support ourselves financially if we suddenly became a widow, got divorced, or lost our job. It made sense to me, although I never thought any of those things could actually happen to us. His wisdom astounded us when all those things really did occur in our family.

Years later, I met up with a childhood friend for dinner. As we reminisced about growing up, she said something that stayed with me. "I wish I had a father like yours," she confessed. "He taught you to go to college. I never had anyone push or encourage me like that, and so I never went to college. Now I really regret it." Her words hit me hard. I realized just how fortunate I was to have a dad who instilled in us the value of education and the drive to pursue it.

All four of us kids followed his advice. Not only did we earn bachelor's degrees, but we all went on to achieve advanced degrees: master's and doctoral degrees. When we told my dad about our academic pursuits, he laughed and said, "Hey, I never said I was going to pay for anything beyond a bachelor's degree!"

Despite his joking, it was clear that he was proud of us. What he had given us was far more valuable than financial support. He had ingrained in us a love for knowledge and an understanding of the doors that education could open. It wasn't about titles or credentials; it was about equipping ourselves to contribute meaningfully to the world and to have the confidence to chase our dreams.

My dad's insistence on education wasn't just a lesson; it was a legacy. His example and guidance didn't just shape our futures; they shaped who we are today. And for that, I will always be grateful. Getting an education is investing in yourself and your future.

Quote

"Education is the most powerful weapon which you can use to change the world." —Nelson Mandela (president of South Africa from 1994 to 1999)[25]

Scripture

"Seek ye out of the best books words of wisdom; seek learning, even by study and also by faith." (Doctrine and Covenants 88:118)

Lesson Learned

A college education and a commitment to lifelong learning are two of the most valuable investments an individual can make in their personal and professional development. These pursuits not only unlock a wealth of knowledge but also pave the way for a fulfilling and prosperous life. In today's rapidly changing world, the importance of acquiring skills, education, and a passion for continuous learning cannot be overstated.

Most companies require their employees to take continuous education classes, attend seminars, or earn specialized certifications in order to stay competitive in today's quickly evolving world. Whether it's through a university experience, a trade school, or an apprenticeship, continued education introduces students to diverse perspectives, cultures, and ideas that they might not encounter otherwise. Through exposure to various disciplines, students develop critical thinking skills and learn to analyze issues from multiple viewpoints. This intellectual growth not only enriches their personal lives but also prepares them to navigate the complexities of the modern world.

Mark Twain, who was an American writer, humorist, entrepreneur, and lecturer stated, "A person who won't read has no advantage over one who can't read."[26] I also love these powerful words I read on an educational poster once:

> The more you read,
> the more you know.
> The more you know,
> the smarter you grow.
> The smarter you grow,
> the stronger your voice,
> when speaking your mind
> or making your choice.[27]

A college degree has long been associated with better job prospects and higher earning potential. According to numerous studies, individuals with a college education earn significantly more over their lifetimes than those without. Beyond financial benefits, a degree often opens doors to more fulfilling and intellectually stimulating careers. Many professions require specialized knowledge that can only be acquired through higher education, making college a crucial step for those aiming to achieve their career aspirations.

One of the most important things going to college teaches you is how to learn. It inspires you to want to learn!

Challenge

The Church of Jesus Christ of Latter-day Saints is so passionate about lifelong learning that it has empowered Brigham Young University to reach out to students of all ages and all over the world, encouraging them to enroll in the Pathway program, which offers certificates and degrees online at an impressively reduced price. BYU also offers Independent Study programs where high school students can simultaneously earn college credits online.

There are so many free ways to get an education today, no matter what you want to learn! Here are some options:

- **Coursera (coursera.org):** Free courses from top universities like Stanford and Yale (pay only for certificates).
- **edX (edx.org):** Harvard, MIT, and more offer free classes.
- **Khan Academy (khanacademy.org):** Great for math, science, history, and career skills.
- **MIT OpenCourseWare (ocw.mit.edu):** Free courses straight from MIT.
- **Harvard Online Courses (pll.harvard.edu):** Some Harvard courses are free!
- **Google Digital Garage (learndigital.withgoogle.com):** Learn digital marketing, coding, and business skills.
- **LinkedIn Learning (sometimes free with a library card):** Business, tech, and creative courses.
- **Codecademy (free tier) (codecademy.com):** Learn coding languages for free.
- **Duolingo (duolingo.com):** Learn a new language for free.
- **Google Scholar and YouTube Lectures:** Tons of university lectures are uploaded for free.

ENCOURAGEMENT

STORY

Earning a doctoral degree is no joke. It's a marathon of research, late nights, and moments when you seriously question why you ever thought this was a good idea. But one of the best parts of my program was the semiannual seminars—intense academic discussions mixed with the perk of staying in a resort hotel. It was a little like a sleepover for overachievers, complete with endless debates that could go from "casual" to "heated" in under sixty seconds.

One afternoon, I was deep in conversation with a classmate when he suddenly stopped mid-sentence, eyes wide like he had just remembered something life-altering. "Wait right here!" he said, then bolted up the stairs to his room.

I stood there, confused and mildly concerned. Did I have something in my teeth and he was going to bring back a toothbrush for me? Had I said something weird? Was he about to return with a whiteboard and a thesis rebuttal? A few minutes later, he came back, grinning from ear to ear, holding a small stuffed puppy dressed in a graduation cap and gown in our university's colors.

"This is for you," he said, proudly handing it over.

I stared at it, speechless. I mean, I wasn't about to turn down a free stuffed animal, but . . . why? He must have noticed my confusion because he quickly explained, "I bought this before the seminar, planning to give it to someone who truly loved learning. And that's you!"

I was floored. First, because he had thought ahead to bring a gift for someone just in case. How thoughtful! And second, he chose me to be the recipient of his kindness! In a room full of brilliant minds, he had noticed my enthusiasm for learning and wanted to celebrate it. Amazing!

That tiny stuffed puppy instantly became one of my most treasured possessions. I kept it on my desk throughout my doctoral journey to inspire me. It's still sitting on my desk! On the days when my motivation wavered, I'd glance at that little scholar pup and remember why I wanted to earn my doctorate. It also reminded me that kindness and enthusiasm go hand in hand and that sometimes, the smallest gestures make the biggest impact.

Years later, I still want to be like that classmate: someone who not only embraces learning but also finds small, meaningful ways to lift others along the way. Because if a stuffed puppy can get me through a grueling doctorate program, surely I could think of something kind that would encourage someone else in this world to reach their goals.

Quote

"A word of encouragement during a failure is worth more than an hour of praise after success." —Unknown[28]

Scripture

"Wherefore comfort yourselves together, and edify one another, even as also ye do." (1 Thessalonians 5:11)

Lesson Learned

Theodore Roosevelt, who was the twenty-sixth president of the United States stated, "Believe you can and you're halfway there."[29] Your mind is a powerful thing. When you fill it with positive thoughts, your life will start to change. I've been teaching at universities for fifteen years and love it. It breaks my heart when students reveal they were told by someone that they were not "college material," so they doubted their ability or wanted to give up.

Sometimes, I feel like my role is more of a cheerleader than a teacher. I'm constantly trying to encourage my students to just take it one day at a time so they're not so overwhelmed. I think we all need a loving cheerleader in our corner, someone who loves us and reminds us that we can do it.

Challenge

Today, try to be that cheerleader for a friend or family member. Your kind words may be just the motivation they need to keep going. You can also be that cheerleader for yourself by repeating positive "I am" statements inside your heart. Replace your negative self-talk with empowering words like "I am smart" or "I am a hard worker and deserve success." We believe the things we tell ourselves, so be gentle with yourself.

If you need an extra dose of encouragement and motivation, check out some of these outstanding YouTube channels:

- **Be Inspired:** This channel features motivational speeches, inspiring stories, and positive content to uplift and encourage viewers.
- **Jay Shetty:** Jay Shetty is a former monk who shares wisdom on mindfulness, relationships, and personal growth, often offering practical advice on how to live a more fulfilling life.
- **Team Fearless:** Team Fearless creates videos that focus on personal development, self-belief, and the importance of taking action toward your goals.
- **Mel Robbins:** Mel Robbins provides motivational talks and strategies to overcome self-doubt, fear, and procrastination, empowering viewers to take charge of their lives.
- **Brendon Burchard:** Brendon shares high-performance habits and personal development techniques designed to help people achieve their goals and live a motivated life.
- **Marie Forleo:** Marie offers motivational content focused on entrepreneurship, creativity, and living a purposeful life, encouraging viewers to follow their passions. (She has a bit of a potty mouth sometimes . . . fair warning.)
- **The Mindful Coach:** This channel combines mindfulness and tech strategies, offering tips for staying positive, focused, and grounded in a digital world.

- **TEDx Talks:** While not exclusively motivational, TEDx Talks feature speakers from diverse backgrounds who share powerful stories of overcoming challenges, making them a great source of inspiration.
- **Simon Sinek:** He's an unshakable optimist who believes in a bright future and our ability to build it together.
- **The Diary of a CEO:** He's a young entrepreneur, author, and podcaster known for his work in personal development and business.

Excuses

Story

Florence Nightingale was born into a wealthy, aristocratic family in 1820. She could have easily lived a life of luxury, sipping tea in elegant drawing rooms, attending social events, and adorning herself in the finest gowns in England. But instead, she felt a calling in her heart, a calling that would not only redefine her life but also transform the world of healthcare forever.

Rather than pursuing the comforts and status that her position in society afforded her, Nightingale chose to dedicate herself to the care of others. She could have used the excuse that it wasn't appropriate for a woman of her status to become a nurse. Instead, during the Crimean War, she volunteered to manage and train nurses to care for British soldiers, making her way to Turkey, where the battlefield hospitals were notorious for their horrific conditions.

She could have given the excuse that she didn't belong in the hospitals because they were overcrowded, filthy, and riddled with disease. Instead, Nightingale's heart broke as she witnessed the conditions, and she was horrified by the lack of proper care.

She could have made the excuse that someone else would take care of the problems, but instead, she took immediate action. She fought to improve the sanitation in the hospitals, arguing for better hygiene, cleaner bedding, and fresh air—simple changes that could drastically reduce the spread of disease. Her boldness and determination were instrumental in saving countless lives.

She also insisted on keeping detailed records of the soldiers' conditions, something that was unheard of at the time. She worked tirelessly, often under the harshest conditions, to bring order to the chaos and show that care, compassion, and science could save lives.

She could have given the excuse that she couldn't make a contribution in a field dominated by men, especially by doctors who often doubted women's abilities to manage reports or handle numbers, but instead, Nightingale defied expectations. She proved not only that she was capable of handling complex data but that her approach to health care was revolutionary. Her skillful use of statistics to track mortality rates, particularly her famous "coxcomb" diagrams, demonstrated the clear correlation between sanitation and health. Her statistical analysis was instrumental in shaping public health policy, and her work is credited with helping to reduce the death rate in military hospitals by two-thirds.

In 1858, Nightingale became the first woman to be elected a fellow of the Royal Statistical Society, a prestigious acknowledgment of her groundbreaking work in the field of statistics. At a time when it was believed that women were ill-suited for analytical or scientific roles, Florence Nightingale shattered that stereotype and proved herself a brilliant and innovative thinker.

Nightingale's influence wasn't just felt during the war. She became a pioneer in nursing education, founding the first secular nursing school in the world in 1860 at St. Thomas's Hospital in London. This laid the foundation for modern nursing as a profession. She is often referred to as the "Lady with the Lamp" because when the workday was over, she continued working through the night to check on her patients while carrying a lamp through the dark halls and rooms. Many nursing colleges award their graduating students with a small lamp to inspire them in their careers. Sweet, right?

Now read the quote below to see how Florence Nightingale became so successful.

Quote

"I attribute my success to this: I never gave or took any excuse." —Florence Nightingale (British social reformer and the "Mother of Nursing")[30]

Scripture

"And Moses said unto the Lord, O my Lord, I am not eloquent, neither heretofore, nor since thou hast spoken unto thy servant: but I am slow of speech, and of a slow tongue. And the Lord said unto him, Who hath made man's mouth? or who maketh the dumb, or deaf, or the seeing, or the blind? have not I the Lord? Now therefore go, and I will be with thy mouth, and teach thee what thou shalt say." (Exodus 4:10–12)

Lesson Learned

Excuses are the enemy of progress. When we justify inaction with reasons like "I'm too busy," "I'm not talented enough," or "I'll start tomorrow," we rob ourselves of growth and opportunity. The truth is that no one ever achieved greatness by waiting for perfect conditions. Success comes to those who push forward despite obstacles.

Challenge

Instead of making excuses, find solutions. If you don't have time, make time. If you lack skill, learn and practice. If fear is holding you back, take one small step forward anyway. Life rewards action, not excuses, so stop waiting and start doing!

While growing up, my siblings and I would often complain when something was hard. When our dad would say, "Suck it up!" we just thought he was mean. He was right though. Chris Fussell is a former US Navy SEAL who wrote a book called *Embrace the Suck.* My dad would have loved that book. Read it!

Fussell uses the phrase "embrace the suck" to refer to the mentality of accepting the tough and uncomfortable challenges that often cause us to use excuses to stop working or trying. The phrase embodies the mindset that discomfort and adversity are part of growth and accomplishment. No more excuses!

Fear

Story

Nelson Mandela's name is synonymous with strength, resilience, and an unwavering commitment to justice. As the first Black head of state and the first person elected in a fully representative democratic election in South Africa, he transformed a nation deeply divided by racial oppression. But his journey to leadership was anything but easy. It was marked by hardship, sacrifice, fear, and a relentless fight against injustice.

From the 1950s to the 1960s, Mandela was repeatedly arrested for his political activism against the apartheid government. His resistance to racial segregation and his call for equality made him a target of the oppressive regime. Despite numerous arrests, he refused to back down, knowing that his cause was greater than his personal freedom. In 1964, he was convicted of sabotage and sentenced to life in prison. Fear of the unknown and what his ultimate fate would be must have been overwhelming.

For the first eighteen of his twenty-seven years behind bars, he was confined to a tiny, cold prison cell on Robben Island, so small that he could barely stretch out. He slept on the floor, had no plumbing, and was forced into grueling labor, breaking rocks in a limestone quarry under the blinding sun. His life was stripped to the bare minimum. He was allowed to write and receive only one letter every six months, and once a year, he was granted a single thirty-minute visit with a loved one.

Can you imagine the isolation? The deprivation? The mental and physical toll? The unending fear and uncertainty? Any ordinary person would have been consumed by anger, resentment, and a thirst for revenge. And no one would have blamed him if he had emerged from prison bitter and hardened.

But Mandela chose a different path. Instead of clinging to hatred or fear, he chose forgiveness. Instead of seeking revenge, he sought reconciliation. When he was finally released in 1990, he walked out of prison not as a broken man but as a symbol of hope. He understood that fear was natural, but he refused to let it control him. He famously said, "I have walked that long road to freedom. I have tried not to falter; I have made missteps along the way. But I have discovered the secret that after climbing a great hill, one only finds that there are many more hills to climb."[31]

Mandela went on to lead South Africa out of apartheid, not by fueling division but by advocating for unity. He proved that courage isn't the absence of fear—it's acting in spite of it. His life is a testament to the idea that even in the face of unimaginable hardship and fear, we always have a choice. We can let our struggles make us bitter, or we can use them to become better. Mandela chose the latter, and in doing so, he changed history.

After all of that, what did Nelson Mandela have to say about fear? Keep reading!

Quote

"I learned that courage was not the absence of fear but the triumph over it. The brave man is not he who does not feel afraid but he who conquers that fear." —Nelson Mandela (president of South Africa from 1994 to 1999)[32]

Scripture

"For God hath not given us the spirit of fear; but of power, and of love, and of a sound mind." (2 Timothy 1:7)

Lesson Learned

Fear is a natural human emotion, but it can also be a barrier that holds us back from growth, happiness, and success. When we let fear control our decisions, we miss out on opportunities and experiences that could shape us for the better. However, fear is not from God. God gives us power, love, and a sound mind to overcome our worries. The key to conquering fear is faith: faith in God, faith in ourselves, and faith in the possibilities ahead. Instead of letting fear paralyze us, we should use it as a signal to trust, step forward, and embrace the unknown with courage.

Challenge

Be brave. If you want to do something but it's super scary, do it anyway. One way to overcome fear is to take small, intentional steps outside your comfort zone. Fear often grows when we avoid what scares us, but facing it little by little helps build confidence. If you're afraid of doing something, so what? Do it anyway!

If public speaking makes you nervous, start by speaking up in small group discussions. If you're afraid of failure, set a small goal and celebrate progress rather than perfection. Each step forward weakens fear's grip and strengthens your courage. Over time, what once seemed terrifying becomes manageable, and you prove to yourself that you're stronger than your fears.

Finding Your Purpose

Story

I absolutely love food. I used to teach classes at the world-famous Le Cordon Bleu Culinary College, and I have the weight gain to prove it. Sadly, the cooking school closed in the United States while I was teaching there, although the one in Paris is still going strong. It's quite expensive and the students would often go into serious debt to attend college there. In fact, the school where I taught in Las Vegas spent $50,000 a year on butter alone! Awww, French cooking!

One day, a young student admitted to me that she thought she made a terrible mistake. She decided that cooking wasn't her passion after all, and she didn't want to be a chef anymore. She felt guilty that she had wasted so much time and money. She worried what the teachers and other students would think of her for quitting. She wondered what her true purpose in life was.

I gave her a hug and assured her that it was okay to take some wrong turns on her journey of self-discovery. I explained that now she knows what she doesn't want to do and be, and that's good information! The process of elimination can be extremely helpful on your journey to self-discovery.

Figuring out who you are and what you want takes time and practice. You have to be willing to make mistakes to get to the answer. If you still don't know what you want to be when you grow up, relax. For most of us, it takes a lifetime to discover who we really are.

The truth is that you don't have just one purpose for your life. You will have many as you go through different phases, such as childhood, going to school, serving a mission, marriage, your career, raising a family, and so on. The Lord gives you clues in your heart and in your patriarchal blessing as you go through each phase of your life. Listen and talk to Him about it!

Quote

"The two most important days in your life are the day you are born and the day you find out why." —Mark Twain (American writer, humorist, and lecturer)[33]

Scripture

"Wherefore, the Lord God gave unto man that he should act for himself. Wherefore, man could not act for himself save it should be that he was enticed by the one or the other." (2 Nephi 2:16)

Lesson Learned

Finding your purpose in life is a journey of self-discovery, faith, and perseverance. It's not about waiting for a grand revelation but about actively seeking what brings you joy, fulfillment, and a sense of contribution to the world. Purpose is often found in service, growth, and aligning your life with your values and beliefs. It may take time, trial, and error, but each experience—both successes and failures—shapes and refines your understanding of why you're here. When you trust that God has a plan for you and take steps forward with faith, you'll find that your purpose unfolds naturally, guiding you toward a life of meaning and impact.

Challenge

Be anxiously engaged in discovering your talents and purpose for life. One way people can find their purpose in life is by trying new things. Be brave and explore all your options! Serving others can help you discover what lights your fire. When you focus on helping, uplifting, and making a difference in the lives of those around you, you gain clarity about what truly matters.

Reaching out to others for mentorship and experiences allows you to discover your strengths, develop new skills, and see the impact you can have on the world. Studying your patriarchal blessing and spending time in prayer can reveal passions and callings you may not have recognized before. Often, our greatest purpose is found in how we bless the lives of others.

It's important to note that your life doesn't have just one purpose. Your age and stage of life naturally present different purposes, so don't feel lost, thinking you can only have one. You are much more layered and complex than that!

Some people take a "gap year" with the hope of finding themselves—traveling, relaxing, or just stepping away from responsibility to figure out who they are or what they want in life. While a short pause can offer clarity, many end up drifting through that year with no real plan, hoping that purpose will somehow fall into their laps. But in reality, identity and direction don't usually emerge from prolonged waiting or soul-searching—they're discovered through action.

Clarity comes from doing. You learn who you are by trying things, facing challenges, working through discomfort, and seeing how you respond. Sitting still or wandering aimlessly might feel freeing at first, but it often leads to more confusion, not less. Forward motion—whether through work, study, service, or building something meaningful—creates momentum. As the saying goes, "Action brings insight." If you want to find yourself, don't waste a year hoping life will reveal your path. Start moving, and the path will start revealing itself.

Food Memories

Story

Surprise dinners were always the most fun meals when I was young, although often the least nutritious! Each "chef" in our family was given a generous five-dollar bill (back then it *was* generous) to spend however our culinary hearts imagined, and then we were allotted secret time in the kitchen to prepare a masterpiece that would be added to the family meal. This activity promoted mysterious creativity in the kitchen and thriftiness at the checkout counter, both of which my husband is grateful that I have, even to this day!

Every time I cook a semi-decent meal and get compliments from a grateful family member, I think of all the burnt dinners my patient parents had to endure while we kids learned how to cook. They put up with a lot of experimentation and almost always ate everything on their plates with a smile. Their critiques were always gentle and very important to the four young blooming gourmets who tried so hard to cook good meals.

The best culinary custom our parents invented was the applause and standing ovation that the cook would receive at the end of dinner for a job well done. What a great tradition! Of course, the best compliment would be when my dad would say, "Isn't food wonderful?" It was and still is.

Many of my favorite memories involve food, and I think that's true for most people. There's something special about breaking bread with others that binds us closer to one another. Studies have even shown that families who eat daily meals together show higher levels of overall happiness than those who don't. Eating together has a magical way of making people open up to one another. Mealtime is sacred time.

A friend of mine once admitted to me that her family didn't have dinners together as often as she knew they should because everyone was always so busy, especially during those years with busy teenagers. One night, she gathered everyone to the dinner table, even though it was just three of them: her husband, her teenage son, and herself. It didn't take very long for her to see that there was something seriously wrong with her son while they began to eat together. He seemed really out of it, so she began to ask him questions about his day. Finally, she was brave enough to ask, "Are you on drugs?" thinking she just needed to rule out that ridiculous idea. She was shocked when he lowered his head and said, "Yes."

What seemed like "just" a dinner together became a medical emergency and a life-changing conversation with her son. She stayed up with him until 2:00 in the morning, monitoring his breathing, hugging him to assure him of her love, and having heart-to-heart talks about everything. It changed and deepened their relationship. Mealtime is sacred time.

Quote

"The family that eats together stays together." —Unknown[34]

Scripture

"Yea, all things which come of the earth, in the season thereof, are made for the benefit and the use of man, both to please the eye and to gladden the heart." (Doctrine and Covenants 59:18)

Lesson Learned

Having family dinners is an invaluable tradition that fosters connection, communication, and a sense of belonging. Sitting down together for a meal allows family members to share their day, discuss thoughts and feelings, and bond over shared experiences. These moments create opportunities for meaningful conversations, especially in a world where busy schedules often make it challenging to connect. The act of gathering around the table promotes a sense of unity, as it becomes a time to nurture relationships and strengthen emotional ties, making family members feel supported and valued.

In addition to the emotional benefits, family dinners also contribute to healthier eating habits and a sense of stability. Families who eat together are more likely to make nutritious choices and engage in mindful eating, as home-cooked meals tend to be more balanced than fast food options. The routine of sitting down to a meal together provides a predictable, comforting structure that can help children feel more secure, especially during times of stress or change. Ultimately, family dinners are more than just about the food—they're a space for love, support, and togetherness, creating lasting memories and a strong foundation for future generations.

Challenge

One way to make family dinners even more special is by introducing a "theme night" once a week, where each meal is inspired by a particular culture, holiday, or family tradition. This not only adds excitement to the dining experience but also opens up opportunities for learning and exploration.

For example, one night could be dedicated to Italian cuisine, complete with learning how to make homemade pasta together and entertaining each other with Italian accents, while another night could include mini umbrellas in tropical drinks while discussing favorite family memories from vacations. This can turn the meal into an event that everyone looks forward to, offering a chance to bond over the preparation and enjoyment of something new and creative. Take turns coming up with ideas; this isn't just Mom's job.

Another way to make family dinners more memorable is by implementing a "gratitude round" where each person shares something they're grateful for before the meal begins. This simple practice helps cultivate a positive atmosphere and fosters meaningful conversations. It encourages family members to reflect on the good moments of their day and express appreciation for one another. By making this a regular part of the dinner ritual, families can strengthen their emotional connections and set a tone of love and appreciation that transcends the meal itself.

A lot of families take turns having everyone share one thing they learned during the day, but that request can often be met with silence. When my kids were growing up, we found flashcards and books with "fun facts" that we'd take turns reading at meals. That always led to laughter and longer conversations.

Other ideas include:

- Ask each person to share one way they served or helped someone
- Encourage family members to constantly look for God's hand in their lives, invite everyone to share a miracle or tender mercy they experienced during the day
- To get the laughter rolling, play verbal games like "Would You Rather" where you give everyone two crazy options to choose between such as "Would you rather have to sing everything you say or dance everywhere you go?"

Friendship

Story

On many occasions, the little house I grew up in would be magically transformed into a Western saloon (complete with swinging doors), a tropical island, or a tennis lover's paradise. My parents didn't just have parties . . . they had extravaganzas! With just a little extra effort and some creativity, a simple party could become a magical moment in time and an escape from the everyday, common world. They loved creating fun events for their hardworking friends to enjoy. Life should be fun! Life is also too short to be so serious all the time.

I was always so impressed with the personalized invitations that my parents would so artistically and cleverly create to pass out to friends. I loved watching the guests enter our home, usually dressed in an appropriate costume to correspond with their theme for the event. They seemed to be having the time of their lives. The best sound was always my parents' laughter. I loved seeing them surrounded by their friends. It taught me how important it is to cherish friends and make time for them.

Sometimes, the parties were just for adults, so we would sneak our heads around the hallway wall to get a peek at the festivities and longingly wish for the day when we would be big enough to join in the fun. And sometimes my parents would give us the honor of being on the "planning committee" where we could see their creativity at work and contribute a few ideas of our own. One time, they even let us help cater the affair, a great privilege for us as teenagers . . . and a great risk for them!

One year at Christmastime, they hired the "Jazz Singers," a very expensive, famous, world-renowned choir . . . which their daughter sang in. (Okay, fine—it was just a small ensemble I was in during high school.) They were thrilled to donate funds to the school and entertain their party guests at the same time, all while giving their daughter some confidence and recognition.

They taught by example how important it is to savor every moment because every minute of our lives is worth celebrating. Those moments are even more cherished when shared with good friends. Friendship is the spice of life.

Quote

"A friend is someone who knows all about you and still loves you." —Elbert Hubbard (American writer, publisher, philosopher, and artist)[35]

Scripture

"A friend loveth at all times, and a brother is born for adversity." (Proverbs 17:17)

Lesson Learned

Friendships are some of the most valuable relationships we can cultivate in life. They provide a sense of belonging, offering emotional support through both the highs and lows of our experiences. True friends are the ones who understand us deeply and stand by us in times of need. Whether it's celebrating victories or facing challenges, a good friend offers encouragement, perspective, and reassurance. Friendships create a sense of connection, reminding us we're not alone in the world.

Through the exchange of ideas and experiences, we learn from one another. Friends challenge us to become better versions of ourselves, offering constructive feedback and holding us accountable. The bond we share with friends encourages us to embrace different viewpoints and understand diverse backgrounds, ultimately broadening our horizons. These relationships teach us empathy, kindness, and the value of compromise, making us more well-rounded individuals.

Friendship reminds us to enjoy the present moment, find joy in the little things, and not take life too seriously. A true friend helps us navigate life's uncertainties with optimism, offering a sense of comfort and safety.

I always encouraged my kids to throw parties at our house, and I enjoyed getting to meet their friends. Whenever I would suggest they invite a specific person I knew didn't get invited to parties very often, they would often hesitate and say, "But I don't know that person very well." I completely understood their reluctance, but I would tell them that's exactly why they should extend the invitation! That's how they could get to know people better and make more friends.

Challenge

Making friends as an adult can sometimes feel challenging. The key is putting yourself in situations where friendships can naturally form. Here are some great ways to build real connections with people:

- Engage in activities where you'll meet like-minded people.
- Join a club or group, like a book club, hiking group, or gaming community.
- Take a class, such as dance, art, cooking, or even a personal development course.
- Go to the gym or a sports league. Shared fitness goals create bonds.
- Volunteer. Helping others is a great way to meet kindhearted people.
- Be active in church activities or study groups.
- Be brave and make the first move. Text or call first; don't wait for others to reach out.

Gratitude

Story

My parents had a way of turning any gathering into something extraordinary. They were masters of hospitality, and their parties became the stuff of legend in our circle of friends and family. The effort they put into every event was impressive—everything from the elaborate invitations to the detailed decorations, to the entertainers and games that made every evening unforgettable. They were the kind of hosts who truly believed in making people feel special, and no detail was too small for them.

The invitation alone was a hint of the fun that awaited, and it made everyone feel like they were about to attend something special. The food was always a showstopper. Together, they created meals that were both delicious and creative, with something for everyone. They catered to dietary restrictions and preferences, always going the extra mile to make sure no one went hungry.

Then, of course, came the entertainment and games. There was always something to capture everyone's attention and keep the energy high. There were always prizes—quirky little trophies or goofy awards that added to the fun. The prizes themselves were always unexpected and playful, like a rubber chicken or a giant inflatable flamingo, just to keep the humor alive. It wasn't about spending money on lavish rewards; it was about making people laugh and feel like they were part of something special.

Despite all the effort they put into these gatherings, there was one thing that always puzzled my parents: the lack of thank-you cards. This may sound extremely old-fashioned, but growing up, they had been taught by their own parents to always send a simple thank-you card after an event, a small token of appreciation for the time and care someone had taken to host an event. It was a simple but important gesture that seems to have been forgotten over the generations.

Because of my parents, I love to entertain too. Like them, I've also been surprised at how few people have ever taken the time to send a thank-you note or even return the favor with a reciprocal invitation. Yes, it may be old-fashioned, but it shows appreciation and class.

Despite their confusion over the lack of appreciation, they never let it change how they hosted. They continued to pour their hearts into every party, every invitation, and every detail. They never expected anything in return, but they couldn't help but wish that the small gesture of a thank-you card might somehow complete the circle of generosity they had set into motion.

Quote

"Gratitude unlocks the fullness of life. It turns what we have into enough, and more." —Melody Beattie (American author)[36]

Scripture

"Two are better than one; because they have a good reward for their labour. For if they fall, the one will lift up his fellow: but woe to him that is alone when he falleth; for he hath not another to help him up." (Ecclesiastes 4:9–10)

Lesson Learned

Expressing gratitude is important because it helps cultivate positive emotions and strengthens relationships. When we take the time to thank others, it shows that we recognize and appreciate their efforts. This not only makes the recipient feel valued but also deepens our connection with them. Gratitude fosters an environment where people feel supported, seen, and heard. It can turn ordinary interactions into meaningful exchanges, building a foundation of trust and mutual respect.

Gratitude also has a powerful impact on our own well-being. Studies have shown that people who regularly express gratitude are happier, less stressed, and more optimistic.[37] When we focus on what we're thankful for, we shift our mindset from scarcity to abundance.

In addition to emotional benefits, expressing gratitude has physical health advantages. Research suggests that grateful people experience lower blood pressure, better sleep, and a stronger immune system.[38] By practicing gratitude, we can reduce the stress and negativity that contribute to physical ailments. The act of thanking others releases feel-good hormones, such as oxytocin, which promote a sense of well-being and reduce the body's stress response.

Gratitude is also crucial for personal growth. When we acknowledge the contributions of others, we gain a deeper understanding of how interconnected our lives are. Recognizing the support we receive from others, whether it's through a kind word or a helping hand, can motivate us to pay it forward. It encourages a cycle of generosity, kindness, and support, creating a ripple effect that spreads positivity throughout communities.

Challenge

Be a good guest whenever someone invites you over for dinner or to any event. Another often forgotten tradition of etiquette is to bring a bouquet of flowers or a small hostess gift. It doesn't have to cost a lot of money; the act of gratitude can simply be a flower from your garden or a card you make yourself. In today's world, it doesn't cost anything to send a thank-you text after the event with cute emojis or photos you took at the event.

If you ever want to stand out from the crowd, all you have to do is say thank you. That's how rare it is in today's world. Crazy, right?

Grit

Story

When Robert Gardner decided to carve his mark on history, he didn't take the easy route. He took the path that involved sweat, blood, and a level of grit that would make a bulldozer look like a paper airplane. Gardner didn't just stumble into greatness—he built it from scratch. This is the man who founded St. George, Utah, for starters. He's the man who didn't just dream up the idea of a thriving town but rolled up his sleeves and laid the groundwork—literally.

He didn't stop at that. Oh no; he built the sawmill in Pine Valley, Utah, too. And not the kind of sawmill you could just knock together in a weekend. This was the kind that would serve as the backbone of a community, processing the logs that would eventually be used to build the iconic St. George Temple.

One day, while Gardner was doing his usual heavy lifting with the logs, one of the big ones came flying down the mountain at full speed—completely out of control—and slammed right into his leg. The log sliced him open badly, bad enough that any sane person would've screamed and fallen to the ground, waiting for help to come. But not Robert Gardner. He looked at the injury, then looked at the steep, treacherous mountain around him, and thought, "Well, this leg's not going to walk itself down the hill."

So with the kind of grit that makes you wonder if this guy had more than just one good leg, he managed to make his way down the mountain, blood dripping from his wound, determination oozing from his soul. He didn't stop to rest or wait for someone to come to the rescue. That's hardcore mountain-man grit.

Enter Porter Rockwell, a legend in his own right and a man who might be just the person you want to stitch you up. As Rockwell tried to help, he fainted. So what did Gardner do? He picked up the needle and thread and stitched himself up. It took over a year for him to fully recover.

He didn't have a fancy education or a degree on the wall, but he had something far more valuable: grit. He made sure that his children received an education, though, because he wanted them to have the tools to succeed that he hadn't. It wasn't about making sure they learned how to build a sawmill or lay out a town; it was about giving them the chance to live their own dreams with the education he'd had to go without.

Fast-forward to today, and you'll find Gardner's legacy all over the place. Gardner Village in Salt Lake City was named after him and his family. If you dig a little deeper, you'll learn that Robert Gardner was also the first cousin of Elder Jeffrey R. Holland. It's safe to say that determination and grit run in the family. Even better, Robert Gardner is my brother-in-law's ancestor! My twin sister's children now share his incredible legacy!

Quote

"It does not matter how slowly you go as long as you do not stop." —Confucius (ancient Chinese philosopher, teacher, and political thinker)[39]

Scripture

"I have fought a good fight, I have finished my course, I have kept the faith." (2 Timothy 4:7)

Lesson Learned

Grit is the relentless determination to keep pushing forward despite obstacles, failures, and setbacks. It's not just about talent or intelligence but about perseverance, resilience, and a strong work ethic.

People with grit don't give up when things get tough; instead, they dig deeper, learn from challenges, and keep striving toward their goals.

Whether in academics, career, sports, or personal growth, grit separates those who dream from those who achieve. It's about having a long-term vision and the discipline to take consistent steps toward success, no matter how difficult the journey may be. Life is hard. So? Nobody said it was going to be easy!

Challenge

One way people can develop more grit in their lives is by setting long-term goals and committing to them, even when motivation fades. Instead of giving up when things get tough, they can practice pushing through discomfort and setbacks by breaking their goals into smaller, manageable steps.

Building resilience through challenges, learning from failures, and staying focused on the bigger picture helps strengthen perseverance. Over time, consistently choosing persistence over quitting will develop grit and the ability to overcome obstacles with determination.

Grit is a habit. Grit is a mindset.

If you're looking for more examples of what grit looks like, check out these inspiring movies!

- ***The Pursuit of Happyness* (2006):** A single father (Will Smith) faces homelessness but refuses to give up on his dreams.
- ***Erin Brockovich* (2000):** A struggling single mother (Julia Roberts) fights a major corporation against all odds.
- ***Hidden Figures* (2016):** The inspiring story of three Black women mathematicians who played vital roles at NASA.
- ***127 Hours* (2010):** Based on a true story, a rock climber (James Franco) survives a harrowing ordeal after being trapped by a boulder.
- ***Unbroken* (2014):** The incredible true story of Louis Zamperini, an Olympic athlete turned WWII prisoner of war.
- ***Rocky* (1976):** The ultimate underdog boxing story about perseverance and hard work.
- ***Rudy* (1993):** A young man with a big dream refuses to give up on playing football for Notre Dame.

- ***Remember the Titans* (2000):** A football coach and his team overcome racial tensions to succeed.
- ***Miracle* (2004):** The story of the 1980 US Olympic hockey team's triumph against all odds.

Habits

Story

About ten years ago, my husband and I, along with two other couples who have been dear friends of ours for many years, embarked on an unforgettable adventure through the stunning landscapes of Greece and Croatia. This journey had been a dream in the making for about a year, and after months of planning, the moment had finally arrived. We were eager to explore the ancient ruins, crystal-clear waters, and breathtaking vistas, but there was a small challenge I hadn't quite anticipated—my fitness level.

As a writer and an online university professor, I spend the majority of my days sitting at a desk, typing away on my laptop, researching, and grading assignments. It's a sedentary lifestyle, and while I'm not exactly proud of it, it's hard to avoid given the demands of my profession. The more I thought about it, the more I began to worry about the amount of hiking we would be doing on our trip. I swim a few times every week at the gym, but I hadn't really done much leg strengthening or weight-bearing exercises to climb European mountains. I was concerned that my legs wouldn't be able to handle the rugged terrain, the steep steps, and the long walks through ancient sites. It was a nagging worry that stuck with me in the weeks leading up to the trip.

To address this, my husband and I came up with a simple plan—one that was doable despite both of our busy schedules. We decided to set alarms on our phones to remind us to do quick, five-minute leg workouts throughout the day, once an hour, every day. We would take turns running into each other's office whenever the alarm would go off.

Squats, lunges, calf raises, and other leg exercises became part of our routine, something we could do in the middle of our workday or while watching TV in the evening. It wasn't much, but it was consistent. I was surprised by how little effort it took to start feeling the difference. Each workout might have been brief, but over time, I could feel my legs getting stronger, and that subtle transformation encouraged me to keep going.

By the time our trip finally arrived, I felt more confident than I had anticipated. We spent our days exploring the ruins of ancient Greece, trekking up hills to reach cliffside villages in Croatia, and walking through olive groves and vineyards that stretched as far as the eye could see. With each step, I felt a sense of accomplishment with surprising energy.

Looking back, I'm so grateful for that simple commitment to consistent, small efforts. The trip was everything we hoped for—beautiful, enriching, and memorable. But more than that, it taught me a valuable lesson: Sometimes the smallest actions—those that require minimal effort but are done consistently—can make all the difference.

Quote

"We are what we repeatedly do. Excellence, then, is not an act but a habit." —Will Durant (often attributed to Aristotle)[40]

Scripture

"Wherefore, be not weary in well-doing, for ye are laying the foundation of a great work. And out of small things proceedeth that which is great." (Doctrine and Covenants 64:33)

Lesson Learned

Developing good habits is essential because our daily actions shape our future. The small things we do consistently, whether positive or negative, accumulate over time, ultimately defining our success, character, and well-being. Good habits, like exercising, reading, expressing gratitude, or being kind to others, create a foundation for a fulfilling life. They help us stay disciplined, overcome challenges, and make progress toward our goals.

On the other hand, bad habits can hold us back, leading to missed opportunities and regret. The key is to start small, stay consistent, and remember that even the tiniest improvements can lead to life-changing results over time.

Challenge

One effective way to develop good habits is to start small and be consistent. Instead of trying to make huge changes all at once, focus on one small, manageable habit at a time. For example, if you want to develop a habit of reading the scriptures more, start by reading just five minutes a day or even one verse. Something is better than nothing!

Once that becomes a regular part of your routine, you can gradually increase the time or quantity. Consistency is more important than intensity. Small daily actions, repeated over time, lead to lasting change.

To reinforce your habit, try linking it to an existing routine. For example, pair a task like memorizing a scripture with brushing your teeth. Combine getting dressed in the morning with saying positive affirmations out loud to yourself. Combine listening to an uplifting podcast about next Sunday's *Come, Follow Me* lesson with doing the dishes. Use reminders or track your progress to stay motivated.

Sometimes we bite off more than we can chew by trying to conquer several New Year's resolutions at the same time. Instead, work on one goal at a time until it becomes a habit. Then move on to conquer the next one!

Happiness

Story

At first glance, you might assume that the happiest athletes at the Olympics would be those who take home the gold. After all, they've reached the pinnacle of their sport, standing atop the podium as the best in the world. But psychological research tells a different story—one that reveals a powerful lesson about happiness, mindset, and perspective.

Studies on Olympic medalists have shown that bronze medal winners are actually happier than silver medalists. Why? Because bronze medalists are simply grateful to have made it onto the podium at all! They recognize how close they came to leaving empty-handed, so they savor their achievement. Silver medalists, on the other hand, often experience what's known as counterfactual thinking—they compare themselves to the gold medalist and dwell on what they almost had. Instead of celebrating their incredible accomplishment, they regret falling just short of the top spot. Gold medalists savor the moment yet immediately feel pressure to repeat their performance, which often robs them of lasting joy.

A striking example of this was seen at the 1992 Barcelona Olympics, where researchers studied the facial expressions of medalists. They found that silver medalists frequently looked disappointed, while bronze medalists beamed with joy. One silver medalist was even caught on camera shaking his head in frustration as he received his medal, while a bronze winner in the same event jumped up and down with excitement.

This concept extends far beyond sports. How often do we focus on what we *don't* have instead of appreciating what we *do*? A mindset of gratitude—like that of the bronze medalist—can dramatically increase happiness. Instead of comparing ourselves to those above us, we can choose to see how blessed we already are.

So next time you find yourself feeling envious of someone else's "gold medal," ask yourself: Am I appreciating my own victories, or am I letting comparison steal my joy?

Quote

"Most folks are about as happy as they make up their minds to be." — Abraham Lincoln (sixteenth president of the United States of America)[41]

Scripture

"Now was not this exceeding joy? Behold, this is joy which none receiveth save it be the truly penitent and humble seeker of happiness." (Alma 27:18)

Lesson Learned

Happiness is a choice. One of the biggest obstacles to true happiness is jealousy. When we constantly compare ourselves to others—what they have, what they've accomplished, or how they look—we rob ourselves of joy. There will always be someone with more money, a bigger house, a better job, or a seemingly "perfect" life. But happiness doesn't come from having more; it comes from appreciating what we already have. The moment we shift our focus from what we lack to what we're blessed with, we start experiencing genuine contentment. Gratitude is the antidote to jealousy, and when we practice it daily, we realize that happiness isn't about *having* everything; it's about *appreciating* everything.

Instead of wasting energy envying others, we should use that energy to become the best version of ourselves. Everyone has a unique path in life, and comparing our journey to someone else's is unfair and unproductive. Rather than feeling bitter about someone else's success, celebrate it! When we lift others up and share in their joy, we create a positive mindset that allows our own blessings to multiply. True happiness comes when we stop worrying about what others are doing and, instead, focus on growing, improving, and embracing the wonderful things in our own lives.

Challenge

For the next seven days, commit to focusing on gratitude instead of comparison. Each day, write down three things you're grateful for in your own life—big or small. Then take it a step further by celebrating someone else's success or happiness. This could be as simple as complimenting a friend on their achievement, congratulating a co-worker on their promotion, or genuinely supporting someone else's good news without comparison. By the end of the week, you'll notice a shift in your mindset: less jealousy, more joy, and a greater appreciation for both your own blessings and the success of those around you.

Here's a list of additional things you can do to feel instant happiness in your day:

Get outside and move your body: Fresh air and physical activity are natural mood boosters.

Connect with people you love: Even a short, meaningful conversation can uplift you.

Listen to music that makes you feel good: Music can shift your mood instantly.

Learn something new: Growth brings energy and a sense of accomplishment.

Smile more—on purpose: It signals joy to your brain, even if you're faking it at first!

Take a break from screens and social media: Comparison is the thief of joy.

Set small, achievable goals: Progress—even tiny steps—fuels happiness.

Try mindfulness or meditation: Even a few quiet minutes a day helps reduce stress.

Serve someone else: Acts of kindness create lasting joy for both giver and receiver.

Make time for creativity or hobbies: Play isn't just for kids; it's essential for adults too.

Hardship

Story

Now, I'm not wishing hardships on anyone. Trust me, they stink. But if I'm being honest, it's during the hardest times in my life that I've grown the most. The struggles, the setbacks, the obstacles—they've all been part of what has shaped me into who I am today. And if you need a perfect example of someone who turned adversity into triumph, look no further than Winston Churchill.

Churchill is widely regarded as one of the greatest leaders in history, especially for his role as the British Prime Minister during World War II. Under his leadership, Britain held strong against the forces of Nazi Germany, and he led his country to victory in one of the darkest periods of history. He was tough, determined, and unflinching in the face of overwhelming odds, which is why, to this day, he's considered a hero by many. He was even voted the Greatest Briton by the people of the United Kingdom. But surprisingly, Churchill wasn't always that popular.

As a child, he struggled academically. In fact, he probably would have been diagnosed with dyslexia or ADHD, and his grades reflected that. He didn't fit the mold of the ideal student, and teachers were often frustrated with him. But if there's one thing Churchill had, it was determination. He was not one to back down from a challenge, and that attitude followed him throughout his life. He once said,

"Success is not final, failure is not fatal: It is the courage to continue that counts."[42]

Churchill's mental health was another struggle he faced head-on. He battled depression, which he famously referred to as the "Black Dog." He didn't shy away from acknowledging it, even though it was an incredibly difficult thing to live with. Today, it's likely that Churchill would have been diagnosed with bipolar disorder, but back then, there were few people who understood or spoke openly about mental health. Even in his darkest moments, Churchill kept going, leading Britain through its most desperate days. My husband and I visited his underground bunker in London where he slept and planned out war efforts while the Nazi bombs continued to drop on the city.

Some historians believe it was his personal battles with mental health and his early struggles that equipped him with the grit to face the challenges that came during World War II. The resilience he developed during his own hardships helped him persevere, and that persistence became a beacon of hope for the British people.

Through it all, Churchill didn't just endure; he thrived. He became an icon of leadership, inspiring millions to push forward, even when victory seemed impossible. His speeches are still remembered today for the unwavering conviction found in them. "Never, never, never give up," he urged.

Here's a man who was told he wasn't smart enough, who fought inner demons every day and yet became a symbol of perseverance and triumph. Maybe that's the lesson for all of us: Sometimes the things that seem like they'll break us are the very things that make us stronger. Churchill didn't let anything stop him. He didn't let his struggles define him; instead, he used them as fuel to push forward, and in doing so, he changed the course of history.

So while hardships aren't fun and no one actively seeks them out, we can always choose how we respond to them. Maybe, just maybe, they're the stepping stones to greatness, just like they were for Winston Churchill.

Quote

"Hardships often prepare ordinary people for an extraordinary destiny." —C. S. Lewis (British writer, university professor, and theologian)[43]

Scripture

"These things I have spoken unto you, that in me ye might have peace. In the world ye shall have tribulation: but be of good cheer; I have overcome the world." (John 16:33)

Lesson Learned

Hardships are some of life's greatest teachers, shaping us into stronger, wiser, and more resilient individuals. When we face challenges, we are pushed out of our comfort zones, forced to adapt, and given opportunities to develop patience, perseverance, and faith. Just like a muscle grows stronger through resistance, our character is refined through trials. Hard times teach us empathy, making us more compassionate toward others who are struggling. They also reveal our inner strength, showing us that we're capable of overcoming more than we ever imagined. We usually realize that those struggles were the very things that prepared us for greater opportunities and deeper joy.

Challenge

Even in the toughest times, taking a moment each day to recognize the good in your life can shift your mindset and help you stay resilient. Whether it's writing down one thing you're grateful for each day or simply pausing to appreciate a small blessing, gratitude can bring strength and hope during hardships.

Here are some things to focus on when life gets hard:

- Be grateful for what you do have
- Lean on a support system
- Drop your pride and reach out for support
- Brainstorm ways to get out of the situation
- Identify what it is exactly that you need

- Pray
- Attend the temple for peace
- Study the lives of people who showed grit and ingenuity to conquer their struggles
- Ask yourself, "What is this teaching me?"
- Remind yourself, "This won't last forever. Better days are ahead."
- Just take the next step
- Journal your thoughts and feelings
- Remember past victories
- Take time for self-care

Honesty

Story

Integrity was at the top of the list of qualities I looked for in the men I dated. I couldn't imagine marrying someone I couldn't trust completely. This story is about my husband, who many call "Mr. Integrity" because of the way he lives his life. The experience he had as a child changed his life and made him commit his life to the principle of honesty. In his words . . .

I learned a lot about my Father in Heaven from my earthly father who was not a member of the Church. My dad never lied. He never cursed. He never argued with Mom. He never turned me down when I wanted to play catch. As far as I can remember, he never did any unfair thing.

This story starts in a first-grade classroom in 1959. A young teacher is sitting at her desk in front, slowly shaking her head and rolling her eyes. Most of the children are working on their assignments as they should be, but there's a boy in the second-to-last row who has sharpened his pencil down to about two inches, because at that length it resembles a rocket ship. Instead of writing with that pencil, he is moving it slowly across his desk on a course for Mars. That boy was me. During those first few weeks of school, I don't think I ever finished an assignment. Somewhere about halfway through my paper, Mars would be calling again, and any focus on learning numbers and letters was gone.

"Great" was my answer when Dad asked daily how I was doing in school. This was a lie. I was doing terrible in school, but I had enough "smarts" to know that my dad would be very disappointed if he knew the truth. Eventually, the day of reckoning came. Our teacher handed each of us a closed envelope to bring home to our parents. I had paid so little attention in class that I didn't even know what a "report card" was. I was soon to find out.

That night, we had what my dad called a "man-to-man talk." First, he had to explain to me what a report card was, then what each of the letter grades meant. The bad grades spoke for themselves. It was devastating to realize I had fallen short in front of my hero, my nearly perfect dad. He said, "It's not so much your poor performance that bothers me. It's the fact that you lied to me. I don't ever want to think of my son as a liar." It felt like those words had been spoken by God Himself as a voice of thunder from Mount Zion: "You lied to me."

Many decades later, I can still feel the sting of that moment, standing in front of my dad as a liar. That moment ended my lying career. It was clear even at six years old that the returns for honesty were greater than any benefit gained from lying. Sure, I had plenty of faults, but year after year, I built a reputation of honesty. Part of the process of repentance is forsaking the sin and never doing it again. We never spoke about it again, but inside I still felt a little bit stained, knowing that my dad would always remember I had lied to him.

Years later, in college, I became a member of the Church and decided to embark on a two-year mission. My bishop asked me to plan my "farewell" sacrament meeting, so I asked both of my parents to speak. Despite the fact that neither had ever been inside a Latter-day Saint church building, both agreed to do so. They both gave fine talks, but there was a particular phrase my dad spoke that thundered in my ears. As he praised me, he stated, "I can honestly say that in his entire life, my son has never lied to me." I was shocked. Had my dad really forgotten about that fateful day when I was a young boy? He truly did.

When the day comes when I stand before my Maker, I hope to hear something similar.

My dad taught me the truth of this promise from the Lord: "Behold, he who has repented of his sins, the same is forgiven, and I, the Lord, remember them no more" (Doctrine and Covenants 58:42).

Quote

"Honesty is the first chapter in the book of wisdom." —Thomas Jefferson (third president of the United States of America)[44]

Scripture

"Lying lips are abomination to the Lord: but they that deal truly are his delight." (Proverbs 12:22)

Lesson Learned

Honesty is one of the most important virtues a person can have. It builds trust, strengthens relationships, and fosters a sense of integrity within ourselves. When we're honest, we show others that we can be trusted and relied on. This trust is the foundation of strong friendships, healthy families, and successful workplaces. On the other hand, dishonesty leads to broken relationships, lost credibility, and a constant need to cover up lies. The truth may sometimes be uncomfortable or difficult to share, but it always leads to greater peace and stability in the long run.

Beyond our relationships with others, honesty shapes our character and self-respect. When we live truthfully, we don't have to carry the burden of deception or worry about being caught in a lie. We can walk with confidence, knowing that we're living in alignment with our values. Honesty also invites personal growth, as it encourages us to own up to our mistakes and learn from them rather than hiding behind excuses.

One reason why we can have faith is simply because God is honest. His promises are sure. We know He's not going to change any of the commandments on us!

Challenge

One way people can commit to being more honest is by practicing self-reflection daily. Taking a few moments each day to evaluate your words and actions can help you recognize areas where you may have been less than truthful—whether with others or yourself.

Keeping a journal to track moments of honesty and dishonesty can also provide insight into patterns that need improvement. By making a conscious effort to be truthful in both big and small matters, honesty will become a natural habit, strengthening your integrity and deepening your relationships.

Even small lies can lead to a habit of dishonesty. Look for honest alternatives when tempted to say something untrue. If you're tempted to lie, consider the pros and cons of what you say. What will the consequences be?

Here are a few habits you can work on to develop your integrity:

- Keep your promises (even small ones). If you say you'll do something—do it. Follow-through is one of the clearest signs of integrity. Your word is your reputation in motion.
- Avoid flattery, exaggeration, or double-talk. Speak clearly and truthfully. People trust those who speak with honesty—not charm.
- Integrity shines brightest in private moments. Ask yourself: Would I still do this if someone I respected were watching me? Character is who you are in the dark.
- Choose friends who value integrity. You become like the people you spend time with. Surround yourself with those who hold high moral standards.
- Resist peer pressure. Stand for your values—even if it means standing alone. Integrity often requires courage. Doing right is rarely easy, but always worth it.
- Align your actions with your beliefs. Let your values guide your choices. Say no to what conflicts with your conscience—even if it costs you something. Integrity is living in harmony with your deepest convictions.

HOPE

STORY

My father's best friend was the kind of person who could light up a room the moment he walked in. Handsome, charismatic, and full of life, Johnny had an infectious energy that made every gathering feel like a party. And when he and my father were together, their bond was something special. It was rare to see two men admire and love each other so openly, and as a child, I found it inspiring. Their friendship was effortless, filled with laughter, inside jokes, and a deep, unshakable loyalty.

Then one day, Johnny called with devastating news: He had cancer. The moment my father hung up the phone, his role shifted. He was no longer just a friend; he became a cheerleader, a rock, the unwavering support his best friend needed. Determined to help in any way he could, he rallied their circle of friends, organizing fundraisers, hospital visits, and emotional support. At first, the response was overwhelming—everyone wanted to help, everyone believed in a miracle.

But as the treatments dragged on and the cancer refused to loosen its grip, that support began to fade. People got busy. Their enthusiasm waned. The harsh reality of a losing battle made it easier for them to quietly step away. I watched as my father grew disappointed, even angry, as friends who had once been so eager to help slowly withdrew their support.

Then came the final attempt. There was one last treatment center, a place that offered a glimmer of hope. But it was expensive—far more than what Johnny could afford. My father once again turned to their circle of friends, asking if they would be willing to contribute. This time, all of them refused. They saw it as a lost cause, a waste of money, a futile effort to prolong the inevitable.

One night, I asked my father the question that had been weighing on my mind. "Why are you willing to spend so much money on another treatment when you know it's not going to work?"

His answer was simple yet profound.

"I'm not just paying for treatment," he said. "I'm buying hope. And everyone deserves to have hope."

That response has stayed with me, long after Johnny passed away. The treatment didn't work, as everyone expected. My father wasn't trying to deny the inevitable. He knew the odds, but he also understood something deeper—that hope is sometimes the only thing a person has left. Fighting for someone, even when the outcome is uncertain, is one of the greatest acts of love.

Through his loyalty, my father taught me what true friendship looks like. He showed me that real love doesn't walk away when things get hard. It doesn't fade when hope seems fragile. It stands firm, even in the face of loss. And while his best friend may have lost his battle with cancer, he never had to face it alone.

Quote

"Hope is like the sun, which, as we journey toward it, casts the shadow of our burden behind us." —Samuel Smiles (Scottish author and reformer)[45]

Scripture

"Now the God of hope fill you with all joy and peace in believing, that ye may abound in hope, through the power of the Holy Ghost." (Romans 15:13)

Lesson Learned

Hope is a powerful force that helps individuals navigate the difficulties of life. It serves as a guiding light in moments of darkness, offering the strength and motivation needed to keep moving forward. Without hope, it can be easy to feel overwhelmed by challenges, loss, or uncertainty.

Hope allows us to believe that things can improve and that our efforts will bear fruit even if progress seems slow. It fuels perseverance and resilience, empowering us to face obstacles with courage and optimism. When we have hope, we're more likely to take positive actions toward our goals and dreams, even in the face of setbacks.

Jesus Christ offers hope to every human being. He has saved us from both physical and spiritual death! No one has ever given a better gift. Knowing we are saved allows us to have hope and believe that other things are possible too.

Challenge

One thing people can do to have more hope in life is to remember that Heavenly Father knows our entire story from beginning to end. We need to have faith that everything that happens is part of His plan and for our eternal good and growth.

By focusing on the positive aspects of life and recognizing the good, even in challenging circumstances, individuals can shift their perspective and foster a sense of hope. Keeping a gratitude journal, where you write down things you're thankful for each day, can help train your mind to look for the good, even in difficult times. This simple habit encourages a hopeful outlook, reminding us that even when things feel tough, there are always blessings and opportunities to appreciate.

Today and every day, don't lose hope. It's more powerful than you know and is the one thing that can make all the difference. Sinking into the depths of despair never solved any problem or made things better. Be hopeful.

Humility

Story

Jack, a family friend of mine, had a way of making life better for people without anyone realizing it was him. He wasn't the type to look for recognition or brag about his generosity. He just quietly stepped in when he saw a need, like a shadowy superhero in everyday life. I always knew he was kind, but it wasn't until years later that I started piecing together just how deeply he cared for others and how far he went to help them.

I remember the day I found out about my cousin's car. We were sitting around the table at a family reunion, sharing old stories and catching up. Out of nowhere, my cousin brought it up, saying, "You know, I wouldn't have gotten through that tough time if it weren't for Jack." I blinked, surprised, because I had no idea what she was talking about.

She went on to explain that, years earlier, when she was struggling financially and her old car finally gave out, Jack had quietly arranged for her to have a reliable vehicle. A friend of our family revealed the exact same thing happened to her too.

I later found out from another friend that Jack had paid for their son to go all the way to Japan for a big wrestling tournament he had qualified for. They couldn't afford it, but it was a once-in-a-lifetime opportunity for their son, who had worked so hard to qualify. Jack stepped in, quietly covering the expenses so the boy could represent his school and country on an international stage. The friend shared how Jack insisted they never tell anyone it was him. "He just said, 'Let the kid have his moment.'"

When I asked Jack about it, he shrugged, as if buying a plane ticket to Japan and helping with travel costs was no big deal. "It was something I could do," he said simply, and that was the end of it.

These stories made me realize that Jack's generosity wasn't just about money; it was about the way he believed in people. He never flaunted what he did because it wasn't about him. He didn't need credit or accolades. His reward was knowing he'd made someone's life a little easier or given them a chance to succeed. Sure, Jack was blessed with wealth, but that's not the point. He made the deliberate choice to use his money to bless others. If he hadn't been financially strong, he would have been generous in other ways.

For Jack, kindness wasn't something you talked about. It was something you did. He showed by example how to serve with love and that serving others is the key to happiness.

Quote

"Humility is not thinking less of yourself; it is thinking of yourself less." —Rick Warren (American evangelical Christian pastor and author)[46]

Scripture

"Humble yourselves in the sight of the Lord, and he shall lift you up." (James 4:10)

Lesson Learned

In a world that often emphasizes personal success, recognition, and material gain, the act of serving others selflessly can feel like a rare and precious thing. Yet helping others without expecting anything in return is one of the most profound ways to bring meaning to life—for both the giver and the recipient.

True service is not about accolades or rewards; it's about lifting others, connecting with humanity, and creating ripples of kindness that extend far beyond what we can see.

When we give without expecting anything back, we tap into a deeper part of ourselves and truly become more Christlike. We will never be able to repay the Savior for what He did for us, yet He willingly did it anyway. Developing humility allows us to become more Christlike. Humility is knowing that everything comes from God, not from us. When we use our gifts and talents and money to help others, we need to be mindful that God has given us those things so that we can help others.

Challenge

Serving others doesn't have to involve money. Here are a few ways you can make a difference in someone else's day:

- Listen to what others need so you know how to better serve them
- Offer your time or talents
- Sign up to feed the missionaries
- Ask your Relief Society president or bishop who might need anonymous help in your ward
- Donate your unneeded items to organizations that could truly use your things to bless others in need
- See what you can do on JustServe.org to see people truly in need (You probably already possess the skills they're in need of)
- Ask Heavenly Father to share ideas of how you can help others (You may be surprised at the creative ideas that pop into your head and heart!)

Hygge

Story

I absolutely love to travel, and I even created a website and Facebook group where I share my travel hacks. I love exploring other cultures, countries, food, music, art, language, and architecture. I am constantly tickled and inspired by what I learn. I love leading tour groups and watching the surprised faces of people discover with delight the places I love.

I used to teach classes at a culinary college and would tell my students that traveling would allow them to expand their knowledge of food and make them a better chef. It's true! A number of years ago, I went to Denmark for the first time and learned a new word that changed how I looked at my home and my daily life. The word is *hygge.* (It's pronounced "hyoo-guh.") It's a delightful word that attempts to describe that cozy feeling you get when you sit down and melt onto your soft couch and pillows near a crackling fire, wearing fuzzy socks and drinking hot chocolate with the one you love. Isn't it cool that there's one word that effectively describes all that?

While in Denmark, I stayed with a lovely Danish family who served me delicious food in their outdoor garden, seated on squishy pillows and warm blankets, with those stylish outdoor lights dangling above our heads from a beautiful pergola. Total hygge. They made me feel so welcome and wanted. Hygge is about that kind of warmth, happiness, and love.

I was inspired by my visit to Denmark to try to recreate that warm, cozy feeling for guests who come to my home in the U.S. Danes try to incorporate hygge into their everyday life: less hustle, more cozy, with genuine warmth and joy. In terms of how this relates to the gospel, hygge describes exactly how Heavenly Father will make us feel when we return to our heavenly home: loved, welcomed, and in a warm embrace.

The topping on that delicious experience is that one of my sons is now dating a girl from Denmark! We absolutely adore her and her terrific family. Hygge forever!

Quote

"Travel makes you realize that no matter how much you know, there's always more to learn." —Malcolm Teasdale (motivational speaker and renowned author of travel books)[47]

Scripture

"And the man said unto him: I am a Nephite, and I know that thou art a holy prophet of God, for thou art the man whom an angel said in a vision: Thou shalt receive. Therefore, go with me into my house and I will impart unto thee of my food; and I know that thou wilt be a blessing unto me and my house." (Alma 8:20)

Lesson Learned

Hygge is a Danish concept that embodies a sense of coziness, comfort, and well-being, often experienced through simple, everyday moments. It's about creating an environment where you feel safe, content, and connected, whether it's through lighting candles, enjoying a yummy drink, or spending quality time with loved ones. The key to hygge is mindfulness: being present in the moment and savoring the little things that bring you joy. It's less about material possessions and more about fostering an atmosphere of peace and contentment. When people embrace hygge, they create a space where they can unwind, relax, and embrace life's simple pleasures.

At its core, hygge also focuses on connection, both to people and to the environment around you. It's about being intentional in how you spend your time, making sure it's spent in ways that nurture your spirit and your relationships. Whether you're enjoying a quiet evening at home, having a heartfelt conversation with a friend, or taking a walk in nature, hygge encourages people to slow down and appreciate the warmth of human connection and the beauty in their surroundings. By embracing hygge, you not only cultivate a peaceful atmosphere in your home, but you also learn to create moments of joy in your everyday life.

A great quote that captures the essence of hygge comes from Danish author Hans Christian Andersen: "Just living is not enough. One must have sunshine, freedom, and a little flower."[48]

Challenge

One way people can incorporate hygge into their life is by creating a cozy, calming environment in their home. This can be done by adding soft blankets, warm lighting (like candles or fairy lights), and comfortable furniture that invites relaxation. It's the opposite of stuffy formality or cluttered mess. The key is to make this environment feel personal and inviting so it becomes a sanctuary where you can truly recharge and enjoy life's simple pleasures.

Light a candle in your home today. Make a cup of hot cocoa to share with someone. Instant hygge! Thanks, Denmark! Be that warm, cozy person that people want to spend time with.

Instruments in God's Hands

Story

It was a typical day in the life of Larry, a hardworking young man with a knack for getting himself into unusual predicaments—and somehow always finding his way out. He was driving long-distance for a construction job, the kind of job that had him zipping along with the sun in his eyes and a radio playing just loud enough to drown out the stress of the day. But as luck would have it, his truck's engine decided to take an early retirement. Just like that, he was stranded in the middle of nowhere. He admits he was young and foolish at the time, so he decided to pull out his thumb and hitchhike home. (Those were safer times.)

He eventually made it home, only to have his dad drive him back out to the same spot to help him fix the truck. After trying for a while, the truck still refused to start. So they hooked up the broken vehicle and began to tow it home. On the way back, something unexpected happened. They passed a young family stranded on the side of the same road, looking as desperate as Larry was when his own truck stopped working. Without thinking twice, Larry's dad pulled over. What followed was something straight out of a feel-good movie. He picked them up, took them home, cared for their children, fed the family, and then went out to buy an alternator for their car. And just to make sure their day turned around completely, he filled their gas tank, hooked up the tow rope, and helped them get their car back on the road.

The family, of course, was overwhelmed by his kindness, expressing their gratitude and humbly admitting they had no money to pay him back. It was one of those moments when you realize that the world isn't all bad, that there are people who still go out of their way to help others—no questions asked.

Now, I don't know what it is about Larry's vehicles, but another one broke down a year later with another lesson in its wake. He and his dad were driving on a dirt road, miles away from civilization, when suddenly—boom!—the car broke down. No cell service, no passing cars, just them and the endless stretch of dirt and dust. They hadn't seen another car for miles and hours in rural Nevada. It was one of those moments when panic starts to settle in, and you begin to wonder, "How on earth are we going to get out of this?"

All they could think of doing was to pray. They knew they couldn't rely on anything else—just a prayer to God, asking for help, because at that moment, He was the only one who could come to their rescue. Within five minutes, a Jeep came driving down the road, towing a rope behind it. The man in the Jeep was the extremely quick and unbelievable answer to their prayer and an obvious message from God that He was aware of Larry and his dad.

Larry's dad didn't just help that young family stranded on the road because he was a nice guy—he was answering a prayer that they whispered to the heavens. The man in the Jeep was the answer to Larry's dad's prayer. It's like a divine game of tag, where God orchestrates everything so perfectly that it feels like fate—when really, it's just His timing and His kindness at work.

In order to make it all work, we need to be willing to help others and be willing to be instruments in God's hands. Sure, God could do it all Himself, but it's way more fun and an honor to be a part of the miracles!

Quote

"Service makes us strong in our faith and useful in His kingdom. Service gives us purpose and courage in life. It brings us closer to God and helps us refine our divine nature." —Elder Carlos H. Amado (Latter-day Saint Seventy)[49]

Scripture

"Our brethren, the Lamanites, were in darkness, yea, even in the darkest abyss, but behold, how many of them are brought to behold the marvelous light of God! And this is the blessing which hath been bestowed upon us, that we have been made instruments in the hands of God to bring about this great work." (Alma 26:3)

Lesson Learned

We are all instruments in God's hands, called to help fulfill His purposes and bring about His work on earth. Whether through small acts of kindness, sharing our talents, or teaching others, God works through us to touch hearts and change lives. As we align our will with His and serve others selflessly, we become vessels of His love and light. By recognizing that our actions and choices can be used for His greater good, we can step into our divine roles with humility and joy, knowing that we are helping to build His kingdom, one person at a time.

What a privilege it is to be a part of His work!

Challenge

One way we can become instruments in God's hands is by serving others with a willing heart, whether it's helping a neighbor, comforting a friend, or offering our time to those in need. When we put aside our personal desires and focus on God's will, we open ourselves up to being His hands and heart in the world.

Another way is by cultivating a spirit of humility and prayer, asking God how He wants to use us in His service. By seeking His guidance and listening to His promptings, we can better align ourselves with His purpose and be ready to act when He calls.

Today, ask Heavenly Father what He needs you to do. Then be willing to do it. I mention the "be willing" part of that process because of an experience I had many years ago. One morning, I woke up with the sincere prayer that I wanted to be an instrument in God's hands that day. I told Him I would be available to do whatever He needed me to do. I truly wanted to serve and I had the time. Later that morning, the Relief Society president called me to ask if I could help out a sister in our ward who needed a ride to a doctor's appointment. I was kind of amazed when the call came because I hadn't told anyone about my prayer! Heavenly Father was really testing me because I instantly had a million excuses for why I couldn't do it. I had to have a heart-to-heart with myself in about four seconds so that I could say yes to the Relief Society president. I could practically hear the Lord laughing at me.

President Spencer W. Kimball stated, "God does notice us, and he watches over us. But it is usually through another person that he meets our needs."[50] Be ready to act when the Lord calls!

Integrity

Story

Very often, a trip to the grocery store for my family was a "sweet" experience, as demonstrated by my dad who would unwrap and savor pieces of candy throughout his journey up and down the food aisles. No need to worry—right along with the many items to be purchased at the checkout counter would be the empty candy wrappers and banana peels, waiting to be paid and accounted for. We always knew Dad would pay for what he had eaten.

Many times during my pregnancies, when I wanted to devour everything in sight, I continued Dad's legacy and example, always thinking of him when I arrived at the checkout counter with several of the contents of my shopping cart opened and consumed! Eating my way through a grocery store helped me survive several pregnancies. His example got me through many hungry moments in the store with his example of delicious integrity.

Quote

"The most important persuasion tool you have in your entire arsenal is integrity." —Zig Ziglar (American author, salesman, and motivational speaker)[51]

Scripture

"The just man walketh in his integrity: his children are blessed after him." (Proverbs 20:7)

Lesson Learned

My dad used to say that integrity means doing the right thing even when no one is looking. Integrity is about staying true to your values, principles, and moral compass, even when there's no external reward or recognition. It's about being honest and dependable and doing the right thing simply because it's right—not because of the fear of consequences or a desire for praise.

Developing integrity is essential for building trust and fostering meaningful relationships, both personally and professionally. In both individual and group contexts, when integrity is present, people feel secure and respected, knowing that they can count on consistent, transparent actions from others. This consistency creates a safe environment for collaboration, growth, and accountability.

In addition to its role in relationships, integrity is crucial for self-respect and personal growth. By practicing integrity, individuals align their behaviors with their values, helping them feel more confident and at peace with themselves.

Challenge

One way to develop integrity is by practicing honesty, even when it's difficult. Being truthful in both our words and actions helps to build a strong foundation of trust with others and reinforces our commitment to ethical behavior. This means not only avoiding lies but also being transparent and open about our intentions, decisions, and mistakes. Over time, consistently choosing honesty strengthens our character and establishes a reputation for being reliable and trustworthy.

Another way to develop integrity is by setting clear personal values and holding ourselves accountable to them. Regularly reflecting on what we stand for and ensuring that our actions align with those values helps us to make ethical choices in challenging situations. Accountability can be reinforced by seeking feedback from trusted mentors or peers, who can offer guidance and hold us responsible for staying true to our principles. This practice helps create a sense of internal consistency and fosters the confidence that we're living in alignment with our highest ideals. While honesty and integrity are closely related, they're not exactly the same. Honesty is about telling the truth. Integrity is about living the truth. Honesty means being truthful in your words, while integrity goes further; it's about aligning your actions with your values, even when no one is watching. Integrity is a way of life, not just a moment. Honesty is a piece of the puzzle. Integrity is the whole picture of living a moral, consistent life.

Joy

Story

I've always prided myself on being a minimalist; there's something about having a clutter-free house that just feels so peaceful and calm. However, my love for a clean, organized space recently collided with my deep affection for quirky little treasures that spark joy.

A dear friend of mine taught me the importance of finding small moments of joy in my days . . . every day. Rather than waiting for big events, special celebrations, or vacations to feel happy, we need to look for and even create small moments of joy every day.

My friend surrounds her work desk in her home office with little mementos from her travels, tiny gifts from thoughtful friends, and oddball trinkets that just make her smile when she looks at them. Gone are the days of strict minimalism! Her desk looks more like an eclectic mini museum of joy.

She lights a candle and has an essential oil diffuser going all day, filling the room with calming scents to help her focus and concentrate on her work. It's her way of trying to "soak in the good vibes." She puts cuttings of fresh flowers from her yard in a vase on her desk so she can be surrounded by beautiful nature.

When the weather is good outside, she opens the window in her home office so she can hear the birds singing outside. She told me about a study published in *Scientific Reports* in 2022 called "The Restorative Effects of Birdsong on Cognitive Performance," which found that listening to birdsong can reduce stress, improve mood, and enhance cognitive performance! What's even more fascinating is that listening to birds singing on a YouTube channel has the same effect. The human ear can't decipher the difference, so you can receive the same health and mental benefits when it's snowing outside and you just have a video playing on your computer or cell phone!

She's intentionally creating little pockets of joy throughout her day because, let's face it, we never really know what tomorrow will bring. As much as I enjoy the serenity of an uncluttered space, I've realized that it's equally important to intentionally surround myself with things that make me laugh and smile throughout my day. Whether it's a travel souvenir, a goofy figurine, or a squirt of my favorite air freshener, I'm learning to use little items around me that spark joy in my day as well-placed reminders that life's too short not to be filled with happiness.

Quote

"The happiness of life is made up of minute fractions—the little soon-forgotten charities of a kiss, a smile, a kind look, a heartfelt compliment in the disguise of a playful raillery, and the countless other infinitesimals of pleasurable thought and genial feeling." —Samuel Taylor Coleridge (English poet, philosopher, and critic)[52]

Scripture

"Adam fell that men might be; and men are, that they might have joy." (2 Nephi 2:25)

Lesson Learned

True joy doesn't come from waiting for life to be perfect or for circumstances to align in our favor. I used to tell myself, "I'll be happy when . . ." but I finally realized I was robbing myself of daily joy. It's easy to fall into the trap of thinking, "I'll be happy when I get that promotion," "I'll be happy when I'm in a better relationship," or "I'll be happy when I reach my goals." Happiness isn't a distant reward waiting for you just around the corner if you work hard enough. Life is filled with imperfections and challenges, and it's those very experiences that shape us, teach us, and help us grow. When we stop waiting for the "perfect" moment to feel happy, we begin to notice the small joys around us: the laughter of a friend, the warmth of the sun on our face, the satisfaction of a job well done, and yes . . . even a funny cat video.

When we die and stand before the Lord, I can imagine Him giving us a big hug and then excitedly asking, "What part of mortal life did you love the most?!" He sent us here to gain a physical body, learn, grow, and have joy!

President Russell M. Nelson shared this profound message during the October 2016 general conference: "When the focus of our lives is on Jesus Christ and His gospel, we can feel joy regardless of what is happening—or not happening—in our lives."[53]

Challenge

Think of this acronym each day as you seek J.O.Y. in your life: Jesus, Others, You. You'll find that when you look for joy in that order of priorities, you'll find it! Let's find joy in the journey!

Today, find some kind of talisman you can put in your car, on your mirror, or anywhere in your home to remind you to find joy in the moment. Remember, it's all about the journey, not the destination.

Many years ago, I struck up a conversation with the saleswoman in the floral department of the grocery store. I complimented her on the little yellow gemstones she had placed in her hair. They made her look so happy and cute. She beamed brightly and instantly took one out of her hair to give to me as a gift! Her kind and generous spontaneity tickled me so much that I put the little gemstone on my car's dashboard once I got back to my car after shopping to remind me to be more like her. It was easy to see that she was surrounding herself with beautiful things that sparked joy and that she was quick to share them with others!

Judging Others

Story

During a study abroad program that my sister and I both did together in college, there was a girl named Shelly who, at first glance, seemed rather unimpressive. With unkempt hair, a few too many pounds, and a wardrobe that never quite matched, she didn't stand out in a crowd. Our classmates often glanced past her, drawn instead to those who had perfect smiles or fashionable attire. Shelly was quiet at first, but we quickly learned she was smart, hilarious, and fun to hang out with. We were surprised that the others in our group didn't take the time to get to know her.

But as the weeks passed, something unexpected began to unfold. Shelly's sharp wit emerged in group discussions. She always had a clever observation or an insightful comment, turning ordinary lectures into lively debates. Her dry sense of humor often caught us off guard, and everyone was amused by her quick comebacks. Beneath her shy exterior, she was a force to be reckoned with—intelligent, thoughtful, and remarkably genuine.

One evening, our group gathered for dinner at a local restaurant. As everyone shared their hopes and dreams, Shelly quietly spoke of her ambition to become a lawyer. She talked about the injustices she had seen in the world during our travels together, how she wanted to fight for those who had no voice, and the years of studying it would take to get there. Her words struck a chord, but most of the students were only half-listening, distracted by the other conversations swirling around us. Shelly was so much more than her appearance, but the rest of the group still hadn't quite realized it yet.

Years later, I ran into Shelly again at a work conference. She had become a successful lawyer, standing tall in a sharp suit, confident and composed. Her eyes still sparkled with the same intelligence and wit, but now she carried herself with a quiet strength that commanded respect. She was the one giving a keynote speech, captivating the audience with her knowledge and passion for justice.

As I watched her speak, I realized how few people had appreciated her when we were together abroad. They had judged her too quickly, focused on the surface, and missed the essence of who she was on the inside. Shelly had grown into someone they all would have been proud to know then, yet they had never fully seen her for who she truly was.

She had outgrown the need for our approval. The woman standing before us was a testament to the power of inner beauty, the kind that grows silently and steadily only to shine through when the time is right. Unfortunately for many in our group, that realization came too late.

It reminds me of how many people underestimated a young man from Nazareth too. Look harder to find the hidden gems of people all around you every day.

Quote

"When we see men of a contrary character, we should turn inwards and examine ourselves." —Confucius (ancient Chinese philosopher, teacher, and political thinker)[54]

Scripture

"Judge not, that ye be not judged." (Matthew 7:1)

Lesson Learned

Judging others is an instinctive reaction for many, but it's one that can often lead to misunderstandings, conflict, and a lack of compassion. The first reason we should avoid judging others is that we lack a full understanding of their circumstances. Every individual comes with a unique set of experiences, challenges, and struggles that may not be immediately visible. By passing judgment without understanding the full context, we risk misrepresenting or misunderstanding their situation. Just as we might desire to be understood and not hastily judged, extending the same grace to others can foster empathy and harmony.

Compassion requires us to look beyond external actions or differences and recognize the shared humanity in all of us. If we judge, we close off the possibility of truly understanding or helping others. Embracing the idea that everyone has a story encourages us to listen and offer support rather than criticism.

The reality is that our judgments rarely reflect the truth of who the other person is but instead reveal our own preconceived notions and imperfections. By letting go of judgment, we open the door to self-reflection and personal growth. Rather than criticizing others for their flaws or differences, we can learn to embrace them as opportunities to connect, grow, and improve.

Challenge

Here are several ways we can develop the habit of refraining from judgment:

- Practice self-reflection
- Ask questions instead of assuming
- Listen to the Spirit
- Challenge negative thought patterns
- Focus on the positive
- Be willing to learn from others
- Focus on your own growth; self-awareness leaves less room for criticism
- Be curious, not critical; understanding someone's why changes how you see their actions.
- Give others the benefit of the doubt; assume good intentions when you don't have all the facts (most people are doing the best they can)
- Avoid gossip and negative talk; choose to build, not belittle
- Remember your own mistakes; when you reflect on your own imperfections, it's easier to extend grace to others
- Ask God to help you see others as He sees them

Kindness

Story

Brooke had always been drawn to nursing, not just for science but for the humanity of the profession. A striking young woman with an infectious smile, she possessed a natural grace and compassion that seemed to put people at ease. As a nursing student (one of my twin sister's students when she taught at a nursing college), Brooke excelled in her studies, mastering the technical skills and knowledge needed for her future profession. Yet she quickly realized that true healing went far beyond IV lines and medication charts.

Her revelation came one afternoon during a clinical rotation. She had been assigned to care for an elderly woman who was recovering from surgery. The woman's hair was tangled, unkempt, and matted from days of lying in bed. As Brooke adjusted the woman's IV, she noticed the patient avoiding her reflection in the small mirror across the room.

"Would you like me to brush your hair?" Brooke asked gently.

The woman's eyes filled with tears as she nodded. "I'd love that," she whispered.

Brooke fetched a comb and began to untangle the knots with care. As she worked, the woman's posture seemed to change; her shoulders relaxed and her face softened. When Brooke finished, she gathered the hair into a simple braid. The woman smiled, touching the braid with trembling fingers.

"Thank you," she said. "I feel like myself again."

That moment stayed with Brooke long after her shift ended. She couldn't stop thinking about how something as simple as brushing someone's hair could transform their spirit. It wasn't about vanity; it was about dignity, about feeling human in the face of illness.

On her next day off, Brooke returned to the hospital—not to work but to serve. Armed with a bag of brushes, combs, and hair ties, she began visiting female patients who were bedridden or too weak to care for their hair. She would pull up a chair, gently brush out their tangles, and style their hair in simple braids or ponytails.

Word quickly spread through the hospital about the "nursing student who does hair." Patients who had been withdrawn and quiet began looking forward to Brooke's visits. She would sit with them, listening to their stories as she worked, and often saw their spirits lift before her eyes.

One woman, who was recovering from chemotherapy, broke into a wide grin when Brooke tied a colorful scarf around her head. "I haven't felt pretty in months," she said, tears spilling over.

For Brooke, these moments reaffirmed why she had chosen nursing. She realized that healing wasn't just about curing the body—it was about nurturing the soul. By taking the time to care for something as simple as a patient's hair, she was offering more than a service; she was offering hope, dignity, and a reminder that they were still beautiful, still valued, still human.

Brooke continued her studies, but her off-hours hair visits became a staple of her hospital routine. She even inspired some of her classmates and colleagues to join her, creating a ripple effect of kindness throughout the hospital.

Looking back, Brooke often said that those hours spent brushing and braiding hair taught her more about nursing than any textbook ever could. She learned that true care lies in the small, simple acts of love—the moments that say "You matter" when the world feels like it's falling apart.

Years later, as a registered nurse, Brooke carried that lesson with her. Whether she was administering life-saving treatments or simply helping a patient feel pretty, she knew that every act of kindness could spark a light in someone's healing journey.

Quote

"No act of kindness, no matter how small, is ever wasted." —Aesop (ancient Greek storyteller and philosopher)[55]

Scripture

"And be ye kind one to another, tenderhearted, forgiving one another, even as God for Christ's sake hath forgiven you." (Ephesians 4:32)

Lesson Learned

Acts of kindness, no matter how small, hold the power to create ripples that can transform not only the immediate environment but also the broader world. When we engage in acts of kindness, we begin to shift the energy around us, fostering a culture of empathy, understanding, and love.

Whether it's a smile, a helping hand, or a word of encouragement, these seemingly small gestures can make a big impact. As we share kindness, we inspire others to do the same, creating a cycle of positivity that spreads far beyond our initial actions. It's through these interactions that the world can gradually become a more compassionate and connected place.

In addition to affecting the world around us, acts of kindness also profoundly impact us. When we show kindness to others, we experience a boost in our own well-being. Research has shown that helping others can increase our feelings of happiness, reduce stress, and even improve our physical health.[56]

Engaging in kind acts releases feel-good chemicals like oxytocin and serotonin, which enhance our mood and promote a sense of fulfillment. This positive reinforcement helps us see the world in a brighter light, making kindness not just a gift to others but a source of personal joy and growth.

Penguins often leave little rocks in nests of those they care about as a sign of affection. It's called "Pebbling." Today, when we forward funny videos or share cute memes with our loved ones, it's also called "Pebbling." I love that! Think of other types of pebbles you could give to others to encourage them or let them know someone cares.

Challenge

You can watch a short video clip about Brooke in the news! Check her out on YouTube.[57]

Here are six ideas for ways we can show acts of kindness to others:

- Offer a listening ear
- Carry water bottles or snacks in your car that you can hand out to homeless people standing on corners
- Write a heartfelt note
- Surprise someone with a thoughtful gift
- Perform random acts of service to strangers
- Offer words of encouragement

The list of ways you can show kindness is endless. Check out www.JustServe.org for more ideas.

Knowledge

Story

One of the most entertaining and inspiring true stories of someone who used knowledge to achieve remarkable success is that of Thomas Edison, the prolific American inventor and businessman. Edison is best known for inventing the practical light bulb, but his journey to success was far from easy, and it was driven largely by his relentless thirst for knowledge and his refusal to give up.

Edison's education wasn't traditional; he only attended school for a few months, as his teachers thought he was "addled" (a term for being slow to learn). However, his mother, a former schoolteacher, believed in him and took it upon herself to educate him at home. Edison developed a lifelong love for reading, often devouring books on science and engineering. His inquisitive mind led him to experiment with a wide variety of projects, including making a telegraph machine at the age of twelve.

Edison's most famous invention, the light bulb, didn't come overnight. In fact, he reportedly failed ten thousand times before he finally developed a practical, commercially viable light bulb. When asked about his many failures, he famously said, "I have not failed. I've just found 10,000 ways that won't work."[58] This mindset of learning from every failure was key to Edison's success. He didn't see his mistakes as defeats but as valuable opportunities to acquire more knowledge and refine his methods.

In addition to his inventing genius, Edison was an exceptional businessman. He founded General Electric, which is still one of the largest companies in the world today. He understood that knowledge wasn't just about science; it was also about how to manage and apply that knowledge to make an impact on society. Edison's ability to harness knowledge, combined with his determination and resilience, not only made him a household name but also changed the course of modern history. Through his example, we see how the pursuit of knowledge, combined with a mindset that embraces learning from both successes and failures, can truly lead to success in life.

Quote

"The secret of success is to know something nobody else knows." —Aristotle Onassis (Greek shipping magnate who became one of the wealthiest and most influential figures in the world during the mid-twentieth century)[59]

Scripture

"And as all have not faith, seek ye diligently and teach one another words of wisdom; yea, seek ye out of the best books words of wisdom; seek learning, even by study and also by faith." (Doctrine and Covenants 88:118)

Lesson Learned

The pursuit of knowledge is admirable, but even more important is to learn how to use that knowledge wisely to bless other people.

If you own your own business or want to be recognized as an authority in your field, try to become an expert at something very specific. In today's business world, the riches are in the niches, as the saying goes. That means discovering something in a unique segment rather than having a generalized knowledge of it.

YouTube is an example of people who have become experts in super-specific things, such as how to solve a math problem with exponents inside the parentheses or how to replace a valve inside a General Electric washing machine. Nowadays, most people are looking for a detailed answer to a very specific problem. You might just be the one who has the answer!

Challenge

Acquiring more knowledge in life is a powerful way to grow and make a meaningful impact. One of the best ways to gain knowledge is through reading. Books, articles, and scholarly papers open up new worlds of information and perspectives. Whether it's delving into subjects you're passionate about or exploring new areas, reading broadens the mind.

Alongside reading, engaging in conversations with others can be incredibly enriching. Conversations provide opportunities to learn from people with different experiences, opinions, and expertise. It's also helpful to ask questions and actively listen.

Another valuable approach is taking courses, whether online or in person, which allows for structured learning and access to expert knowledge in a specific field. Setting aside time for reflection and critical thinking is essential. Taking moments to digest what you've learned, ponder how it fits into your life, and connect new insights to your own experiences will deepen your understanding and help integrate knowledge into your daily life.

Today, think about something unique you can offer the world. Be an expert at something. What is your passion? What do you want to share with the world?

Laughter

Story

Several years ago, I taught an online math course at Brigham Young University for international students who were also learning English. Now, let's be honest—math isn't exactly everyone's idea of a good time. For many students, tackling formulas and problem sets is about as enjoyable as stepping on a Lego while barefoot. So to lighten the mood, I started a tradition. Every Wednesday, I posted a funny math comic in the course announcements and called it the "Midweek Math Laugh." It was a simple way of reminding students that yes, calculus can make you cry, but at least we can laugh while learning it!

One day, I received an email from one of my international students in Nigeria who wanted to thank me for those little moments of humor. He wrote, "I am screwing my head off with laughter."

I had to read it twice. Screwing his head off? For a split second, I pictured him sitting at his desk, literally unscrewing his head like a light bulb while laughing uncontrollably. Clearly, something had been lost in translation. But I couldn't help it; I burst out laughing. It was one of the best emails I had ever received from a student.

This got me thinking about the power of laughter. Have you ever heard of laugh therapy? It's a real thing! Science backs it up.[60] Laughter reduces stress, boosts your immune system, and even burns calories. (So technically, watching funny dog videos could count as exercise, right?) It's why people say laughter is the best medicine—well, that and actual medicine, of course.

I like to think of laughter as being similar to changing a diaper. It doesn't solve the problem permanently, but it sure makes things more bearable for a while. So whether it's a math comic, a funny email, or a moment of sheer ridiculousness, don't underestimate the power of a good laugh. Because sometimes, all you need to get through the week is a little humor . . . and maybe a screwdriver, just in case your head starts coming loose.

Quote

"If laughter cannot solve your problems, it will definitely *dissolve* your problems so that you can think clearly what to do about them." —Dr. Madan Katarina ("Guru of Giggling" and the founder of the Laughter Yoga Clubs movement)[61]

Scripture

"A merry heart doeth good like a medicine." (Proverbs 17:22)

Lesson Learned

Intentionally look for moments that make you laugh every day. Laughter is more than just a response to something funny; it's a powerful tool for maintaining both mental and physical well-being. It has been shown to reduce stress, improve mood, and even boost the immune system.

Laughter helps us cope with difficult situations by providing a moment of relief and perspective, making challenges feel more manageable. It strengthens relationships by creating bonds of connection and shared joy with others. Ultimately, laughter reminds us that despite life's hardships, we have the capacity to find lightness and joy in the midst of it all, improving our overall quality of life.

That said, be mindful of what you're laughing at. Don't ever make others the brunt of your jokes. What you laugh at is a mirror to your soul, reflecting what you cherish, what you dismiss, and where your heart truly finds its joy.

Challenge

One great way to include more laughter in your daily life is to intentionally seek out moments that bring you joy. This could mean watching a funny video, listening to a comedy podcast, or spending time with people who have a great sense of humor.

You could even create a "laughter jar" where you write down things that make you laugh and read one of them whenever you need a pick-me-up. By incorporating these small, intentional moments of laughter, you're not only improving your mood but also making it a habit to find humor throughout your day. Choose to fill your day and attitude with laughter. Surround yourself with things that make you smile and laugh each day.

Even better, become the type of person that makes others laugh with joy. Memorize a few good jokes you could share with others or simply learn to point out the bright side of any bad situation. Be the light in the room for others.

Many of us take life way too seriously. We all make mistakes, so why do we think everything has to be or is going to be perfect? Learn to roll with imperfection and celebrate this crazy earthly experience. Look for the humor in every situation, and be sure to laugh every day!

Leadership

Story

Mission presidents come in all types: Some are strict, some are laid-back, some are obsessed with numbers, and some seem to think we should all be fluent in the local language within three weeks. My sister's mission president was the perfect mix of fatherly love, spiritual mentor, accomplished businessman, motivational leader, and fun-loving support. During one of her one-on-one interviews with him, he leaned forward with a serious expression and asked, "What do you think is my biggest concern?"

She said she froze for a second. This felt like a test. She mentally ran through all the mission priorities: baptisms, reactivating less-active members, improving fellowshipping efforts. Surely it had to be one of those. "Um . . . baptisms?" she guessed hesitantly.

He shook his head, "No."

"Uh . . . making sure companionships get along?" my sister guessed again.

Another shake of the head.

"Uh . . . making sure missionaries wake up on time?" (Because let's be real, that was an ongoing battle.)

He laughed and then said something that she would never forget: "Nope! It's *you*."

She stared at him, confused. She wasn't expecting that. But he meant it. His biggest concern wasn't the numbers, the goals, or the mission statistics—it was the missionaries themselves. He didn't just see them as missionaries; he saw them as individuals—young adults figuring out life, trying their best, and needing support, encouragement, and sometimes just a reminder that they were doing better than they thought.

One of the most genius things he did was open the mission home on preparation days. Any missionary who needed a break, a pep talk, or just a little time to feel human again was welcome. He'd throw on inspirational movies and training clips, letting them recharge spiritually and emotionally before sending them back into the field. After a long week of doors slammed in their faces by people who absolutely did not want to hear a message about Jesus, people pretending not to be home, and the occasional dog chase, those moments of renewal were everything.

Now don't get me wrong—he *did* care about numbers. A lot. He had a favorite saying: "If you track the statistics of a missionary, I'll show you the #1 mission in the world." And he meant it. He firmly believed that tracking progress was the key to improving, and he wanted his missionaries to be disciplined and accountable. But at the end of the day, his real focus was never just on baptisms or retention rates. His focus was on the missionaries—their growth, health, happiness, and success as disciples of Christ, both in the mission and beyond.

Looking back, my sister realized that his leadership style wasn't just about making the missionaries better missionaries; it was about making them better people. He taught her that numbers matter, but people matter more. He showed her what true leadership looks like—not someone who demands results at any cost but someone who lifts, inspires, and genuinely cares about those they lead.

Quote

"If your actions inspire others to dream more, learn more, do more, and become more, you are a leader." —John Quincy Adams (sixth president of the United States)[62]

Scripture

"Whosoever will be great among you, let him be your minister; And whosoever will be chief among you, let him be your servant: Even as the Son of man came not to be ministered unto, but to minister, and to give his life a ransom for many." (Matthew 20:26–28)

Lesson Learned

People are more important than statistics. Leadership is not about holding a position of power or authority; it's about serving and inspiring others to achieve a common goal. True leaders understand that leadership is rooted in humility, selflessness, and a commitment to the well-being of those they lead.

A good leader listens, communicates effectively, and motivates others by example. They don't simply dictate from the top, but rather they empower others to contribute, grow, and thrive. Effective leadership requires emotional intelligence, resilience, and the ability to adapt to challenges and changes. Leaders must also be willing to take responsibility for their decisions and lead with integrity, always striving to do what's best for the greater good.

One of the most important qualities of a great leader is the ability to inspire trust and loyalty in others. This trust is built through consistent actions, transparency, and a commitment to shared values. Leadership is about more than just setting a direction; it's about walking alongside others as they navigate their own paths. It's about encouraging them when they falter, celebrating their successes, and helping them find the courage to face the inevitable obstacles that arise.

True leadership uplifts and transforms both the leader and those they lead, creating a lasting impact that extends far beyond the immediate goal or project.

Challenge

Becoming a servant leader requires a shift in mindset from focusing on personal gain or recognition to prioritizing the growth and well-being of others. One of the first steps to becoming a servant leader is to practice active listening. By truly listening to the needs, concerns, and aspirations of others, leaders can understand how to best support and guide them. This not only helps build trust but also fosters deeper connections.

Instead of just giving orders, servant leaders demonstrate the values and behaviors they wish to see in others. They model integrity, hard work, and humility, showing that they're willing to put in the effort alongside their team. Servant leaders also encourage personal and professional growth by investing in others, whether through mentorship, training, or simply providing opportunities for others to shine.

If you want to better understand and develop qualities of great leadership, simply make a list of what Jesus Christ did! Jesus Christ is often cited as a model of servant leadership, emphasizing humility, compassion, and service to others. Here are ten ways He demonstrated this leadership style, based on biblical accounts:

Washing the Disciples' Feet (John 13:1-17): Jesus humbly washed His disciples' feet, a task typically done by servants, to show that true leadership involves serving others selflessly.

Teaching with Humility (Matthew 5-7): In the Sermon on the Mount, Jesus taught values like meekness, mercy, and peacemaking, emphasizing leadership through example rather than authority.

Healing the Sick (Mark 1:29-34, Matthew 8:1-17): Jesus served by healing people, such as curing Peter's mother-in-law and lepers, prioritizing others' well-being over His own comfort.

Feeding the Multitudes (John 6:1-13): Jesus fed 5,000 people with five loaves and two fish, demonstrating care for physical needs and leading through provision.

Associating with the Marginalized (Luke 5:29-32): Jesus dined with tax collectors and sinners, showing that servant leadership includes uplifting those society rejects.

Sacrificing His Life (John 15:13, Matthew 27:32-56): Jesus's ultimate act of service was His crucifixion, laying down His life to redeem others, embodying selfless leadership.

Empowering His Disciples (Matthew 10:1-8): Jesus gave His disciples authority to heal and preach, equipping them to serve others and extend His mission.

Showing Compassion to the Lost (Luke 15:1-7): In the parable of the lost sheep, Jesus illustrated His commitment to seeking and serving those who are lost or struggling.

Forgiving Others (Luke 23:34): Even on the cross, Jesus forgave those who crucified Him, modeling leadership through forgiveness and grace.

Living Simply (Matthew 8:20): Jesus lived without material wealth, saying, "The Son of Man has no place to lay His head," demonstrating that leadership focuses on service, not power.

Lifelong Learning

Story

When I graduated from high school, so many students celebrated, saying it would be the last time they'd ever have to read a book. Strange, right? Sad too. There's a whole lifetime of learning to do! When I graduated from college, I felt like I was being kicked out because I wanted to stay and keep taking classes!

The stories of people who didn't achieve their goals and success until an older age are countless. Those who keep learning and growing can do remarkable things. For example, Colonel Harland Sanders was sixty-two years old when he franchised Kentucky Fried Chicken (KFC). By age seventy-three, he sold KFC for $2 million (about $18 million today) but still continued to work as the brand's spokesperson!

Laura Ingalls Wilder was sixty-five when she published her first *Little House on the Prairie* book, which later became a popular TV show. Frank McCourt won a Pulitzer Prize for writing *Angela's Ashes* at age sixty-six. Grandma Moses started painting at age seventy-eight and became a world-renowned folk artist.

Another great true story that illustrates the importance of keeping your brain active for both health and happiness involves the life of Rita Moreno, a legendary actress and dancer best known for her role in *West Side Story*. In her later years, she found herself at a crossroads, facing some common challenges of aging.

Instead of allowing herself to slip into the "retirement" mode that many seniors fall into, she made a conscious decision to keep her brain engaged. She started learning new skills, took on new roles, and even returned to school to take classes and earn her doctoral degree. Her most striking transformation came when she began taking up new languages, challenging her mind in ways that she hadn't in decades. Dr. Moreno found that one of the keys to maintaining her happiness and mental sharpness was consistently pushing her brain outside of its comfort zone. She said, "I keep learning new things. I think it's important for your brain, and I think it keeps me happy." Her dedication to keeping her mind active helped her maintain a strong sense of joy and excitement for life, even as she entered her nineties. She's currently ninety-three years old!

I've been trying to learn Mandarin and admit I'm terrible at it. Two of my grandchildren are half Chinese! It's such a fascinating language that has rich lessons and insights embedded in the words. For example, the word "learning" is made up of two characters. The first one, pronounced "shoo-eh" (Xue), stands for "learn," and the second one, pronounced "shee" (Xuexi), means "to practice." In other words, to truly learn something, you have to practice it. You can't expect to know something after only one attempt. Every habit you want to create takes daily practice. Each day, you are changing and becoming more proficient at that skill, as well as becoming a new type of person.

Quote

"Happiness consists in activity: such is the constitution of our nature; it is a running stream, and not a stagnant pool." —John M. Good (English writer)[63]

Scripture

"A wise man will hear, and will increase learning; and a man of understanding shall attain unto wise counsels." (Proverbs 1:5)

Lesson Learned

All humans need stability in order to be happy, but we also need a certain level of uncertainty; otherwise, we become bored and restless. Variety is the spice of life.

Science has concluded that keeping active, both physically and mentally, has numerous benefits, including lessening the likelihood of getting Alzheimer's disease.[64] Beyond that, a love of learning can fill our lives with purpose, meaning, and awe. There are so many amazing things to learn about this world we live in!

Challenge

Today, think of something you have always wanted to learn how to do and start doing it! YouTube is one of the easiest and least expensive teachers out there! Pick a topic and subscribe to a newsletter that keeps you informed on the latest discoveries in that field. Become an expert in something new!

Listening Better

Story

There's a lesson my dad taught me that has stuck with me my whole life. It was something so simple yet so powerful: "Talk less about yourself and get others talking about themselves."

I remember him saying it one afternoon, right before I went to a party. I had been anxious about making a good impression, unsure of what to say or how to fit in. I asked him for advice, and without hesitation, he shared his secret: "At a party, don't focus on yourself. Ask other people questions about their lives, their stories, their interests. People love talking about themselves, and when you let them, they'll go home thinking, 'Wow, she was such a nice person.'"

It sounded too easy to be true, but I took his advice. At the party, I did exactly what he said, asking people about their jobs, classes, hobbies, favorite books. I barely mentioned myself; instead, I listened. By the end of the night, I noticed that people were gravitating toward me. They seemed genuinely happy to have shared their stories with someone who was interested in them. I learned a lot, and I felt a warmth in the way they spoke to me. They left with big smiles, and a few days later, I heard from some of them, saying how nice it had been to meet someone who was so easy to talk to.

Years later, I realized my dad's lesson wasn't just about parties; it was about making people feel important. I've seen it over and over in my life. People loved my dad because he made them feel like they were the center of attention, not by talking about his own accomplishments but by showing genuine interest in theirs. His ability to make others feel valued was a gift. And because of it, he was always surrounded by friends and admirers, not because he had the most to say but because he knew the value of listening and making others feel seen.

My dad didn't just tell us about this secret to being liked; he showed us. Whenever we were together and he wanted to prove his point, he'd say, "Watch this," and give us a wink. It was his little way of signaling that a lesson was about to unfold before our eyes.

I remember one particular afternoon at a family gathering. My sisters and I were sitting around, talking about how we could make new friends at school, and Dad overheard us. He leaned in, gave us that signature wink, and approached one of the guests, someone he didn't know very well but who seemed to be standing alone.

We all watched as he struck up a conversation with them. At first, it seemed like small talk, but then, as the minutes passed, it became clear that he wasn't doing much talking at all. He asked questions, listened intently, laughed, put his hand on their shoulder, and nodded as the other person shared stories about their life. My dad was just there, making them feel important.

By the end of the conversation, that person was practically glowing. They walked away with a big smile, almost as if they had just shared their deepest secrets with a best friend. We couldn't help but laugh because it was exactly what Dad had promised. He didn't have to be the center of attention, although he often was. He didn't have to boast about his achievements or talk about himself. Instead, he let the other person shine, and in doing so, he made them feel heard and valued.

It didn't matter where we were—a family gathering, a party, or even at the grocery store—Dad would always manage to put his lesson into action. And sure enough, every time, the person he spoke to would walk away smiling, feeling like they'd had the best conversation of their life. It was like magic, and it wasn't until later that I realized how powerful that simple gesture of listening could be. Some say it like this: Be interested, not interesting.

Quote

"We have two ears and one mouth so that we can listen twice as much as we speak." —Epictetus (Greek Stoic philosopher)[65]

Scripture

"Let every man be swift to hear, slow to speak, slow to wrath." (James 1:19)

Lesson Learned

Most of us are so busy thinking about what we're going to say in a conversation that we don't hear what the other person says. One of my faults is that I often get excited and then jump in before the other person has even finished. I really am trying to work on that.

Several years ago, I got my ham radio license. I thought it would be a fun hobby and an important part of my emergency preparedness efforts. One thing I really like about it is that while one person is pushing the button to talk, no one else can butt in. Everyone involved in the conversation has to listen. Before speaking, you identify your call sign so that everyone knows who you are. If it's unclear what was said, you repeat back what you think you heard. We can learn some important lessons from those ham radio rules to improve our everyday communication. George Bernard Shaw, who was an Irish playwright, critic, and political activist, jokingly said, "The single biggest problem in communication is the illusion that it has taken place."[66]

Getting people to like you isn't about pretending to be someone you're not or using manipulative tactics to win affection. Instead, it's about being genuine, approachable, and emotionally intelligent. It's about creating an environment where people feel comfortable, valued, and respected. Genuine listening builds relationships and trust.

Challenge

Starting conversations with people can often be scary. Here are some simple tips to remember:

- Show genuine interest in others
- Practice active listening

- Smile and use positive body language
- Give sincere compliments
- Be empathetic and understanding
- Be humble and avoid bragging
- Find common ground
- Instead of yes-or-no questions, ask open-ended questions that get the other person talking

Here are a few questions you can ask someone to start a conversation:

- What's something you're really passionate about?
- How did you get into your line of work?
- What's your favorite book or movie?
- What has been your favorite travel destination so far?
- Do you have a favorite family tradition?
- If you could learn any new skill, what would it be?
- What's something that always makes you laugh?
- What's the most interesting thing you've learned recently?
- Do you have a favorite quote or motto that inspires you?
- What's your favorite thing about where you live?
- Do you have any pets, or would you like to have one?
- What's something you've always wanted to try but haven't yet?

Making People Feel Wanted

Story

When I was a young girl, there was an experience that will forever live in family lore. My oldest sister came bursting through the front door of our house one afternoon after school, glowing with excitement. "We've been invited to dinner at my friend's house!" she announced, as though we had just been invited to dine with royalty.

Naturally, the entire family jumped into action like we were preparing for the Oscars. We all got dressed up, and I was proud of my sister for snagging such a generous friend to invite us all. My parents had recently divorced, so I was looking forward to a home-cooked meal with a "real" family again.

When we finally arrived at the friend's house, her mother opened the door and . . . froze. The look on her face was a mixture of shock, panic, and confusion, like she had just opened the door to a marching band she didn't hire. After a long, awkward pause, she managed to stammer out, "Oh . . . um . . . this is unexpected. Only your sister was invited. We don't have enough food for everyone."

Cue the most cringe-inducing silence in the history of social interactions. My dad, always the diplomat, chuckled nervously and said, "Well, we must've misunderstood. Sorry for the confusion!" As my older sister was escorted into the house, the rest of us shuffled back to the car, our fancy outfits and enthusiasm feeling very out of place. Nobody spoke, but the embarrassment and rejection hung in the air like fog. Then my dad turned around with a sparkle in his eye and said, "Well, we're all dressed up, so let's go somewhere fun to eat!"

And just like that, we found ourselves at a nice restaurant. We had the time of our lives eating food that was not mac and cheese from a box while my dad shared one of his famous life lessons. "Remember this, girls," he said, gesturing with a breadstick for emphasis. "Never make people feel unwanted. That mother could've thrown together a simple meal, even if we all had to share a potato. It's not about the food—it's about making people feel welcome."

I've always remembered that lesson and tried my hardest to make guests in my home feel wanted. I also learned another lesson that day. Instead of feeling angry or depressed by the rejection, my dad turned it into a fun event that stretched my stomach and my heart.

Quote

"The deepest principle in human nature is the craving to be appreciated."—William James[67]

Scripture

"Remember the worth of souls is great in the sight of God." (Doctrine and Covenants 18:10)

Lesson Learned

It's a fundamental human need to feel valued and wanted. When someone feels unwanted, it can erode their confidence, damage their emotional well-being, and leave lasting scars. Whether it's in personal relationships, at work, or in casual interactions, the way we treat others can profoundly impact their sense of belonging. Showing kindness, attentiveness, and appreciation can make a world of difference.

Everyone deserves to feel seen, heard, and cherished, regardless of their circumstances. When we actively show others that they matter, it strengthens relationships and promotes mutual respect. This can be as simple as listening attentively, expressing gratitude, offering encouragement, or welcoming someone into your home for dinner.

Challenge

For one week, challenge yourself to give a genuine compliment or positive affirmation to at least one person every day. Whether it's praising a colleague's work, appreciating a friend's kindness, or acknowledging a stranger's effort, your words can make them feel valued and accepted. Keep it sincere and specific to show that you truly see them.

Identify someone in your circle who might feel left out—whether it's a new colleague, a quiet classmate, or a distant acquaintance—and invite them to join an activity or conversation. It could be as simple as asking them to lunch, including them in a group chat, or striking up a conversation.

Making Time for the One

Story

I had never felt more nervous or proud than I did when wearing my formal, light blue gown at the Velvet Turtle restaurant while sitting across from the most eligible bachelor in the San Francisco Bay Area: my dad. Even though he could have been out to dinner with any of the women who were interested in dating him, he had asked *me* out to dinner and made me feel important and special. We talked about things that were important to a twelve-year-old, and I felt like my dad truly saw me.

Because I'm a twin, it was more common for me to be grouped as "one of the twins," so a dinner date alone with my dad was truly special. I've tried to have date nights with each of my children over the years too. What a great tradition for parents to have with their kids and grandkids.

I remember seeing a long spider web attached to a chandelier high above our heads in the elegant two-story ceiling of the restaurant. As waiters would rush by us to deliver delicious meals to guests, my dad and I would watch the spider web sway from the gusts, wondering where it might end up. My dad was so tickled by that. It made me feel special that I could be a part of that memorable evening that we laughed about for years after.

He did a great job of introducing us to different cuisines over the years and always encouraged us to be willing to try new foods. To encourage us kids to try tasting baby octopus for the first time, he allowed some of the legs to intentionally dangle from his lips, eliciting laughter and an eagerness to try the unique delicacy. Smart man, right?

QUOTE

"To love and be loved is to feel the sun from both sides." —David Viscott (American psychiatrist, author, and radio host)[68]

SCRIPTURE

"What man of you, having an hundred sheep, if he lose one of them, doth not leave the ninety and nine in the wilderness, and go after that which is lost, until he find it?" (Luke 15:4)

LESSON LEARNED

Making time for our kids is vital. Making people feel important and seen is a simple yet powerful way to build connection and trust. When we take the time to acknowledge others, whether through a kind word, active listening, or just giving them our undivided attention, we communicate that they matter.

In a world where many often feel overlooked or unheard, the act of truly seeing someone can be a profound gesture. It doesn't require grand gestures or elaborate compliments; it can be as simple as asking how their day is going and genuinely caring about their response. When people feel heard, they begin to feel valued, and this often leads to stronger, more meaningful relationships.

Beyond words, making people feel important involves recognizing and appreciating their unique qualities and contributions. It's about celebrating who they are rather than what they do or how they look.

CHALLENGE

One way to make people feel special is by taking the time to remember details about their lives, such as their interests, preferences, or significant events. It shows that you care about them as an individual. Whether it's a thoughtful message acknowledging an achievement or a small surprise that reflects something important to them, these acts of recognition can make someone feel deeply valued. Personal attention makes people feel seen and appreciated, beyond generic interactions.

Most of us are terrible at remembering people's names, so simply getting better at that can go a long way to making someone feel like they matter. After you meet someone, say their name out loud. A person's name is like music to their ears. When you get a chance, write a note to yourself on your cell phone about them and their name and then review it later so you don't forget.

When my husband and I are in social situations, we play a game that challenges our memorization skills: He's in charge of memorizing the men's names, while I have to learn the women's names. Then we compare notes and teach each other what we learned.

When trying to remember someone's name, connect it to something memorable like a rhyme, a celebrity, or a unique trait. Silly or visual associations make names stick in your memory easier. For example, if you meet Mark and learn that he loves to read books, repeat in your mind, "Mark, the bookmark!"

Mind Over Matter

Story

I have a friend who really struggles when others achieve success. It's not that he's a bad person; he just has a tough time feeling happy for others when they're doing well and he isn't. In fact, he says it makes him feel worse about himself. He's honest about his jealousy; he feels like if someone else is succeeding, that somehow means there's less success left for him. And it's not just in big, life-changing events; it's even watching TV shows like *America's Got Talent.* He can't help but feel a bit down when someone else gets the praise or wins the big prize that he secretly wishes for.

It's a bit of a backward way of looking at things though. Instead of feeling worse, I think we should let the success of others inspire us. If someone else can do something amazing, why not let that spark a fire in us? It's like seeing a friend get their dream job—rather than thinking, "Well, there goes my shot," we should think, "Hey, if they can do it, why can't I?" Their success doesn't take anything away from us. In fact, it can make us more motivated to pursue our own goals and dreams.

One of the most inspiring examples of this comes from the world of sports. For centuries, the idea of running a mile in under four minutes was considered absolutely impossible. Experts said the human body just wasn't capable of it. Enter Roger Bannister. In 1954, he broke that barrier, becoming the first man to run a mile in under four minutes. You would think that after such an extraordinary feat, the record would stand for years, right? Wrong! Just forty-six days later, another man, John Landy, did the same thing. And then, a year later, *three* more runners broke the four-minute barrier in a single race! Rather than be jealous, they chose to be inspired!

In less than a year, running that fast went from being thought of as physically impossible to becoming a reality for several athletes. Today, more than 1,000 runners have broken the four-minute mile. The impossible became possible, and now it's a goal that countless athletes chase and achieve. The success of one person didn't limit the success of others—it actually made the world more open to achieving what was once unthinkable.

Quote

"Who is the happiest of men? He who values the merits of others, and in their pleasure takes joy, even as though 'twere his own." —Johann Wolfgang von Goethe (German writer, poet, naturalist, and philosopher)[69]

Scripture

"But this much I can tell you, that if ye do not watch yourselves, and your thoughts, and your words, and your deeds, and observe the commandments of God, and continue in the faith of what ye have heard concerning the coming of our Lord, even unto the end of your lives, ye must perish. And now, O man, remember, and perish not." (Mosiah 4:30)

Lesson Learned

This principle doesn't just apply to sports; it applies to all aspects of life. When you see someone else succeed, whether it's in their career, in their relationships, or in achieving a personal goal, don't feel threatened. Let it motivate you. The fact that someone else can succeed doesn't mean there's less success to go around—it means there's even more potential for all of us. It means that barriers are there to be broken and dreams are there to be chased. So instead of feeling jealous, let's choose to be inspired. If someone else can do it, then maybe, just maybe, we can too.

Our minds possess far more power than we often give them credit for. The thoughts we choose to focus on shape our attitudes, behaviors, and even our physical well-being. By harnessing the power of positive thinking, mindfulness, and visualization, we can overcome obstacles, push past limitations, and transform our lives in ways we never thought possible.

Our minds not only influence our emotions and reactions, but they can also impact our bodies, as seen in the mind-body connection that plays a role in healing and resilience. In fact, studies have shown that our beliefs and mindset can affect our health, success, and overall happiness.[70] When we realize that we hold the key to shaping our reality through our thoughts, we can begin to use that power to create meaningful, lasting changes in our lives.

Challenge

Today, try to develop an attitude of abundance. There are plenty of opportunities for success and happiness and even money in the world. Celebrate someone else's victory as an achievement for humankind.

To avoid feeling jealous of others' accomplishments, view it as inspiration, not competition. Someone else's success doesn't diminish your own potential. Jealousy often comes from feeling insecure or inadequate. Choose to be inspired to improve yourself.

Every single time I have been jealous of someone else for their success, looks, house, money, or whatever, I always find out something about their life that I would absolutely *not* want in my life. Every single time. Focus on the good you have in your own life. Someone is probably secretly jealous of you!

Missionary Work

Story

It absolutely breaks my heart that so many Jews and Romans rejected the Messiah when He was standing right in front of them. The same is true today. I'll never forget a moment on my mission that taught me a profound truth about why some people accept the gospel and others do not.

It was a hot summer day in Spain, and my companion and I were in our little apartment eating lunch. I walked into our bedroom and heard a fluttering sound. I followed the soft pattering and looked behind a huge, heavy armoire. I noticed that the bedroom window was open to let the breeze in, and then suddenly I saw a tiny bird stuck between the wall and the big piece of furniture. My arm couldn't reach the bird, and I wasn't strong enough to move the armoire by myself.

Trying to think outside the box, I quickly retrieved a long broom and thought I could nudge the frightened bird up and out to freedom, but whenever the broom handle would get near the bird, it would chirp in fear. I quietly tried to explain to my new feathered friend that I wanted to help it, save it. But the more I tried, the more frightened the bird became. I recruited the help of my companion, and together we tried to move the heavy furniture away from the wall to give the bird room to escape. We pushed and heaved for ten minutes, trying to assure the bird that we were trying to help it, when suddenly my companion and I looked at each other, realizing that this familiar scenario was how we were spending each and every day of our mission—trying to help others learn of Christ and be free from their sins.

So many people we talked to were afraid of us and would slam their doors when we came knocking. So many of them didn't understand that we just wanted to help and make their lives better. They didn't know that our efforts were to save them from spiritual bondage. They just couldn't *see*. Nevertheless, we kept trying. Every day we went out into the world and continued to invite people to hear our message. We couldn't be angry with those who rejected our message because they simply didn't understand what we were offering. Our job was to open our mouths and keep trying. I realized that I probably wouldn't convert the entire country of Spain, but I could love and invite. That's what Jesus Christ did on His mission, and I could do the same thing.

The bird story has a happy ending. Eventually we were able to push the huge armoire away from the wall enough that the bird was able to quickly fly away. Did it thank us? Of course not. We didn't get angry for its lack of gratitude. We didn't judge the bird for getting into that predicament in the first place. We just worked and helped to save one little sparrow. You know how the Lord feels about sparrows, right? He created them and is mindful of their needs (see Luke 12:6–7). Matthew 10 says that the Lord knows the very hairs on your head and that you are of even more value to Him than His precious sparrows. You are His family.

So it is with the world. There will be many who reject the prophets and also you. That's okay. They have their agency to choose. Your job as one of Christ's followers is to keep loving and continue to invite others until you find the ones who are sincerely seeking truth and light. Just keep standing in holy places, and when the Lord comes again, you'll be ready!

Quote

"Preach the gospel at all times, and if necessary, use words." —St. Francis of Assisi (Italian Catholic friar, deacon, and preacher who founded the Franciscan Order)[71]

Scripture

"[Be] willing to mourn with those that mourn; yea, and comfort those that stand in need of comfort, and to stand as witnesses of God at all times and in all things, and in all places that ye may be in, even until death, that ye may be redeemed of God, and be numbered with those of the first resurrection, that ye may have eternal life." (Mosiah 18:9)

Lesson Learned

There is a unique and profound joy that comes from sharing the gospel of Jesus Christ with others. When we invite others to experience the love, hope, and peace that Jesus offers, we are not only extending a message of faith but also helping them discover a life filled with purpose and direction. The joy we feel in these moments goes beyond the simple act of teaching; it is a deep, soul-enriching satisfaction that comes from knowing we are participating in something eternal.

Whether it's through a conversation, a simple act of service, or inviting someone to learn more, the act of sharing the gospel becomes a personal mission that brings us closer to Christ and to others in ways we never expected.

As we share the gospel, we often find that our own faith is strengthened. Seeing the light of understanding and hope in someone else's eyes when they hear the message of Christ is an experience unlike any other. When we witness others grow spiritually and embrace the love of Jesus, we realize that this joy is not just about us helping them; it's about all of us coming closer to Christ and becoming better disciples together.

Challenge

There are many ways people can share the gospel of Jesus Christ with others, and each method can be tailored to fit one's personal strengths, circumstances, and relationships. Here are a few:

- Living by example
- Sharing personal stories about gospel principles with others
- Inviting others to church or activities

- Sharing scriptures or inspirational messages on social media
- Offering service
- Posting your testimony about a certain gospel principle on social media
- Starting a YouTube channel or podcast about the Church and your beliefs
- Sending referrals to the missionaries
- Doing genealogy work

Money

Story

As an online university professor, I truly love what I do. One of my favorite topics to teach is financial management in my life skills class. It's always a treat when students come up with unique ways to express key concepts. I remember when one of my international students who was learning English wrote something that made me smile. He said, "Your pillow will be softer when you are wise with money."

Isn't that a poetic and clever way to put it? It's like he found the key to inner peace hidden in a financial spreadsheet! And he's right! When we're careful and thoughtful with our money, we can rest easier at night. Instead of losing sleep over unpaid bills and mounting credit card statements, you get to lay your head on that pillow, knowing you're in control of your money.

The feeling of being out of debt is downright delicious. It's like the weight of the world is lifted off your shoulders. Or, maybe more accurately, it's like taking off a 500-pound backpack that's been digging into your skin for years. No one wants to walk around with a financial noose around their neck. But here's the reality—according to Comet.com, 80 percent of Americans are carrying some form of debt, whether it's from a mortgage, car payment, student loan, credit card, or medical bills.[72]

So if you fall into that group, you're not alone, but it might be time for an honest financial self-assessment. Take a good look at your assets and liabilities. Your future, and that soft pillow, will thank you!

You have two simple choices if you want to get ahead financially: spend less than you earn, or earn more money.

QUOTE

"Money does not dictate your lifestyle. It's what you do to get it and how you manage your finances that determine your lifestyle." —Wayne Chirisa (American businessman)[73]

SCRIPTURE

"Do not spend money for that which is of no worth, nor your labor for that which cannot satisfy." (2 Nephi 9:51)

LESSON LEARNED

Being wise with money starts with creating a budget that helps you manage your income and expenses effectively. It's important to track where your money is going and make conscious decisions about your spending habits. Set financial goals that are realistic and achievable, whether it's saving for an emergency fund, paying off debt, or saving for future goals like retirement or a home.

Learn to prioritize needs over wants and avoid impulse purchases by sticking to a plan. By controlling your spending and being intentional with your finances, you can build a strong foundation for financial security and peace of mind.

Stop comparing yourself with what others have. They may appear to have it all—the big house, the expensive car, the stylish clothes, etc.—but what they might also have that you can't see is crippling debt and constant arguments over money. Appearances can be deceiving.

Another key component of financial wisdom is saving and investing for the future. Start by setting aside a portion of your income for savings, even if it's a small amount at first. Consider contributing to a retirement account, building an emergency fund, and exploring low-risk investment options to grow your money over time.

Educate yourself on the importance of debt management, making sure to pay off high-interest debt quickly, and avoid accumulating more. Being wise with money also involves understanding the value of money, resisting the temptation to compare yourself to others, and practicing contentment with what you have. By making informed decisions and planning for the future, you can feel more peace and sleep better at night!

CHALLENGE

Today, take an honest look at your finances. Start by tracking your expenses this week . . . every penny. Then you can plan a strategy for cutting back on unnecessary expenses. All those pretty pennies add up.

Be in control of your money so that it doesn't control you. Here are a few things people can do to be wise with their finances:

- Create and stick to a budget
- Build an emergency fund
- Pay off high-interest debt
- Save and invest for the future
- Live below your means
- Educate yourself about finances
- Consider a side hustle job
- Stop scrolling and believing everything you see on social media

Morning Rituals

Story

For a long time, my mornings started with checking my emails the moment I woke up. I thought I was being productive—staying on top of things, responding quickly, and keeping everything moving. But over time, I realized that I was starting each day in a reactive mode. Instead of focusing on my own priorities, I was immediately pulled into other people's requests, problems, and expectations. My inbox was essentially setting my agenda for the day, and my most important tasks kept getting pushed aside.

I'm not saying email isn't valuable—it's an essential tool for communication. But I've learned that how and when I use it makes a huge difference in my productivity and focus. Instead of letting emails dictate my day, I created a morning ritual centered on what truly mattered first. Now, I begin my day by focusing on my highest-priority tasks—whether it's deep work, creative projects, or personal growth. Only after making meaningful progress on my goals do I then check my inbox.

One of the best strategies I've found is blocking out dedicated time for emails on certain days rather than constantly reacting to them. This shift has been a game changer. It ensures that I stay in control of my time and energy rather than letting my inbox dictate my productivity. If you want to perform at a higher level, consider structuring your mornings around what truly moves the needle in your life. It's a simple but powerful habit that will help you focus on your priorities—rather than letting others decide them for you.

Quote

"You have to be able to set boundaries; otherwise, the rest of the world is telling you who you are and what you should be doing." —Oprah Winfrey (American media executive, TV producer, and philanthropist)[74]

Scripture

"Counsel with the Lord in all thy doings, and he will direct thee for good; yea, when thou liest down at night lie down unto the Lord, that he may watch over you in your sleep; and when thou risest in the morning let thy heart be full of thanks unto God." (Alma 37:37)

Lesson Learned

George Lorimer, who was an American journalist, author, and publisher of *The Saturday Evening Post*, once said, "You've got to get up every morning with determination if you're going to go to bed with satisfaction."[75]

Do you have a morning ritual? High-performance men and women have a morning ritual. It's a thing! Of course, they're all different, and yours also needs to meet your unique needs and situation. It might include listening to an inspiring podcast while you get dressed or writing in a gratitude journal to create a positive mindset for the day.

As you create disciplined morning rituals, push yourself, but also be gentle with yourself. Don't expect perfection. The goal is to improve yourself step by step. If you need to start with baby steps, do that. If you're ready to jump to your "Next-Level Self," go for it!

Challenge

Look at your daily routine and discover what's working for you and what's not. Create a morning ritual that allows you to decide who you are and what you need to do.

Be guarded about your precious time and where you choose to spend it. Think about some things you can include in your morning to help you wake up refreshed and energized.

Be energized by your morning ritual. Include habits that get you excited about waking up and starting your day.

Starting the day off right with a meaningful morning ritual can set a positive tone for the rest of the day. Here are some ideas to consider:

- Pray and/or meditate
- Read scriptures
- Memorize inspirational quotes while you get dressed
- Recite positive affirmations in your mind while you brush your teeth
- Move or exercise
- Journal
- Hydrate
- Eat a healthy breakfast
- Set goals for the day
- Practice mindfulness, setting intentions for the day
- Engage in deep breathing
- Stand outside in the sun for 5 minutes to get natural Vitamin D and signal to your body that it's time to wake up and get moving
- Stretch or do yoga poses to get your blood circulating
- Hum a happy tune to stimulate your Vagus nerve to lower stress and enhance emotional regulation
- Identify 3 things you're grateful for to instantly elevate your mood and perspective
- Set an intention for the 3 most important tasks you need to accomplish today
- Make your bed
- Limit phone use for the first 30 minutes to protect your peace

Nature

Story

Several years ago, I got to walk around Walden Pond in Concord, Massachusetts, just a short drive outside of Boston. Author Henry David Thoreau famously lived at Walden Pond for two years, two months, and two days in an experiment in simple living. Thoreau built a tiny cabin on a piece of land that his friend, author Ralph Waldo Emerson, owned in the 1840s. Thoreau's goal was to completely disconnect from society and explore how a person could live self-sufficiently in harmony with nature. He wanted to strip away unnecessary material possessions and obligations to focus on what was truly essential to human happiness and personal fulfillment.

His time at Walden Pond was not just about personal introspection but also a critique of the materialism and consumerism of society, urging people to live more thoughtfully and with greater awareness of their impact on the world. His reflections focused on the beauty of a simple life, which he later wrote about in his well-known book *Walden*. After reading his book many years prior, I had always wanted to go there to see the beauty he wrote about. I was so glad when a business trip finally took me there!

I remember it was a cold November afternoon, and I shuttered to imagine Thoreau sitting in his cold cabin without a heater! It was so cold that day that I didn't want to walk all the way around the lake, even though I had dreamed of walking along the very same path Henry David Thoreau surely did each day over a hundred years ago. My husband reminded me of my goal and guided my wavering thoughts by saying, "You're going to regret it if you don't walk all the way around!" I knew he was right, so I pushed on in the cold with my teeth chattering. Despite the weather, it was magical, and I was so grateful I took action on my dream.

Henry David Thoreau was a great American essayist, naturalist, poet, abolitionist, and political philosopher. He said, "If you have built castles in the air, your work need not be lost; that is where they should be. Now put foundations under them."[76] In his quote, "building castles in the air" refers to daydreaming or imagining "what if" scenarios for the future. Instead, he challenged us to not just dream but to take action. There's still a place for dreams because everything needs to be created spiritually before it can be created physically, but at some point, we need to do the work to make our dreams come true.

Quote

"The creation of a thousand forests is in one acorn." —Ralph Waldo Emerson (American essayist, philosopher, poet, and lecturer)[77]

Scripture

"All things denote there is a God; yea, even the earth, and all things that are upon the face of it, yea, and its motion, yea, and also all the planets which move in their regular form do witness that there is a Supreme Creator." (Alma 30:44)

Lesson Learned

Nature has a remarkable way of soothing the soul, offering a sense of peace and renewal that's hard to find anywhere else. The sound of rustling leaves, the smell of fresh pine, or the sight of a glassy lake can immediately calm the mind and ease the weight of the world. In a fast-paced, technology-driven society, we often forget how much we need the grounding presence of nature.

Stepping outside, whether for a walk in the park or simply lying on the grass beneath the stars, allows us to reconnect with something timeless. It serves as a reminder of the beauty and simplicity that often gets lost in the noise of everyday life. Nature offers us a pause, an opportunity to breathe deeply and remember that we are part of something much bigger than our worries.

Spending time in nature provides more than just a temporary escape from stress; it rejuvenates our spirits and gives us the clarity and energy we need to face life's challenges. It's a balm to our souls, not only in the moment but in its lasting effects on our well-being. We need it—perhaps more than we realize—to feel whole and connected to both ourselves and the world around us.

Challenge

Make plans to spend time outdoors:

- Go on a walk outside
- Practice mindfulness outdoors by listening to the birds or rustling leaves
- Read outside
- Have a picnic
- Garden or plant something
- Watch the sunrise or sunset
- Stand in the sun in the morning to help your body wake up and get that important vitamin D!
- Get down on your knees to pull some weeds and pray at the same time
- Do deep-breathing exercises while inhaling that fresh air
- Gather fresh flowers for your home or to give to a friend
- Walk on the grass barefoot to feel childlike wonder again
- Sit down with your back against a tree to feel truly grounded
- Create rock formations while you consider how to gain more balance in your life

Parenting

Story

I admit it: I was a clueless mother. Not in the forgot-to-pack-lunch or sent-my-kid-to-school-in-pajamas kind of way, but in the I-had-no-idea-what-my-kid-was-destined-for kind of way. And one of my sons is the perfect illustration of the important lesson I learned.

When he was little, all he wanted to do was play video games. Morning, noon, night—he was glued to that screen, fingers flying, eyes locked in intense focus. As a *good* mother, I did what any responsible parent would do: I nagged him. I limited screen time. I warned him about wasting his childhood, rotting his brain, and dooming himself to a life of underachievement. I dispensed wisdom like "You can't spend your life playing video games! Go develop some real talents for a future career!"

He also loved drawing, but to me, that was just another hobby. You know, the kind of thing kids do before they get serious about *real* jobs. Of course, I told him he was talented and amazing—because, obviously, I'm a supportive mom—but deep down, I worried. Was he spending his time wisely? Would he ever do something productive with his life? Was he doomed to be a starving artist?

Well, guess what he does for a living now?

Yep. He designs video games at one of the largest video game companies in the world. He took the very thing I thought was a distraction and turned it into a wildly successful career, making impressive money and having a blast doing what he loves. And here I was, worried he'd end up living in my basement, surviving on instant ramen and nostalgia.

Now, not only does he have a dream job, but he's introduced me to an entire industry I didn't even know existed. (Did you know people watch other people play video games online? And the people who make those videos get paid for it? My son could have told me this years ago, but I was too busy telling him to go outside and get some fresh air.)

Sometimes the thing that looks like a distraction today is actually the foundation for a brilliant future. And sometimes, as a parent, you just have to sit back, eat a slice of humble pie, and admit that your kid knew better all along.

Ready for a laugh? One of my other sons is also working in the video game industry now. On top of their full-time jobs, the three of them have created their own studio together called Nekomata Games, and have launched several games into the world. In other words, as parents, we can guide our children to what we think is a solid career, but their hearts will also direct them to what they were possibly born to do.

Quote

"If you want to change the world, go home and love your family."
—Mother Teresa (Catholic nun, missionary, and humanitarian)[78]

Scripture

"Train up a child in the way he should go: and when he is old, he will not depart from it." (Proverbs 22:6)

Lesson Learned

So what did I learn from this? First, never underestimate the power of passion. Second, maybe *I* should have played more video games! And third, as parents, we simply cannot—and should not—project what *we* think is right onto our kids. Sure, we can guide them, offer advice, and steer them away from *actual* danger, but we also need to stop forcing them into our neatly labeled boxes of success. The world has changed since I was a kid and so has the path to successful careers.

Good parenting is a blend of love, discipline, and guidance. It's about creating an environment where children feel safe, valued, and heard while also providing the structure they need to grow and develop into responsible, compassionate individuals. At the core of good parenting is the ability to model positive behavior, teaching children through both words and actions. Parents who show kindness, patience, and respect for others set a powerful example, helping children learn how to treat those around them. It's not about being perfect but about being present, listening, and offering support, all while helping children navigate the complexities of life.

Another key aspect of good parenting is setting clear boundaries and expectations. Children thrive when they understand what's expected of them and the consequences of their actions. This helps them build self-discipline, make good choices, and understand that their behavior affects others. But good parenting isn't just about discipline; it's also about being their biggest cheerleader. Encouraging children to pursue their passions, reassuring them during setbacks, and celebrating their achievements create a strong foundation of self-confidence.

Ultimately, good parenting involves balancing love with accountability and providing the right tools for children to succeed in life, knowing they're supported every step of the way. I've always thought that a "good" parent's job is to expose their children to as many things as possible so that they know their options, have experience with a variety of things, and can then choose what's best for them. After all, I was the one who bought them their first video game system!

Challenge

Parents can always find ways to improve their approach to raising children. One effective way is by focusing on active listening. Taking the time to truly hear what children are saying, validating their emotions, and responding thoughtfully can strengthen relationships and foster trust. When children feel understood, they're more likely to open up and seek guidance when needed.

Another way parents can improve is by modeling emotional intelligence. Showing children how to express their feelings in a healthy way, manage stress, and problem-solve when conflicts arise teaches them critical life skills. The way parents handle their own emotions and reactions can serve as a powerful example for children to follow.

Lastly, consistency is key. Ensuring that rules and expectations are clear and followed regularly helps children feel secure, which can also build their self-discipline and resilience. When parents make an effort to be consistent, they also reinforce the values and behaviors they want to instill in their children.

Commit yourself to encourage others on their path. Our journey is different from everyone else's.

Persistence

Story

My oldest son was fortunate to get his first job at age fifteen because the owner of a local movie theater was a member of the Church who hired him. My son worked hard and accepted all the crummy tasks, and by the time he was sixteen, he already had a strong employer reference to put on his résumé for future jobs. One of his friends also wanted a job there, but the owner wasn't hiring anyone else at the time.

One day, a super popular movie was being released, and the movie theater had a big carnival to attract more customers. Now, you're going to think I'm making this up when you read this next part. My son's friend just showed up and volunteered to help out at the carnival for *free*. He helped clean up, passed out free samples of ice cream, greeted guests, and was so willing to do anything that the boss ended up hiring him at the end of the day! They were so impressed by his eagerness to work and his positive attitude, and they knew they wanted an employee like that and would make room for him in their company. He got the job while other kids who wanted to work there just dropped off their résumé and waited to hear back from the manager.

In other words, go out there and get what you want! Be prepared to work for it and be persistent.

Sometimes we get discouraged when we look at people who have achieved the level of expertise and recognition that we want, but we have to remember that they were once beginners too. We usually see others at the finish line and forget that it took many years of hard work, practice, and even failures to achieve what they have.

William Shakespeare, the English playwright and dramatist, wisely stated, "To climb steep hills requires a slow pace at first."[79] Whenever we start a new project at work, home, or school, it usually takes a while to get started, possibly because of procrastination or simply not knowing exactly how to begin. Sometimes the finished outcome seems very far away, so we drag our feet and our enthusiasm wanders. That first step is often the hardest. But I've noticed that once I finally get going, I start to gain momentum and even confidence.

This may sound silly, but I recently bought one of those super expensive, handy-dandy blenders and then didn't touch it for a week. It looked complicated, and I didn't think I had the time to read the huge manual and recipe book that came with it. But once I finally took it out of the box and learned how simple it was, I became obsessed, and now I make yummy things with it every day. It's a dumb example, but I'm surprised at how often I do that with other new things in my life. Take action and be persistent.

Quote

"It does not matter how slowly you go as long as you do not stop." —Confucius (ancient Chinese philosopher, teacher, and political thinker)[80]

Scripture

"Wherefore, ye must press forward with a steadfastness in Christ, having a perfect brightness of hope, and a love of God and of all men." (2 Nephi 31:20)

Lesson Learned

Persistence is one of the most powerful qualities one can develop in life. It's a driving force that helps individuals push through obstacles and keep moving forward, even in the face of difficulty. Life is rarely a smooth path, and setbacks are inevitable. Whether in our personal goals, careers, or relationships, challenges will arise. However, it's how we respond to these challenges that defines our success. Those who are persistent do not allow obstacles to stop them but instead see them as opportunities to grow stronger and more determined.

One of the key benefits of persistence is that it enables us to develop resilience. When we encounter failure or setbacks, it's easy to become discouraged and give up. But persistence teaches us to keep going, even when progress is slow or when the results are not immediately apparent.

It's through continued effort that we eventually find success. Every time we push through a challenge, we build the mental and emotional strength to handle future obstacles more effectively. Persistence reinforces the idea that setbacks are not permanent; they're simply part of the journey toward achieving our goals.

Success rarely comes overnight, and it's the consistent effort over time that leads to achievement. It's important to remember that the most successful people are often those who faced the greatest challenges but chose to persist when others gave up.

Challenge

Talk to someone who has already done what you want to achieve and ask them for success tips and motivational reminders for when you get discouraged. Choose a goal or something you want, and be intentional about your plan to get it. Breaking down large tasks into smaller, achievable parts can make the journey feel more manageable and keep us from feeling overwhelmed.

Another challenge is dealing with negative self-talk and doubt, which can undermine our persistence. It's natural to question our abilities when faced with difficulties, but succumbing to these doubts can cause us to give up prematurely. To counter this, we need to know that difficult times *will* come, and we should plan for how we're going to handle them before they happen!

Surrounding ourselves with supportive people who encourage us and remind us of our capabilities is also vital. Don't be surprised if those supportive people are not your family. If that happens, find others and be prepared to be your own cheerleader. By acknowledging our progress and maintaining a positive internal dialogue, we can continue moving forward, even when doubts arise.

In our fast-paced world, we are often accustomed to instant gratification, but achieving long-term goals takes time. Developing patience is key to persistence, as it helps us stay the course without becoming discouraged by slow progress. By focusing on the process rather than rushing toward the outcome, we can develop the endurance needed to persist through even the toughest challenges.

What would have happened if Jesus had given up the first time someone criticized Him for performing a miracle or giving a sermon? Mic drop.

Perspective

Story

Helen Keller was an American author and political activist. She is best known for being the first blind and deaf person to earn a Bachelor of Arts degree and, of course, for inspiring the world with her determination. Helen Keller's life is a true testament to the power of perspective and resilience. Born in 1880, Helen lost her sight and hearing at just nineteen months old due to an illness. Many might have thought that her life was over before it even started, but she proved that a disability does not define a person's potential.

One powerful story that illustrates the importance of keeping things in perspective happened when Helen was a young girl, still struggling to communicate. Her teacher, Anne Sullivan, had been working with her for years, teaching her to read and write using sign language, but Helen's frustration was growing. She had become angry and resistant to learning, feeling like she couldn't make sense of the world around her. It wasn't until Anne took her to the well one day and allowed her to feel the water running through her hand that everything changed.

As the cold water flowed over her palm, Anne spelled the word "w-a-t-e-r" into Helen's other hand. For the first time, Helen realized that words were connected to things and that there was a whole world out there waiting for her to understand. But rather than immediately feeling elated or excited, Helen's first response was to feel overwhelmed and even resentful.

She later wrote, "I felt as if I were a child who had suddenly received an overwhelming, bewildering gift, and I was not sure whether to accept it."[81] Helen didn't feel immediately empowered or grateful. She was confused, even upset, as she grappled with the magnitude of what she had just discovered. But Anne persisted, and over time, Helen's perspective shifted. She learned that understanding the world was a gradual process, that she could handle whatever came her way, and that new challenges didn't necessarily have to be feared—they could be faced with patience and a willingness to keep learning. She knew she could learn through other perspectives too: She could taste, smell, and touch.

Helen Keller's story reminds us that even when we think life is unfair or too difficult, sometimes we just need to shift our perspective. What seems impossible or frustrating can be the very thing that shapes us into the person we're meant to become. And just like Helen, we must recognize that everything is a process. Each new discovery, even if it feels overwhelming, is just one step in our growth. By shifting our perspective, we can turn struggles into opportunities for learning and transformation.

Helen Keller had so many challenges to conquer that I find it hard to find anything in my life to complain about. And yet I do. Sometimes we want something so badly that we spend way too much time mourning when things don't work out. Sometimes another opportunity comes along and later we recognize how much better it was.

I used to get worked up over things when they didn't go my way. Over the years, I've finally learned to embrace the word "Whatever." Now, that may not sound very empowering, but for me, it has been. It's much easier for me to let go of things now. I toss out a lot of fishing poles in life, which is what I call attempts at opportunities or experiences I would like to have. Some of them pull up wonderful things, but others result in nothing. And that's okay. When I don't get the opportunity I want, I simply toss out another fishing pole.

QUOTE

"When one door of happiness closes, another opens, but often we look so long at the closed door that we do not see the one that has been opened for us." —Helen Keller (American author, activist, and lecturer who was blind, deaf, and mute)[82]

SCRIPTURE

"For our light affliction, which is but for a moment, worketh for us a far more exceeding and eternal weight of glory; While we look not at the things which are seen, but at the things which are not seen: for the things which are seen are temporal; but the things which are not seen are eternal." (2 Corinthians 4:17–18)

LESSON LEARNED

If we change the way we look at things, the things we look at change. Perspective shapes how we experience life. Two people can go through the same challenge, yet one may feel defeated while the other finds strength and growth. The difference isn't in the circumstances but in the way they choose to see them. When we adopt a broader, more eternal perspective—what President Russell M. Nelson calls "thinking celestial"[83]—we recognize that our trials are temporary and often serve a greater purpose. Instead of dwelling on setbacks, we can ask, "What can I learn from this?" or "How is this shaping me into who God wants me to become?" By viewing life through a celestial lens, we gain peace in the present and confidence in the future, knowing that everything is in God's hands.

"Thinking celestial" also helps us focus on what truly matters. In a world filled with distractions, it's easy to get caught up in temporary worries—money, status, or the opinions of others. But when we align our thoughts with eternal truths, we prioritize faith, family, and service. We remember that this life is just a small part of our eternal journey. Choosing a higher perspective allows us to let go of frustration, comparison, and fear, replacing them with trust in God's plan. The more we train our minds to "think celestial," the more joy and clarity we'll find, no matter what challenges come our way.

Challenge

So today, think of a fishing pole (something you want) that you could toss out to the world. If nothing bites, it's okay—at least you tried. Look for the good in your situation. If you focus on what's good, you'll see more good. Next, toss out another fishing pole. Sometimes it just takes a little longer for that big fish to bite.

Be gentle with yourself. Not everything works out the way you want or how you want. Be more mindful of your expectations. One powerful way to improve your eternal perspective is to spend time daily in the scriptures and prayer, focusing on God's plan for you. When you immerse yourself in His word, you begin to see beyond the immediate struggles of life and recognize the bigger picture.

The scriptures remind us that trials are temporary and that God is always working for our good. Prayer deepens that understanding, helping us align our will with His. Instead of asking, "Why is this happening to me?" we can ask, "What does God want me to learn from this?" That question brings instant and insightful perspective!

As we consistently turn to Him, our thoughts shift from worldly worries to eternal priorities, bringing more peace, purpose, and direction into our lives. God sees everything, so we need to make sure we're checking in with Him often to help us improve our eternal perspective.

Playfulness

Story

When some people remember seeing the first man walk on the moon, they have feelings of pride, awe, respect, or often patriotism. When I think of that great and historic moment, a different memory comes to mind . . .

As a family, we often lounged around the swimming pool to enjoy the summer evenings in our backyard. This momentous afternoon was no exception, although this time, a small black-and-white TV accompanied our poolside gathering so that we could watch the first moon landing. I was too young to fully understand the significance of this major event on TV, but I knew by the look on Daddy's face that it must be important.

Without trying to disturb Daddy on his pool chair just inches from the water, I quietly tried to maneuver myself past him to get a glass of lemonade from the table opposite him. Without even moving his eyes from the small TV, Daddy simply tapped his foot on my shoulder, instantly sending me into the pool below.

I remember the dress I was wearing (white with colored polka dots) and how it wrapped around my head as I sunk into the pool. My mother had lovingly sewn that dress for me. Now she stood next to the pool with a shocked expression on her face, trying to hold back her laughter.

After I shed a few tears and changed into some dry clothes, we all laughed . . . and I vowed at that moment I would be more careful where I was going! Now that I'm older, I often wonder if I would have even remembered the day the first man walked on the moon. What I do remember is how playful and mischievous my dad was, always trying to create happy memories of fun and laughter.

He could have yelled at me to express his annoyance when I got in his way, but instead, he was playful and created a funny memory for the entire family.

Quote

"Life is too important to be taken seriously." —Oscar Wilde (Irish poet and playwright considered to be one of the greatest writers of the nineteenth century)[84]

Scripture

"If thou art merry, praise the Lord with singing, with music, with dancing, and with a prayer of praise and thanksgiving." (Doctrine and Covenants 136:28)

Lesson Learned

Developing playfulness is a powerful way to tap into the joy of life and release the constant pressure of being serious all the time. When we embrace playfulness, we allow ourselves to let go of rigid expectations and explore new ways of thinking and interacting.

Being playful invites creativity, spontaneity, and a sense of wonder into our everyday lives, fostering connection with others and encouraging us to approach challenges with a lighthearted mindset. Playfulness isn't just for children; it's a mindset that can help adults break free from stress, find humor in difficult situations, and reconnect with their sense of fun.

Being less serious also means giving ourselves permission to make mistakes, fail, and learn without judgment. It's about finding the balance between responsibility and enjoyment, recognizing that life doesn't always have to be perfectly structured to be meaningful. A playful attitude helps us not only relax and have fun but also build resilience as we approach life's ups and downs with a more flexible, open mindset.

Whether through play, laughter, or creativity, choosing playfulness can lead to a more fulfilling, joyful existence, where the pressure to always "get things right" fades into the background. I often find myself being way too serious about everything, so I'm grateful for a father who helped me embrace laughter.

CHALLENGE

Often, we get caught up in our routines and worries, forgetting to notice the small, joyful details around us. By taking time each day to focus on what's happening around us, we can rediscover the lightness and creativity that comes with being fully immersed in the present. Mindfulness encourages us to let go of rigid plans and embrace the unpredictability of life, making space for playful, spontaneous moments to emerge.

Another way to cultivate playfulness is by engaging in activities that encourage creativity and imagination, such as trying new hobbies or playing games. These activities, whether it's drawing, dancing, playing sports, or solving puzzles, allow us to tap into a sense of fun and curiosity that often gets lost in adulthood.

By stepping outside of our comfort zones and embracing new experiences, we break free from the seriousness of daily life and open ourselves up to joy. The more we practice incorporating playful activities into our routine, the easier it becomes to approach life with a more lighthearted attitude.

PRAYER

STORY

When my brother-in-law was a teenager, his parents had a brilliant idea to sign him up for a ten-day summer camp called "Devil Pups." It was sponsored by the Marines and designed to give teenagers a taste of what a real military boot camp was like. He's not sure if his parents were hoping it would be the cure for his teenage attitude or if they were just looking for some peace and quiet at home. Either way, there he was, signed up for this intense program.

Now, "Devil Pups" was not your average summer camp. It wasn't about arts and crafts or roasting marshmallows around a campfire. No, no. This was a military-style camp where teens learned discipline, teamwork, and how to never complain. Some of the boys were sent there as an alternative to rehab, others as part of their football team's conditioning program, and then there was my brother-in-law—just a regular teenager who thought he was signing up for a few days of physical fitness. And by the way, there were about 300 boys, all of whom looked like they were ready to march in formation and maybe even conquer a mountain, while he just wanted to survive a few days without embarrassing himself.

Four of his friends were supposed to go with him to this camp, but they all bailed at the last minute. So there he was, all alone . . . alone with 300 teenage boys and the drill sergeants who, let's just say, weren't going to win any "World's Nicest People" awards. On top of that, he had to drive himself to the camp, which meant an entire night of solo driving through the mountains, at the end of which he arrived at the camp, absolutely exhausted and filled with dread about what was to come.

As soon as he stepped out of his car, he was greeted by a barrage of yelling drill sergeants who, as it turns out, were experts in both volume and intimidation. They wasted no time throwing all the boys into what can only be described as a full-throttle boot camp experience. You know, the kind where you start questioning your life choices. No mercy whatsoever.

After a pleasant few hours of getting screamed at for everything from the way they stood to the way they breathed, it was finally lunchtime. A small reprieve. They were given about ten minutes to sit on the grass and shove their food into their faces as quickly as humanly possible. My brother-in-law quickly realized he was out of his element; this wasn't a camp—this was a survival test.

Before eating his sandwich, he took his teeth retainers out and stored them safely in his brown lunch bag so he wouldn't lose them. He had already lost two sets of retainers in the past, so his mother made it very clear that if he lost these, she wasn't buying him any more.

But as luck would have it, right after lunch, the drill sergeants made their grand announcement: "Everybody get up and *run*! We're going to the building to get your hair cut!" Everyone jumped to their feet and sprinted to the designated building.

You can probably guess where this story is headed, right? As my brother-in-law was getting his hair buzzed off, he suddenly realized he had left his lunch bag with his precious retainers in it. He tried to ignore the panic rising in his chest, but it was too late. When he finally accepted the reality of his dire situation, he approached one of the drill sergeants and sheepishly confessed, "I left my retainers in my lunch bag, and now they're in the dumpster." With a disgusted look, the drill sergeant pointed toward the dumpster and told him to find the bag in ten minutes . . . or else.

And so there my poor brother-in-law was, sitting in a very gross dumpster, sifting through 300 bags of food wrappers and old sandwiches in search of his retainers, trying to suck back the tears and fear of what "or else" could possibly mean. If there was ever a moment to pray, this was it. He prayed like he had never prayed before—asking God for help and a miracle. "Please, *please*, just let me find these retainers. If you help me, I'll never complain again. (Well, maybe not as much.)"

The very next bag he touched was the miracle he had prayed for. In that moment, he felt a deep sense of peace and comfort. He knew that God was aware of him, and from that day forward, he felt His presence beside him, even as he continued to get yelled at by drill sergeants.

The next ten days of boot camp were still hard, but he knew that no matter how tough things got, he wasn't alone.

Quote

"The object of prayer is not to change the will of God, but to secure for ourselves and for others blessings that God is already willing to grant, but that are made conditional on our asking for them." —Latter-day Saint Bible Dictionary[85]

Scripture

"And whatsoever ye shall ask the Father in my name, which is right, believing that ye shall receive, behold it shall be given unto you." (3 Nephi 18:20)

Lesson Learned

God really hears our prayers! Prayer is how we connect with God, express our thoughts and emotions, and seek guidance in times of need. It's more than just a ritual—it's an open line of communication with our Heavenly Father. Through prayer, we can seek peace, comfort, and strength, especially during challenging times.

When we humble ourselves and ask for help, God listens and responds, often in ways we may not immediately recognize. The power of prayer lies not only in receiving answers but also in the process of aligning our hearts with His will, trusting that He knows what is best for us, even when we don't fully understand.

Challenge

There are simple things we can all do to improve our prayers and our ability to hear God:

- Be specific
- Listen more and talk less
- Be patient
- Pray regularly and with faith, knowing that God really does hear you
- Brainstorm with God and take action on how you can solve the problem
- Express gratitude
- Follow the commandments to be worthy of blessings the laws are predicated on
- Pray for others by name, not just yourself an brainstorm ways you can be a blessing to them
- Pray for one unique insight before you study the scriptures for the day
- Fill your prayer with only gratitude, not requests
- Incorporate words like "Prince of Peace" or "Jehovah" to bring reverence and richness to your words
- Keep a prayer journal to record how your prayers are answered

Priorities

Story

Many years ago, I attended the Governor's Conference for Women in California, where thousands of amazing women gathered to improve themselves and their businesses. Several impressive women gave presentations, and then they opened it up for questions and answers from the audience. I'll never forget one of the questions that was asked by a frustrated woman in the audience: Can a woman really "have it all"? One by one, the panelists talked about how amazing they were and how all it took was determination and hard work. I thought to myself, "Of course they can do it all. If I had personal assistants, a nanny, a private chef, a chauffeur, a business coach, a life coach, and a personal trainer, I could do amazing things too!"

Finally, it was Meg Whitman, the CEO of eBay, who gave the most realistic and reassuring answer I heard during that entire event. She simply said, "It's a lie. You can't have it all *at the same time*." Having balance is a moving target. She explained that you could rock it one day in business, but your family life might suffer that particular day because you're putting in more hours at work. You can excel in physical fitness one day, but then you might not have time to serve at your church because you're spending so much time in the gym. You can cook an amazing dinner and have a meaningful family activity afterward, but that's fewer hours you'll have to clean the house or do your other work. It's a balancing act that fluctuates from day to day, based on which tasks are most urgent.

She talked about the importance of balance and perspective. You *can* have it all, but there are ebbs and flows in life that everyone in your family must recognize with patience. Some days, it's simply easier to balance everything than on other days when urgent matters mess it all up!

Quote

"Nobody's life is ever all balanced. It's a conscious decision to choose your priorities every day." —Elisabeth Hasselbeck (contestant on the TV show *Survivor* and talk show host on *The View*)[86]

Scripture

"But seek ye first the kingdom of God, and his righteousness; and all these things shall be added unto you." (Matthew 6:33)

Lesson Learned

Setting priorities is essential for creating a life of purpose and balance. When we establish clear priorities, we're able to focus our energy on what truly matters instead of getting distracted by less important tasks or goals. Prioritizing allows us to direct our time and resources toward the things that align with our values, ensuring that we live intentionally rather than simply reacting to life's demands.

It also provides clarity, making decisions easier to navigate because we already know what takes precedence in our lives. Without setting priorities, we can easily feel overwhelmed, scatterbrained, and unsatisfied with our progress, as we spread ourselves too thin trying to manage everything at once.

Additionally, setting priorities helps us maintain emotional and mental well-being. By focusing on what matters most, we reduce stress and avoid burnout. It also helps us create space for self-care, relationships, and personal growth. When we set and honor our priorities, we feel more confident in our choices and more fulfilled with how we spend our time.

All that being said, a supportive family will recognize that urgent matters simply need to be attended to every so often and accept the fact that the regular routine and balance might be disrupted. Be gracious and patient with one another. No one day will ever be completely perfect.

Challenge

One effective way to help people learn how to set priorities each day is to encourage them to start with a simple "to-do" list and then rank each task by importance and urgency. Begin by writing down all the tasks they hope to accomplish, no matter how big or small. Then guide them to categorize each item into one of four groups:

- **Important and Urgent:** Tasks that need immediate attention, like deadlines or emergencies.
- **Important but Not Urgent:** Long-term goals or personal projects that require attention but aren't due right away.
- **Not Important but Urgent:** Tasks that feel pressing but don't contribute significantly to their overall goals.
- **Not Important and Not Urgent:** Low-priority tasks or distractions that can often be eliminated.

Once the tasks are sorted, encourage them to tackle the "Important and Urgent" tasks first, followed by the "Important but Not Urgent" ones. This method helps people see where their focus needs to be, reduces overwhelm, and fosters better time management. It's a daily practice that, with time, helps them consistently make thoughtful decisions about where to invest their energy.

Choose your priorities and remember that you're going to have to do it all over again tomorrow. Be selective of what you do. Choose your tasks based on your highest priorities.

Punctuality

Story

It was a crisp spring evening, and my twin sister and I were buzzing with excitement. The end-of-year banquet and awards night for our high school drill team we were on was one of the highlights of our dance season.

We had rehearsed our hair flips in the mirror, debated over what outfit to wear for the evening, and somehow managed not to strangle each other during the process. But there was one obstacle we couldn't overcome: Dad.

Among the many talents our father possessed was the ability to be late for everything. His consistent tardiness could rival the sunrise in its reliability. If he said "five minutes," we knew we had at least twenty minutes to wait for him. It was adorable and infuriating all at the same time.

The night of the banquet was no different. "Daddy! We're going to be late!" my sister hollered down the bedroom hallway. "It's fine, girls," he said while trying to find the car keys. "The banquet won't start without us."

Spoiler alert: It totally did.

By the time we finally piled into the car, my sister and I were stewing in silent fury. As Dad puttered along at what felt like the slowest speed legally possible, we both glanced at the clock and cringed. How embarrassing to always be late, not due to our own fault but our dad's!

When we arrived, the event had already started, so we hurried through the doors to see our drill team director standing at the microphone, announcing "And now for our next award, the 'Always Late Award,' goes to . . . "

My twin sister and I froze in horror. What timing! The room erupted in laughter as the spotlight hit us. We felt completely humiliated, yet we could also recognize the humor in the moment. I mean, you couldn't plan that timing any better, right?

To this day, we wonder if our father knew about the award and had timed it to play out like that. Because he was such a prankster, that wouldn't surprise me. He always loved making a big entrance!

Quote

"Punctuality is the soul of business." —Thomas Chandler Haliburton (Nova Scotian politician, judge, and author)[87]

Scripture

"Let all things be done decently and in order." (1 Corinthians 14:40)

Lesson Learned

Despite my dad's flaw in punctuality, he taught me that being on time demonstrates respect for others' time and commitments. I knew I never wanted to make people feel the way I did when my father made us late for events. Whether in the workplace, school, or social settings, punctuality reflects discipline and responsibility, qualities that can enhance one's reputation and opportunities. Arriving on time shows that you value others and are dedicated to meeting your obligations, creating a positive impression that can open doors to new prospects and strengthen existing connections.

When you adhere to a schedule, you allow yourself adequate time to prepare, execute tasks, and transition smoothly between activities. This minimizes last-minute rushes and the anxiety that comes with tardiness. In professional contexts, punctuality can enhance teamwork and productivity by ensuring that projects and meetings proceed without unnecessary delays.

CHALLENGE

One of the biggest challenges in becoming more punctual is mastering effective time management. Many people underestimate the amount of time tasks will take or fail to account for unexpected delays. Note: There will almost always be delays.

If you have kids to get ready, double that time! If you struggle with tardiness, review which tools you're currently using, like calendars, cell phone reminders, alarms, Alexa messages, and other time-tracking apps. Use them!

As a university professor, I've seen that the number one skill that can make or break student success in college is time management. Here are some tips to improve that skill, not only for students but for all of us:

- Start each day by identifying your top 3 most important tasks (Don't prioritize your schedule—schedule your priorities)
- Divide big projects with deadlines into bite-sized actions you can complete each day
- Limit distractions by silencing your phone, closing extra tabs on your computer, and guarding your focus
- Use time blocks to chunk tasks for focused work, scheduled breaks, errands, and family time
- Focus on one important priority at a time (Multitasking often leads to poor results and more stress)
- Before going to bed, make a to-do list and schedule for the next day
- Take time to reflect on what's working and what's not

Pursuing Your Dreams

Story

It takes incredible courage to believe in a dream, but it takes even more courage to actually take action on that dream, especially when it feels like the world is telling you no. We live in a world full of cynicism. People can be quick to mock others who aim high or chase after the seemingly impossible. But here's the thing: Reach anyway. And there's no better example of this than the story of Walt Disney, a man who turned his vision into an empire despite almost every obstacle you could imagine.

People told Walt Disney he wasn't cut out for business. He had only an eighth-grade education, and his formal art training was almost nonexistent. In fact, early in his career, he was fired from a Kansas City newspaper because his boss said he "lacked imagination." Crazy, right? But Disney didn't let that stop him. When he dreamed of creating a feature film based on *Snow White*, his wife and brother tried to talk him out of it. They thought it was far too risky, both financially and creatively. And when he pitched the idea to people in Hollywood, they dismissed it. No one believed in his dream, and his idea became known as "Disney's Folly."

But Disney had something more valuable than formal education or approval from others: He had belief in his own vision. He wasn't afraid to dream big and, perhaps more importantly, he wasn't afraid to put in the work. He poured everything he had into the project, taking huge financial risks and even mortgaging his home. And when *Snow White and the Seven Dwarfs* debuted in 1937, it became a groundbreaking success, forever changing the animation industry and the entertainment world as a whole.

Disney believed that persistence was the key to success, and if there's ever been a more fitting testament to that belief, it's his own story. Persistence isn't easy; it requires the courage to keep moving forward even when you don't have the answers, when the naysayers grow louder, or when it feels like everything is stacked against you. But if you have a dream and the persistence to follow through on it, no matter what, the world can't stop you.

It takes courage to pursue a dream, and it takes even more courage to persist when the odds seem insurmountable. But if you're willing to take that step—if you're willing to continue even when others tell you it can't be done—your dream just might become the next great story of success.

So when people mock you for reaching for the stars, don't let that stop you. Reach anyway. Like Walt Disney, believe in your vision, persist through the challenges, work hard, and let the world be amazed by what you create.

Quote

"All our dreams can come true if we have the courage to pursue them." —Walt Disney (co-founder of Walt Disney Productions)[88]

Scripture

"Delight thyself also in the Lord; and he shall give thee the desires of thine heart." (Psalm 37:4)

Lesson Learned

Making your dreams come true requires a mix of faith, persistence, and action. Dreams don't just happen; they are built step by step through hard work, resilience, and belief in yourself. Challenges will come, and at times, you may feel like giving up, but the key is to keep moving forward, even when progress feels slow. Surround yourself with supportive people, seek guidance from God, and stay focused on your vision. Success doesn't come overnight, but when you stay committed and trust the process, you'll look back and realize that every small effort brought you closer to making your dream a reality.

Challenge

Be specific about what you want and define your dream clearly so you can visualize what success means. Break your big goal into smaller, achievable goals so you don't feel overwhelmed. Find a mentor, someone who has already done what you want to achieve, and surround yourself with people who encourage you.

Anyone can dream big, but not everyone is willing to work hard to make their dreams come true. Take action; even imperfect action leads to progress and gets the momentum going. Work for what you love and don't let fear allow you to give up your dream.

Accept that setbacks are a part of the process. Be flexible but persistent.

Heavenly Father knows you better than you even know yourself, so include Him in your brainstorming sessions! He often speaks to our souls by putting dreams in our hearts as a way to find our potential and reach for the stars.

Reputation

Story

One summer, my brother-in-law's family piled into the car, hitched up a trailer, and set off for their much-anticipated Matthews family reunion. Here's the lesson he learned in his own words:

As we rolled into the small town where the reunion was being held, we were already buzzing with excitement, ready for a weekend filled with laughter, questionable potato salad, and relatives we barely remembered but still hugged like long-lost friends.

Then, flashing red and blue lights in the rearview mirror ended the happy anticipation for fun.

A police officer pulled us over, casually strolling up to the driver's side window. "You're missing a taillight on that trailer," he said, arms crossed and brow furrowed. "Where are you all headed?"

"We're on our way to the Matthews family reunion," we answered, half expecting a lecture or, worse, a ticket.

Instead, the officer's face broke into a wide grin. "Oh! The Matthews? Now that's a great family! Go have fun!" He waved us off without so much as a warning, as if having the last name Matthews was a VIP pass to law enforcement leniency.

We arrived at the reunion feeling on top of the world, eager to spend time with the great Matthews family, reveling in all the usual family reunion traditions: kids running wild, aunts gossiping over casseroles, and at least one uncle falling asleep in a lawn chair with a plate of ribs balanced on his belly. It was, in every way, a fantastic gathering.

But all good things must come to an end, and eventually, we packed up and hit the road. As we were leaving town, déjà vu struck; sirens blared behind us once again. Another police officer. Another stop. Another moment of worry. We hadn't taken the time to fix that doggone broken taillight all day.

This time, the officer was a little more serious as he approached our car. "Where are you all coming from?" he asked.

Without hesitation, we proudly declared, "The Matthews family reunion!"

And just like before, the officer's demeanor shifted instantly. His face lit up, and he clapped a hand on the car door. "Oh! The Matthews! What a great family! You all have a good day!"

No ticket. No warning. Just a friendly wave and a free pass out of town.

As we drove away, we couldn't stop laughing. Two traffic stops. Two officers. Zero tickets. All because of the power of a good reputation.

That day, I learned an important lesson: Live your life in a way that, when people hear your name, they smile. Because if you do it right, your family name might just be worth more than you know.

Quote

"Your reputation is more important than your paycheck, and your integrity is worth more than your career." —Ryan Freitas (American product designer)[89]

Scripture

"A good name is rather to be chosen than great riches, and loving favour rather than silver and gold." (Proverbs 22:1)

Lesson Learned

Having a good reputation is one of the most valuable assets a person can possess. It's the foundation of trust in relationships, both personal and professional. When people know they can rely on you to be honest, kind, and hardworking, doors open, opportunities arise, and respect is naturally given.

A good reputation often precedes us, and it can be the deciding factor in whether someone chooses to work with us, become our friend, or place their trust in us. Proverbs 22:1 reminds us that a good name is more precious than wealth because, unlike money or possessions, a reputation built on integrity, and kindness is something that endures over time. It reflects who we are at our core and influences how others perceive us in every aspect of life.

Maintaining a good reputation requires intentional effort. It's not something we can take for granted, nor is it built overnight. Our words, actions, and decisions contribute to the image others have of us, and sometimes one misstep can tarnish what took years to build. That's why it's essential to be mindful of how we treat others, handle difficult situations, and honor our commitments. When making choices in life, imagine that people are watching . . . because they are.

Challenge

If your actions align with your words, people will begin to rely on you and view you as dependable. If you're a parent, gather your family to talk about what kind of reputation you all currently have as a family. Are you happy with it, or would you like it to be better?

Talk about creating a family theme song, motto, or handshake that reinforces those values. My twin sister's married surname is Long. Their motto was "Long for home. Together forever!" They were able to write a sweet song and sing it every night before bed. Cute, right?

Well, I have four sons, so there was no way they were interested in anything cutesy like that, and singing wasn't their thing, so guess what our family's motto is? "Barfing builds character. Don't be a wimp!" No, I'm not kidding. We then put our fists together and grunt like testosterone-filled gorillas. Still not kidding. My husband and I were trying to allow our kids to have an equal vote in the election of our family's theme, and my motherly suggestion of "Boices making good choices!" got outvoted.

Resilience

Story

In a rehabilitation center nestled in the heart of Texas, a group of soldiers gathered every morning for therapy. They came from different places, served in different units, and fought in different wars, but they shared one thing in common: They had all returned home missing parts of their bodies. Some had lost legs to roadside bombs, others lost arms to shrapnel, and some both. For many of them, the initial days after their injuries were dark, filled with frustration, grief, and a sense of betrayal by the bodies they had once relied on to protect and serve.

One soldier had lost both legs above the knee. He had been a marathon runner before his deployment and had always prided himself on his speed and endurance. "When I woke up in the hospital and looked down, I couldn't recognize the person I had become," he recalled. "I didn't know how to be me without my legs."

Another had been a skilled guitarist before losing his left arm. "Music was my identity," he said. "Without my hand, I felt like I'd lost my voice."

For weeks, the soldiers struggled to adapt. Every task, from brushing their teeth to walking, felt like a monumental challenge. They wrestled with prosthetics, endured grueling physical therapy, and fought against the despair that threatened to consume them. But slowly, the bonds they formed with one another began to shift their perspectives.

One day during group therapy, a soldier shared something that had been weighing on him. "I miss running," he admitted, his voice cracking. "But I've been thinking . . . maybe I haven't lost everything. I still have my heart. My mind. My drive. Maybe I can find new ways to move forward."

His words struck a chord with the group. Over time, they began to reframe their losses, focusing not on what they had lost but on what they still had—and what they could still achieve.

The musician-loving soldier, inspired by the hope he had felt in that session, started experimenting with adaptive equipment for his guitar. It was slow, frustrating work, but one day, he managed to play a simple melody. The sound was imperfect but beautiful. "I realized then that my music didn't end with my arm," he said. "I just had to learn a new way to create it."

The former marathon runner began training with prosthetic running blades. The first time he strapped them on, he fell—hard. But he got back up. Day after day, fall after fall, he pushed himself until he could run again. The first time he crossed a finish line on his blades, he broke down in tears. "It wasn't the same as before," he said, "but it was still me. I could still run. I could still be free."

The group's transformation didn't stop there. Together they started volunteering, visiting schools to talk to kids about resilience, and mentoring newly injured soldiers. They shared their stories of loss and recovery, showing others that life didn't end with an injury—it just changed.

The message was clear: Their bodies might not look or move the same as before, but they were still strong, capable, and worthy of admiration.

As one soldier put it, "I've learned to stop mourning what I lost and start celebrating what I have. My body isn't perfect, but it's mine. It's a part of my journey, and I'm proud of it."

Their new lives became a testament to the power of resilience, adaptability, and self-love. These soldiers taught others and themselves that true strength isn't about physical perfection. It's about the courage to embrace who you are and to honor your body for what it can do.

Quote

"Our greatest glory is not in never falling, but in rising every time we fall." —Confucius (ancient Chinese philosopher, teacher, and political thinker)[90]

Scripture

"And not only so, but we glory in tribulations also: knowing that tribulation worketh patience; And patience, experience; and experience, hope." (Romans 5:3–4)

Lesson Learned

Despite our best intentions and wishes, life happens and doesn't always go our way! Resilience is the ability to bounce back from challenges, setbacks, or hardships. It means adapting, growing stronger, and continuing forward despite difficulties. It's like a tree that bends in the wind but doesn't break—it may sway, but its roots hold firm.

Taking action, even in small steps, is an effective way to overcome struggles. It's easy to feel overwhelmed by a large problem, but breaking it down into manageable tasks makes it more approachable. These incremental victories can build momentum and help you stay motivated during challenging times.

When you focus on taking one positive step forward at a time, rather than dwelling on the enormity of the struggle, you begin to shift your energy from frustration to determination, allowing you to make meaningful progress toward your goals.

When I first watched the movie *Frozen 2,* I thought Anna's song "The Next Right Thing" was pretty dark for a kids' movie, but then the pandemic happened and I realized how the timing for that scene couldn't have been more perfect. Children and adults all over the world learned the importance of resilience and moving forward, even if it's just one small step at a time.

Challenge

Developing the quality of persistence begins with your mindset. Know ahead of time that things will *not* always be perfect. If you expect perfection, you'll always be disappointed. Plan ahead of time how you will handle mishaps and obstacles so that you don't have to melt down when they happen.

Whenever I travel, I ask my travel buddies (family, friends, kids, etc.) what their expectations are for the trip. That way, we can better manage what everyone's goals and priorities are. I've learned that anger and frustration are often the result of not being clear about expectations, not just during vacations but in life in general.

Embracing a mindset of patience and persistence is key to overcoming struggles and fostering growth. Trust that the effort you put into overcoming challenges is building your inner strength and resilience, even if the results aren't immediately visible.

Be patient with yourself and allow room for setbacks, knowing that each experience contributes to your growth in some way. With persistence, time, and a positive outlook, you can learn to embrace even the most difficult challenges as opportunities for growth, ultimately becoming a stronger, more empowered version of yourself.

Respect for the Human Body

Story

At age twenty-one, Claire was at a crossroads in her life. A promising nursing student by day and an aspiring adult performer by night, she navigated two wildly different worlds. The entertainment industry dazzled her with its allure: glittering lights, fame, and fortune. But it also cast shadows, pressures she hadn't anticipated.

"You need to fix your nose," her manager said casually, as though it was a matter of changing a hairstyle. The words struck Claire like a cold wind. She had always thought her nose was fine—a little bump from a childhood fall, sure, but it was hers. Yet in this world, where beauty was currency, her natural self was deemed insufficient.

For weeks, she wrestled with the decision. The mirror became her tormentor, reflecting not just her face but her insecurities. The voice of the industry grew louder: "If you want to succeed, you have to conform." Eventually, Claire gave in.

The surgery was brutal. The pain, swelling, and bruising were far worse than she'd imagined. Her recovery was isolating, marked by days spent staring at a swollen face that didn't feel like her own. When the bandages came off, the mirror revealed a stranger. Her reflection was polished, symmetrical—perfect, some would say. But to Claire, it was a lie.

One evening, as she sat alone in her apartment, she caught a glimpse of her college textbooks that she had once purchased to pursue a different career. She had given up because working in the adult entertainment industry was so lucrative, and she convinced herself a college degree wasn't that important. She opened one of the science books and ran her fingers over the pages, filled with diagrams of organs, bones, and muscles. Here was a world that celebrated the complexity of the human body—not its perfection but its function and resilience.

The contrast was stark. She had once thought she'd like to go into nursing, and she saw something the entertainment industry lacked: authenticity. Nurses didn't ask their patients to change who they were. They embraced people at their most vulnerable, offering care, compassion, and respect for their individuality.

Claire realized that the entertainment industry's obsession with appearance was a fleeting pursuit. How long could she keep changing herself to meet its demands? And at what cost? She didn't want to be valued for a nose or a waistline; she wanted to be valued for her mind, her skills, and her heart.

With newfound clarity, Claire made the hardest and easiest decision of her life. She left the entertainment industry. Pursuing a degree in nursing school felt like coming home. She threw herself into her studies, finding joy in learning how to heal, how to care, and how to see beauty in every body.

Years later, as a nurse, Claire often reflected on her journey. The pressure to alter her appearance had taught her a profound lesson: The human body is miraculous, not because it's perfect but because it's unique. Her nose—bump and all—had been part of her story, a story she no longer wanted to erase.

When patients shared their insecurities with her, Claire would lean in and say, "Your body tells your story. Every scar, every line, every imperfection is a testament to your life. And that's something to be proud of."

I had the great pleasure of meeting Claire on a medical mission trip in Colombia. She's a wonderful nurse now!

Quote

"Take care of your body. It's the only place you have to live." —Jim Rohn (American entrepreneur, author, and motivational speaker)[91]

Scripture

"Know ye not that ye are the temple of God, and that the Spirit of God dwelleth in you? If any man defile the temple of God, him shall God destroy; for the temple of God is holy, which temple ye are." (1 Corinthians 3:16–17)

Lesson Learned

The human body is an extraordinary creation, intricately designed and capable of remarkable things. Respecting the body begins with recognizing its inherent value as a gift from God or, for some, as a marvel of nature. It serves as the vessel through which we experience life, enabling us to feel, think, and act. Treating the body with care honors its importance and reflects gratitude for the opportunities it provides. When we respect our bodies, we develop a deeper appreciation for life and the responsibilities that come with stewardship over our physical selves.

Maintaining physical health is one of the primary ways to show respect for the body. This involves making conscious decisions about nutrition, exercise, sleep, and hygiene. By taking care of our bodies, we ensure that we can function at our best, both physically and mentally. Neglecting the body, on the other hand, can lead to preventable illnesses and diminished quality of life. A healthy lifestyle not only allows us to enjoy life more fully but also equips us to serve and support others effectively.

Respecting the human body also extends to how we view and treat others. Every person, regardless of appearance, ability, or condition, deserves dignity and respect. Judging others based on superficial attributes diminishes their humanity and erodes our own. Celebrating diversity in body types, sizes, and abilities fosters a culture of acceptance and inclusivity. By valuing the physical uniqueness of others, we contribute to a more compassionate and understanding society.

In addition to physical care, respecting the body involves guarding it against harm and exploitation. This includes being mindful of substances that can harm the body, such as drugs or excessive alcohol, and avoiding situations that might compromise physical safety. It also means understanding and honoring personal boundaries, as well as advocating against any form of abuse or mistreatment. Protecting the body reflects a commitment to its sanctity and worth.

Many faith traditions view the body as a temple, a sacred space that should be treated with reverence. Whether through modesty, mindfulness, or acts of self-care, honoring the body becomes a reflection of honoring the Creator. When we respect our bodies, we align our actions with values that uphold the sanctity of life and human dignity. In doing so, we not only enrich our own lives but inspire others to view the human body with the respect it truly deserves.

Challenge

One effective way people can learn to respect their bodies more is by practicing mindfulness and self-compassion. This involves paying attention to how their body feels and how they treat it, without judgment. Start by tuning into your body's needs—whether it's getting enough sleep, eating nourishing foods, or moving in ways that feel good to you. Make small, positive changes and recognize the importance of caring for yourself both physically and emotionally.

Respecting your body also means giving it the proper rest it needs, learning to set boundaries with stress, and recognizing the importance of mental health. Practice self-love by speaking kindly to yourself, acknowledging your worth, and treating yourself with the same compassion you would offer to a loved one. The more you honor your body and its needs, the better equipped you'll be to live a life that reflects that respect.

When you look in the mirror, don't you dare say terrible things about your body. It's one of God's most magnificent creations!

Responsibility

Story

As a little girl, I was an expert in the fine art of procrastination—especially when it came to doing the dishes. There were always more exciting things to do: playing outside until the streetlights flickered on, creating imaginary worlds with my dolls, or simply getting lost in the joy of childhood. Washing dishes? That could wait. And so whenever it was my turn to do the dishes, I would conveniently "forget" my chore, telling myself I would do it later. But later never came.

By the time bedtime rolled around, I was far too tired. My eyelids would grow heavy, and my cozy bed would call my name. With the sink still full of dishes, I would slip under the covers, assuming the task would magically disappear by morning.

But my father had other plans.

Just as I drifted into a deep sleep, I would suddenly feel a hand on my shoulder, gently shaking me awake. "Wake up. Get up," my father would say, his voice firm but calm. In my half-asleep state, I felt like I was being ripped from a dream, convinced it must be the middle of the night—surely 2 or 3 a.m. But in reality, it was probably only 9 p.m.

I remember stumbling into the kitchen, eyes barely open, grumbling under my breath. The dishes sat there, waiting for me, as if mocking my earlier decision to ignore them. In that moment, I thought my father was so mean. Why couldn't he just let me sleep? Why did he have to be so strict about something as insignificant as dirty dishes? I saw myself as the victim of a great injustice, forced to scrub plates while the rest of the world peacefully slept.

But over time, I began to understand the lesson he was teaching me. It wasn't about the dishes. It was about responsibility and following through on my commitments. My father was teaching me the value of discipline, the importance of keeping my word, and the necessity of meeting my obligations—even when I didn't feel like it.

As I grew older, I carried those lessons with me. I learned to take ownership of my responsibilities, whether in school, work, or life in general. As I grew older, I no longer saw my father as mean but as a man who loved me enough to teach me the hard lessons, the ones that would shape me into a reliable, hardworking adult.

And now, when I find myself tempted to procrastinate, I think of those late-night dishwashing sessions. I smile, roll up my sleeves, and get to work—because I know that doing the hard things builds strength of character.

When I did homework, my dad always counseled me to start with the hardest assignment first. That way, it wouldn't hang over my head like a noose. Instead, all the other assignments would seem easy, and I would have the confidence to tackle them quickly. Over the years, I've learned that I should pay less attention to how I *feel* about tasks and focus more on the goal I want to reach. For example, I rarely *feel* like going to the gym to exercise, but I do want to reach the goal of a healthy and fit body. Today's society seems to be all about our feelings and emotions, but there comes a time when you have to *think* and dig in to accomplish what it is you truly want.

Quote

"The price of greatness is responsibility." —Winston Churchill (British statesman, military leader, writer, and Prime Minister of the United Kingdom during World War II)[92]

Scripture

"For behold, it is not meet that I should command in all things; for he that is compelled in all things, the same is a slothful and not a wise servant; wherefore he receiveth no reward." (Doctrine and Covenants 58:26)

Lesson Learned

Taking responsibility for our choices is an essential aspect of growing up. When we own our decisions, both good and bad, we gain a sense of control over our lives. We no longer blame others or external circumstances for our situations, and in doing so, we empower ourselves to make better decisions in the future.

By accepting responsibility, we acknowledge that our actions have consequences, and we begin to see that we are the architects of our own destiny. This awareness encourages thoughtful decision-making and leads to more intentional living. Taking responsibility for our actions also fosters trust and respect in our relationships. Responsibility shapes the way we navigate life's challenges and ultimately defines the kind of people we become.

Challenge

When my kids were young, we gave them opportunities to be in charge of various things, which they would have to report back on during our monthly family council meetings. We gave them goofy titles such as "Family Home Evening Tsar," "Chairman of Service Projects," "King of Chores," "Scribble Scribe," "Vacation Emperor," "Chef Boiceardee," and so on. They would take turns rotating through the various positions to see what each responsibility included. It gave them a chance to think about the family and have their opinions heard about issues.

If you're a parent trying to teach your kids to be responsible, work with them on these basic steps:

- Set clear goals
- Learn how to identify priorities
- Own your actions and mistakes
- Create consistent routines
- Seek feedback and be open to improvement
- Be accountable to others

Self-Care

Story

Emma had always been praised for her looks. Strangers commented on her long, flowing hair, her delicate features, and her slender frame. Friends would whisper enviously about how she always seemed effortlessly thin, calling her "the lucky one." But Emma knew the truth—the kind of truth that hid behind smiles and kept her awake at night.

Her battle was invisible, cloaked beneath the very image that others admired. From her teenage years, Emma had struggled with Crohn's disease, a chronic condition that wreaked havoc on her digestive system. Eating wasn't just a necessity; it was a gamble. Each meal came with the possibility of crippling pain, hours spent doubled over in agony, and endless trips to the bathroom. Slowly, food became her enemy.

To avoid the pain, Emma stopped eating as much. The less she consumed, the less she suffered—or so she thought. What began as a survival mechanism morphed into an eating disorder. Hunger became a familiar companion, but it felt safer than the alternative. She told herself she was in control, but in reality, her illness was controlling her.

Externally, Emma's thinness was celebrated. "You look amazing!" people would say, their eyes filled with admiration. "What's your secret?" they'd ask, as if she held some magical answer. But Emma's beauty was an illusion, a facade masking the toll her body was taking. Her hair began to lose its shine, her energy waned, and her reflection in the mirror became a haunting reminder of her fragility. She was trapped in a body that others idolized but that she herself despised.

When Emma married, she dreamed of building a family, of nurturing a child and finally giving her body a purpose beyond its perceived perfection. But her past choices and her condition had left scars deeper than she realized. Month after month, she faced the heartbreak of infertility. Doctors explained the toll that years of malnutrition and inflammation had taken on her body. Her dream of becoming a mother seemed to drift further away with every failed attempt.

It was during one particularly dark moment, after another negative pregnancy test, that Emma broke. She looked in the mirror and saw what others couldn't: a woman barely holding on. She realized she was chasing the wrong kind of perfection, a standard that had cost her health, her happiness, and now, perhaps, her chance at motherhood.

Emma made a decision that day. She would fight—not against food or her body but *for* them. She sought help, learning how to nourish herself and accept the complexities of her condition. It wasn't easy. Each bite was a challenge, each meal a test of courage. But with time, Emma began to rebuild her relationship with food, her body, and herself.

Years later, Emma welcomed a baby into the world—a miracle she never thought possible. Holding her child for the first time, she felt a deep sense of gratitude for her body, imperfections and all. The same body that had endured so much had also given her the greatest gift of her life.

Emma often reflected on the irony of her journey. People had envied her thinness, unaware of the pain it concealed. They admired her outward appearance, not knowing the battles she fought within. She wished she could tell them, "Beauty is not worth the cost of your health."

Today, Emma uses her story to inspire others. She reminds them that true beauty lies in a body that is loved, nourished, and cared for—not in a number on a scale or the approval of others. Her journey taught her a profound truth: Health is the most beautiful thing of all.

Quote

"Taking care of myself doesn't mean 'me first.' It means 'me too.'" —L. R. Knost (author and parenting expert)[93]

Scripture

"Know ye not that ye are the temple of God, and that the Spirit of God dwelleth in you?" (1 Corinthians 3:16)

Lesson Learned

In this society of quick fixes and limited warranties, it's easy to replace most anything. Any material object can be replaced when it's worn out and used, from automobiles to furniture to electronics. There's only one possession that cannot be replaced: the human body. How we treat it carries the marks of our abuse, misuse, or habits throughout our entire life. We cannot change it for a better model as the fashions change.

Despite the amazing medical technologies and advances in plastic surgery, our body is still, in essence, our very essence. It does, however, come with a lifetime warranty (because it will literally last you your lifetime), but the quality is not guaranteed. That is up to you. Self-care is essential for maintaining our overall well-being and living a balanced life.

In today's fast-paced world, it's easy to prioritize work, responsibilities, and others' needs above our own. Mothers are especially guilty of doing that. However, neglecting self-care can lead to burnout, stress, and a diminished quality of life. Taking time to care for ourselves—whether physically, mentally, emotionally, or spiritually—is crucial for staying healthy and happy. Self-care isn't just about indulgence or pampering; it's about recognizing our own needs and making sure we're in the best possible condition to handle life's challenges. If we don't care for ourself, we might not be able to care for others. It's the same principle as a parent putting on their oxygen mask first on an airplane in an emergency before they can then put it on their child's face.

One of the most important aspects of self-care is physical health. Our bodies are the foundation of everything we do, and when they're neglected, we feel the effects in every part of our lives. Regular exercise, proper nutrition, hydration, and rest are essential for maintaining energy levels and reducing stress. When we prioritize our physical health, we improve not only our body's performance but also our mental clarity, emotional resilience, and overall mood. Taking care of our body ensures that we have the strength and vitality to meet the demands of daily life.

Mental and emotional well-being are just as crucial as physical health. Practicing self-care involves taking time to relax, unwind, and manage stress. Activities like meditation, journaling, reading, or simply taking a walk in nature can help clear the mind and alleviate anxiety. When we make time for these practices, we allow ourselves to process emotions, reflect, and reenergize. This makes us more emotionally stable and better able to face challenges with a calm and clear mind. Prioritizing mental and emotional self-care also means setting healthy boundaries, saying no when necessary, and avoiding overcommitment.

Spiritual self-care is another important aspect to consider. Taking time for personal reflection, prayer, or spiritual practices can nourish the soul and provide a sense of peace and purpose. It helps us reconnect with our values and deeper sense of meaning, providing strength and guidance during difficult times. Spiritual self-care doesn't have to be tied to any specific religious practice; it's about finding what helps you feel grounded and connected to something greater than yourself.

Lalah Delia, who is a spiritual writer and wellness educator, said, "Self-care is how you take your power back."[94] Lalah's core message is that vibration plays a contributing role in our lives. I believe it. Everything is energy, and as we vibrate higher, we attract equally edifying things into our life. Now, that might sound kind of hippie-dippy, but I've seen it in my own life. When I'm down and depressed, all I see in the world is bad, and just keeps me vibrating at that low level. When I try to be positive and grateful for the good in my life, it's amazing how many more good things come my way. Yes, we'll all have ups and downs in life, but if we intentionally try to vibrate higher, we'll feel more peace and joy. How exactly does one "vibrate higher"? The list is surprisingly simple: show kindness, do service for others, express thanks, smell flowers, laugh, pray, use your talents, and even exercise. It's doing all those self-care things that make your heart sing.

Challenge

Consider creating a morning and evening ritual. Write them down to remind you because you'll forget when you're sleepy! They could include things like deep breathing exercises, flossing, stretching, prayer, scripture reading, smiling at yourself in the mirror, memorizing something inspirational, reciting positive affirmations, standing outside with the sunlight on your face for five minutes, listening to music, writing in your journal, writing a kind note to someone to spread cheer, reviewing your planner so you know what to anticipate, identifying five things you're grateful for . . . and on and on! There are so many cool things you can add to your list, but don't overwhelm yourself. Start small.

Making self-care enjoyable and meaningful is essential for sustainability. Choose activities that you genuinely look forward to rather than ones you feel obligated to do. For example, if traditional meditation feels daunting, try a moving meditation like yoga or a creative outlet like painting that provides a similar sense of mindfulness. Experiment with different practices to discover what resonates with you, and don't be afraid to adapt your routine as your preferences or circumstances change. When self-care feels like a reward rather than a chore, it's easier to maintain.

The choices you make today determine the quality of the rest of your life. Read that sentence again. It's *huge*!

Self-Confidence

Story

Like any good father, Daddy often let us "help" him with whatever project around the house he was working on. As a parent myself, I now know that little hands can often be more work than help. I remember one afternoon when Daddy was in the garage, painting a piece of furniture. To my young eyes, that looked like the most fun thing ever, and yet I also sensed it was a very important task since the man of the house was doing it.

After endless minutes of probably tormenting him with my requests to help, he finally consented and handed me a paint brush. Before he let me dip my brush into some real paint and begin my art career, he described every painting technique he could think of (to kill time) and then skillfully demonstrated with each stroke. I listened in awe and watched the master at work, basically unaware that I had still not painted a single stroke. By this time, the job had been completed and Daddy thanked me for helping.

He praised me so much for my willingness to assist with the task and for my speed of learning that I actually thought I had been helpful. He never wanted to make me feel like I was a bother, although I now recognize I most surely was. I hope I can always make others feel more important than any task.

Quote

"Confidence in yourself is the first step to success." —Unknown[95]

Scripture

"I can do all things through Christ which strengtheneth me." (Philippians 4:13)

Lesson Learned

Helping children develop self-confidence starts with fostering a positive and supportive environment. Children need to feel loved and accepted for who they are, which means offering consistent encouragement and praise for their efforts rather than just their outcomes.

Recognizing small achievements, whether academic, athletic, or personal, helps build a child's belief in their abilities. It's also essential to create a space where children can express themselves without fear of judgment, whether through creative outlets like drawing or speaking their minds. This can help them feel valued and validated, which is a crucial step in nurturing self-confidence.

In addition to emotional support, it's important to model confidence and resilience in front of children. When they see adults handle setbacks with a positive attitude and problem-solving mindset, they learn to do the same. Encouraging children to take on challenges that push them slightly out of their comfort zones helps build their resilience and teaches them that mistakes are part of learning, not failures.

Gradually, as they experience success in overcoming obstacles, their self-esteem grows and they develop a sense of empowerment. By combining emotional validation with practical experiences of overcoming challenges, children can learn to trust themselves and their abilities.

Challenge

One way people can challenge themselves to help children develop self-confidence is by actively practicing patience and understanding. Rather than stepping in immediately when a child faces a challenge, adults can encourage them to try solving problems independently. Don't rush in to rescue or be an "enabler." By resisting the urge to "fix" everything, parents, teachers, and caregivers create opportunities for children to experience a sense of accomplishment when they succeed. This also helps children feel more capable and empowered, teaching them that it's okay to struggle, as overcoming difficulties builds strength and confidence.

Another way to challenge oneself is by being intentional about offering constructive feedback. Instead of focusing on what a child did wrong, adults can shift their language to highlight effort, perseverance, and progress. For example, praising the process of problem-solving rather than just the end result helps children internalize the value of trying hard and learning from their mistakes. By making this shift in their own approach, adults help children develop a growth mindset, where they begin to see their abilities as something that can be improved with practice and persistence rather than as fixed traits.

Talk to your kids about the growth mindset versus the fixed mindset. Help them to see that our mindset is an active choice we make every day.

Self-Respect

Story

While growing up, my dad often taught us lessons on what was right by showing us examples of what was wrong. The "S.L.O.B." song is an example of his reverse psychology. It went like this:

> S. L. O. B., a slob, that's me.
> S. L. O. B. forever.

Short and to the point, wouldn't you say? I remember laughing and singing this song with Dad while my mother would be having a fit, convinced that Dad was warping us for the rest of our lives and that because of his silly song, we would all be disgusting slobs as adults. Although at times my house would prove otherwise, I'd like to say that we've all grown up feeling the importance of keeping our surroundings and selves clean and tidy!

At mealtimes, my dad would remind us to put our napkins on our laps by playing a game to see who could do it the fastest. If we ever had our elbows on the table, he would yell, "Who has their elbows on the table?" and playfully tap whatever arms he could find in the wrong place.

Dad would often take us to his rental properties to help clean them up for future leases. We would always stand in one of his houses or apartments in amazement at how badly some people took care of their things. I often wondered if all renters were like that or if Dad intentionally made the point of taking us to the worst properties as an example of how we should never live! He always said, "You can learn manners from those who have none."

Self-respect means making your bed and cleaning your kitchen, even if no one ever sees it. *You* see it. Show yourself you're worth the effort.

Quote

"The way you treat yourself sets the standard for others." —Sonya Friedman (American psychotherapist, author, and relationship expert)[96]

Scripture

"And let us not be weary in well doing: for in due season we shall reap, if we faint not." (Galatians 6:9)

Lesson Learned

Learning manners and etiquette is essential because they help create positive, respectful interactions in both personal and professional settings. Good manners foster an environment where people feel valued and comfortable, which can lead to stronger relationships and smoother communication. They reflect an individual's consideration for others, helping to build trust and goodwill.

Etiquette, whether in casual or formal situations, also serves as a universal language, allowing people from different backgrounds to connect with ease and understanding. This social grace encourages collaboration, kindness, and the kind of atmosphere where mutual respect can thrive.

Challenge

One way to learn manners from those who have none is by observing their behavior and identifying the negative impact it has on their relationships and interactions. By witnessing how rudeness or a lack of consideration can lead to misunderstandings, conflict, or discomfort, we gain a clearer understanding of why good manners are so crucial.

This contrast can motivate us to adopt more respectful and thoughtful behavior, ensuring that we don't replicate those same mistakes.

One way to teach children to learn manners is by pointing out the consequences of their actions. When we see someone being inconsiderate, we can reflect on how it might feel to be on the receiving end of such behavior. This reflection encourages us to act with kindness and respect because we recognize the emotional impact that our words and actions can have on others. Through this awareness, we not only avoid undesirable behavior but also strengthen our ability to be compassionate and understanding.

My kids used to love it when we would do role-playing. My husband would act out all the bad ways we shouldn't behave in various situations, while my kids rolled on the floor with laughter. Then it was my job to show them the correct way to behave. Yeah, my way wasn't nearly as funny, but the exercise made an entertaining point, and I'm proud to say I raised four gentlemen.

Self-Talk

Story

Brenda stood in front of the mirror, her hands gripping the edges of the bathroom sink. The familiar voice in her head started its usual commentary: Your hair looks awful today. Your thighs are too big. Why can't you just be better?

For years, this had been her ritual—a few minutes in front of the mirror, cataloging flaws and berating herself. It always set the tone for her day, draining her confidence before she even walked out the door. But today was different.

Brenda had just returned from a weekend retreat where the speaker shared a simple challenge: What if your mirror became your cheerleader instead of your critic? The idea had stuck with her. It sounded ridiculous at first—talking to herself like she was her own best friend—but something deep inside her wanted to try. She took a deep breath, meeting her own gaze in the mirror. Her reflection stared back, uncertain but willing.

Her reflection didn't argue. Brenda gave herself a small smile. "Okay, so maybe your hair's not perfect. But look at those eyes—they've seen so much. And those legs? They carry you through every single day."

The critic in her head didn't know what to say. It was used to tearing her down, not being silenced by kindness. Brenda took it a step further, raising her hand to the mirror. "High five," she said, pressing her palm to her reflection. She felt a little silly, but it also felt . . . good. Powerful even.

As the days turned into weeks, her morning ritual changed. Instead of criticizing, she started thanking her body. "Thank you, hands, for working so hard today." "Thank you, shoulders, for carrying my burdens without complaint." Some days were harder than others. There were mornings when the critic tried to make a comeback, whispering doubts into her mind. But Brenda found that if she spoke louder—if she reminded herself of her worth—she could drown it out.

One afternoon, a friend complimented her. "You've been glowing lately. What's your secret?" Brenda smiled. "I stopped letting my mirror bully me." Her friend laughed, but Brenda wasn't joking. She realized she had spent years giving her reflection the power to define her worth, and now she was taking it back.

Over time, her confidence grew. She started taking risks, speaking up in meetings, and trying new hobbies. And every time she looked in the mirror, she saw not just her reflection but a friend. The mirror didn't change who she was—it reminded her of who she had been all along: strong, capable, and enough.

Quote

"The only person you are destined to become is the person you decide to be." —Ralph Waldo Emerson (American essayist, lecturer, philosopher, and poet)[97]

Scripture

"Finally, brethren, whatsoever things are true, whatsoever things are honest, whatsoever things are just, whatsoever things are pure, whatsoever things are lovely, whatsoever things are of good report; if there be any virtue, and if there be any praise, think on these things." (Philippians 4:8)

Lesson Learned

The power of self-talk is undeniable; it shapes our perception of ourselves, influences our actions, and ultimately impacts our outcomes. Positive self-talk can be a tool for empowerment, helping us to navigate life's challenges with confidence and resilience. When we speak kindly to ourselves, we reinforce the belief that we are capable and worthy. For instance, telling ourselves "I can do this" or "I am strong enough" provides the encouragement needed to take on difficult tasks, tackle challenges, and persevere in the face of adversity. Positive self-talk builds a mindset of possibility, enabling us to approach obstacles as opportunities for growth rather than as insurmountable barriers.

On the other hand, negative self-talk can have a detrimental effect on our mental and emotional well-being. The constant barrage of thoughts like "I'm not good enough" or "I'll never succeed" can erode our self-esteem and self-confidence. Over time, these negative messages can shape our beliefs and actions, often preventing us from even trying to reach our goals. When we engage in negative self-talk, we may find ourselves paralyzed by fear or self-doubt, which can hinder our progress and perpetuate a cycle of failure. It's essential to recognize the impact of these thoughts and challenge them before they take root.

The good news is that we have the power to change the way we speak to ourselves. Just as we can cultivate positive self-talk, we can also replace negative thoughts with constructive ones. This shift in mindset requires intentional effort, but the results are well worth it. By consciously focusing on our strengths, our achievements, and our potential, we can begin to reframe negative thoughts and replace them with affirmations that foster growth and self-love. For example, instead of thinking "I'll never be able to do this," we can reframe the thought as "I might face challenges, but I'm capable of finding solutions." This subtle shift helps open up new possibilities and fosters an attitude of resilience.

Positive self-talk not only enhances our mental health but also influences the way others perceive us. When we project confidence and optimism through our internal dialogue, we naturally radiate those qualities outwardly. People are drawn to individuals who are self-assured and capable of handling adversity with grace. By reinforcing positive beliefs about ourselves, we invite others to see us in the same light. This, in turn, can lead to stronger relationships, greater opportunities, and an increased sense of connection with others.

Challenge

When you say negative things about yourself, you're insulting one of Heavenly Father's beloved children. You are one of His finest creations!

Here are five things we can do to change negative self-talk into positive self-talk:

- Practice self-awareness
- Challenge negative thoughts
- Reframe your thoughts
- Use positive affirmations
- Surround yourself with positivity

Another powerful yet easy way to switch your negative talk to positive is to simply add the word "yet." For example, consider this change: "I'm not good at remembering people's names . . . yet" or "I'm terrible at cooking, *yet* I know I can improve."

Sisterhood

Story

Sophia had always been fascinated by the intricacies of the skin. While others saw it as just a surface, she viewed it as a living canvas—one that told stories of resilience, health, and beauty. As a nursing student, her passion for dermatology wasn't just about acne creams or beauty routines; it was about helping people feel confident in their own skin, quite literally.

Her love for this often-overlooked aspect of health followed her when she joined a medical mission trip to a small rural village. The days were long, filled with treating wounds, administering medications, and educating the locals about basic hygiene and care. But it was in those stolen moments of connection that Sophia found her true calling.

One afternoon, after treating a patient with a severe rash, Sophia noticed a group of women standing nearby, whispering among themselves and avoiding eye contact with her. Their faces bore scars, blemishes, and the evidence of years under a relentless sun—marks that seemed to burden them with shame. It was clear that they felt invisible, as if the world had deemed them unworthy of being seen.

Sophia's heart ached for them. She rummaged through her supplies and pulled out what she had brought from home—a gentle cleanser, some towels, and a nourishing moisturizer. With a warm smile, she motioned for the women to sit down.

One by one, she began giving them facials, her hands moving with care and intention. She spoke softly as she worked, sharing how the skin renews itself, how scars tell stories of survival, and how caring for their skin wasn't vanity but an act of self-respect.

At first, the women were hesitant. They had spent years internalizing the idea that their faces were flawed, that they didn't deserve attention. But as Sophia cleaned their skin, massaged their temples, and applied soothing treatments, something extraordinary happened. Their guarded expressions began to soften. Eyes that once avoided hers now held her gaze. For the first time in years, they felt seen—not for their scars or imperfections but for their humanity. When Sophia handed them small mirrors to look at themselves, tears welled in their eyes.

One woman, her face weathered by both time and hardship, whispered, "I didn't think my skin could feel this soft again." Another, running her fingers across her cheeks, said with quiet amazement, "I feel . . . beautiful."

For Sophia, those moments were transformative. She realized that honoring the body wasn't just about treating illness or preventing disease; it was about nurturing the parts of ourselves that the world often overlooks. It was about showing people that their worth isn't diminished by their scars, their wrinkles, or their imperfections.

The joy on their faces was unlike anything Sophia had ever seen. They didn't just leave with cleaner skin; they left with renewed respect for themselves, for the stories their faces told, and for the bodies that had carried them through life's trials.

That evening, as the sun dipped below the horizon, Sophia reflected on the power of touch and the beauty of connection. She knew she wanted to spend her life not just healing bodies but also restoring the dignity and self-love that illness, hardship, or time could take away.

Sophia returned from the mission trip forever changed. She carried with her the belief that every face, no matter how weathered or scarred, deserves to be honored. And through her work, she would continue to remind people that their skin—their beautiful, imperfect, resilient skin—was worth cherishing.

Quote

"The success of every woman should be the inspiration to another. We should raise each other up." —Serena Williams (American former professional tennis player)[98]

Scripture

"Who can find a virtuous woman? for her price is far above rubies." (Proverbs 31:10)

Lesson Learned

Women's friendships with other women are vital to emotional well-being and personal growth. These bonds provide a space for women to share their thoughts, dreams, and struggles with those who understand them deeply. A strong friendship between women fosters trust and empathy, allowing each woman to feel supported, encouraged, and validated in ways that other relationships may not. Having a close-knit group of women to lean on can provide a sense of community and belonging, which is essential for emotional resilience and mental health.

Plus, we girls just need to talk about everything, and our husbands simply can't sit through all of that! Through these friendships, women can feel empowered to be their authentic selves, knowing they're accepted and loved for who they truly are.

No one can relate to a woman like another woman. Many years ago, a woman's husband in our ward died suddenly. Her home quickly filled with the bishopric and home teachers who gathered to offer a priesthood blessing and anything the shocked sister needed. She put on a brave face and thanked them profusely. While that was incredibly sweet and greatly needed, it wasn't until another woman from the ward walked into the door that the widowed sister was able to sink into her arms and cry.

By building strong, supportive friendships with other women, they can break barriers together, share experiences, and make meaningful contributions to each other's growth and success. These bonds remind women that they're not alone in their journey, and together they can face life's challenges with strength and confidence.

Challenge

One way women can develop friendships and experience sisterhood is by joining or creating groups that align with their values, interests, and goals. Whether it's a book club, a fitness class, or a volunteer organization, engaging in shared activities provides a natural setting for women to bond and support one another.

If groups like that don't exist in your area, start one! Here are a few ideas:

- Cooking club
- Home evening lesson swap
- Crafting club
- Book club
- Bunko group
- Yoga club
- Babysitting swap
- Cookie swap
- Tamalada day (a tamale-making party)
- Scrapbooking club
- School study buddies
- "Later Is Greater" lunch group for women over 50
- Scripture study group

Stop and Smell the Roses

Story

One day in elementary school, I was called to the principal's office. Now, the principal's office was a place where bad kids went, not me. I was as squeaky clean as the hand sanitizer they made us use before lunch. I hadn't done anything bad—at least not that I could remember. But I guess that's what guilty people think too, so naturally, I started panicking. When I cautiously stepped into the principal's office, I saw my two sisters already sitting there, looking just as confused as I felt. Their faces said it all: What did we do wrong?

Before we could whisper accusations at each other, in walked our dad. Dad?! The plot thickened. He had his serious "Dad face" on, which only made things worse. I thought "Oh no! What does he know? Did I accidentally confess to a crime in my sleep?"

Without a word, he marched up to the principal's desk, signed some paperwork, and motioned for us to follow him. You could've heard a pin drop as we trailed behind him in absolute, terrified silence. Were we expelled? Transferred? Sold to another family?

When we got outside, we saw our mom waiting in the car at the curb. But wait—she wasn't wearing her normal "Mom face." She had a big smile plastered on, and the car was loaded with beach chairs, towels, and a cooler.

That's when it hit us: We weren't in trouble—we were going to the *beach*! We were stunned and excited to officially play hooky with our parents' permission!

The three of us let out a collective sigh of relief so dramatic, it could've been mistaken for a gush of wind in a tornado. As it turned out, our parents decided we all deserved a little "mental health day" and pulled us out of school without any warning to surprise us.

The best part? Mom said, "We didn't tell you ahead of time because you probably would've blabbed to your friends and ruined the surprise." She wasn't wrong. That day, we built sandcastles, ate sandwiches with a little too much sand in them, played in the waves, and admired how creative our parents were. Who knew they could keep such a fun secret from us?

Quote

"Slow down and enjoy life. It's not only the scenery you miss by going too fast—you also miss the sense of where you are going and why." —Eddie Cantor (American comedian, actor, singer, and dancer in the mid-twentieth century)[99]

Scripture

"To every thing there is a season, and a time to every purpose under the heaven: A time to be born, and a time to die; a time to plant, and a time to pluck up that which is planted; A time to weep, and a time to laugh; a time to mourn, and a time to dance." (Ecclesiastes 3:1–4)

Lesson Learned

In the hustle and bustle of modern life, it's easy to get caught up in our endless to-do lists and the pursuit of productivity. However, stopping to "smell the roses" is a powerful reminder to pause and appreciate the present moment. This simple act can have profound effects on our well-being, helping us reconnect with the beauty around us and grounding us in gratitude.

Taking time to notice a blooming flower, a radiant sunset, the salty smell of ocean air, or even the laughter of a loved one can remind us that life's most meaningful moments often happen in the quiet everyday experiences we might otherwise overlook.

Embracing this mindset isn't just about enjoying life more; it's about improving our emotional health and wellness. Studies show that practicing mindfulness and cultivating an awareness of our surroundings can reduce stress, improve mental clarity, and boost emotional resilience.[100] When we allow ourselves to savor life's small joys, we create space to recharge and find balance amid life's challenges. Stopping to smell the roses is a gentle act of self-care, teaching us to slow down and treasure what truly matters before those fleeting moments pass us by.

Challenge

Take five minutes each day to capture a "gratitude snapshot" of your surroundings. This could mean mentally noting three things you find beautiful or taking an actual photo of something that brings you joy: a vibrant flower, a cozy corner of your home, or a heartfelt moment with a loved one. At the end of the week, reflect on these snapshots to remind yourself of the beauty in ordinary moments. This exercise helps train your mind to seek and appreciate the positives in your daily life.

Another idea is to dedicate one hour each day to go device-free (gasp!) and immerse yourself in the present moment. Use this time to connect with your environment, go for a walk, enjoy a meal without distractions, or engage in a favorite hobby. The goal is to create space to simply be free from the noise of notifications and tasks. This practice encourages mindfulness, making it easier to notice and cherish life's simple joys.

Strength through Stretching

Story

When people think of Michael Jordan, they see one of the greatest basketball players of all time: six-time NBA champion, five-time MVP, and an icon of the sport. But what many don't realize is that his success wasn't just the result of natural talent; it came from constantly stretching himself beyond his limits and overcoming trials.

In high school, Jordan wasn't the standout player everyone assumes he was. In fact, he was cut from the varsity basketball team as a sophomore. Most teenagers would have been devastated, and Jordan was no exception. He went home, locked himself in his room, and cried. But instead of accepting defeat, he used that moment as motivation.

From then on, he pushed himself harder than ever. He showed up early to practice, stayed late, and worked relentlessly to improve his game. While other players relied on their existing talent, Jordan stretched beyond his comfort zone, challenging himself to be better every single day.

Years later, when he entered the NBA, Jordan was already a star, but he refused to stop pushing himself. He trained harder than anyone, demanding more from himself in practice than even in games. He worked tirelessly on his weaknesses—his jump shot, his defense, his leadership—until they became strengths.

One of the biggest stretches of his career came in 1993 when he shocked the world by retiring from basketball to pursue professional baseball. He struggled in the minor leagues, facing constant criticism and self-doubt, but he never gave up. Though his baseball career was short-lived, it reinforced his ability to adapt, learn, and push himself into new challenges.

When he returned to the NBA, he didn't just regain his form; he led the Chicago Bulls to three more championships, proving that his success wasn't about talent alone. It was about his willingness to stretch beyond what was comfortable, to outwork everyone around him, and to never settle for less than his best.

Jordan once said, "I've failed over and over and over again in my life. And that is why I succeed."[101] His story is proof that real growth comes when we push past our failures, stretch beyond our limits, and commit to becoming better than we were yesterday.

Quote

"Happiness does not come from doing easy work but from the afterglow of satisfaction that comes after the achievement of a difficult task that demanded our best." —Theodore Isaac Rubin (American psychiatrist and author)[102]

Scripture

"Brethren, I count not myself to have apprehended: but this one thing I do, forgetting those things which are behind, and reaching forth unto those things which are before, I press toward the mark for the prize of the high calling of God in Christ Jesus." (Philippians 3:13–14)

Lesson Learned

Stretching ourselves to learn, grow, and achieve success is essential for personal development and fulfillment. Growth doesn't happen by staying in our comfort zones; it occurs when we push ourselves to try new things, face challenges, and learn from mistakes.

Every obstacle is an opportunity for growth, and every bit of effort to improve brings us closer to our potential. Success, whether personal, professional, or spiritual, requires a willingness to stretch beyond our limits. It means embracing discomfort as a tool for progress, developing resilience, and remaining focused on our goals, no matter the setbacks. The journey of learning and growing isn't easy, but it is incredibly rewarding, helping us realize our strengths and accomplish things we never thought possible.

We were not sent here to this earth to lounge around all day sipping tropical drinks (although that's super fun to do on vacation). Our muscles don't get stronger until we work and push them. That's true for our mind and heart too.

Challenge

One powerful way to stretch yourself is by setting goals that push you beyond what you think is possible. Start with something that challenges you but is still achievable with effort. Break the goal into smaller steps, making sure each step takes you out of your comfort zone. For example, if you want to learn a new skill, such as public speaking or mastering a complex subject, commit to practicing regularly and seeking feedback.

Stretching yourself in this way requires consistent effort, but it builds confidence, increases your knowledge, and improves your abilities over time. The key is to stay persistent, keep pushing forward even when it feels difficult, and celebrate the small victories along the way. Each stretch, whether big or small, moves you closer to success.

Success

Story

My father loved fishing. The rest of the family? Well . . . let's just say we tolerated it. Fishing trips were less about catching fish and more about standing at the river's edge, swatting mosquitoes, and wondering how much longer we had to pretend we were having fun. But my dad? He was in his element. We used to joke that the fish practically surrendered the moment he stepped into the water, flopping straight into the basket he carried on his hip.

For me, fishing as a little girl meant one thing: magic. And my dad was the magician.

He had a sneaky little trick he loved to play—one I fell for every single time. He would wade into the river, standing patiently for what felt like an eternity (probably ten minutes, but time moves differently when you're young and bored). Then, just as my attention started drifting toward the clouds or the dragonflies buzzing by, he would turn to me and say, "Here, Sweetheart, hold this for a second."

Like clockwork, the moment my tiny hands gripped the pole, I'd feel it—a sudden, thrilling tug on the line. My heart would race as I squealed with excitement, convinced I had single-handedly hooked a monster fish. "Daddy! I got one!" I'd shriek, reeling with all my might, visions of being the next great angler in the family.

Of course, I hadn't really caught anything. My dad had already done the hard part, hooking the fish before casually handing me the rod. He'd just smile, cheer me on, and act like he had never seen such an incredible display of fishing expertise in his life.

As much as I loved those moments as a child, I found even greater joy in watching him play the same trick on my own kids years later. He executed it flawlessly, just as he had with me—handing over the pole at the perfect moment, letting them experience the thrill of success. They beamed with pride, just as I had, believing they were born to fish.

But here's the thing—it was never really about the fish. It was about something much bigger.

My dad understood something profound: Success breeds success. Confidence isn't something you just wake up with one day; it's built, little by little, through moments where you feel capable, strong, and accomplished. He had a way of making us believe in ourselves, of giving us those tiny wins that turned into bigger victories over time.

Quote

"We are, each of us, angels with only one wing; and we can only fly by embracing one another." —Luciano De Crescenzo (Italian author, actor, director, and engineer)[103]

Scripture

"By small and simple things are great things brought to pass." (Alma 37:6)

Lesson Learned

I really love Luciano De Crescenzo's elevated idea of us as angels in that quote above. In fact, this is one of my all-time favorite quotes. We often admire and even praise the qualities of independence and self-reliance, yet the truth is that we really do need each other. If you look at a successful person, you will more often than not also see a team of people supporting that successful person. No matter what your goals are, you can attain greater heights with help.

Challenge

Thank the people who have helped you get where you are. If you're still climbing that ladder to success and achievement, surround yourself with others who can help you build your dream. Find people who have achieved what it is you want in life. Find a mentor who can teach you the steps you need to take to get where they are now. Map out a plan that breaks down the long-term goal into smaller steps you can work on each day.

Identify the types of people you need around you to level up to your next best self. For example, do you have a friend who could serve as a study buddy, accountability partner, mentor, muse, or wingman? Consider people you currently have in your life who could play those roles. If certain roles aren't filled, explore ways you could find and bring those people into your circle of influence.

Be strategic when choosing your team, and develop a willingness to help others on their path. When you recognize that you need others in your life to help you be successful, you will naturally develop an attitude of humility and gratitude, two qualities that will fill your life with happiness. Surround yourself with good people who can support you along the way. Be a team player.

Taking Time to Do It Right the First Time

Story

This is a story a dear friend of mine wanted to share about something he learned over the years:

My father-in-law had a unique way of building my confidence. He never gave long speeches about my potential or showered me with empty compliments. Instead, he showed his belief in me through action. Whenever we were up at the family cabin, he would give me projects to work on to make me feel like a real part of the family. He encouraged me to share my ideas, to solve problems, and even to take the lead.

This was no small thing. My father-in-law had decades of experience in real estate and construction. He knew more than I could ever hope to learn, yet he never made me feel small in comparison. Instead of lecturing or taking over, he listened to my input, treating my thoughts as valuable contributions. In his eyes, I wasn't just an extra set of hands; I was someone capable, someone with potential. And because he believed it, I started to believe it too.

One particular project stands out in my memory. We were working together, just the two of us, building something that required both speed and precision. I held the nail gun, while he steadied the two-by-fours, trusting me to get the job done right. We had a lot to accomplish, and I was determined to work quickly, eager to prove myself.

You can probably guess what happened next.

In my rush, I lost control for just a second—but a second was all it took. The nail gun slipped and slammed into his finger. Blood sprayed everywhere.

I froze in horror, dropping everything as my stomach twisted into knots. I had hurt him. My father-in-law, the man who had always lifted me up, was now bleeding because of my mistake. We scrambled to patch him up before heading to the nearest hospital, where he needed stitches.

I felt awful, but in true form, he never once made me feel bad about it. In fact, he laughed about that incident for years, retelling the story with a grin and holding up his finger as proof. But he didn't just make it a funny memory; he turned it into a lesson.

"If you go too fast," he'd say, "you'll end up having to stop and fix the damage. It's always smarter to take your time and do it right the first time."

That lesson stuck with me—not just in construction but in life.

How often do we rush through things, eager to check them off our list, only to find ourselves backtracking and fixing the mistakes we could have avoided? My father-in-law's words remind me to slow down, to be intentional, and to do things with care.

But more than that, his unwavering belief in me shaped the way I see myself today. He didn't just teach me how to build things with my hands—he helped build my confidence, my patience, and my understanding that sometimes the best leaders are the ones who know how to listen.

Quote

"Whatever is worth doing at all is worth doing well." —Philip Stanhope (fourth Earl of Chesterfield)[104]

Scripture

"And see that all these things are done in wisdom and order; for it is not requisite that a man should run faster than he has strength." (Mosiah 4:27)

Lesson Learned

Taking the time to do things right the first time is not only a sign of excellence; it's also an investment in long-term success. In today's fast-paced world, it's easy to rush through tasks to get them done quickly, but this often leads to mistakes that require additional time and effort to correct.

Taking a bit more time to do it right ensures that you avoid unnecessary revisions and can be proud of your results. Quality work requires focus, patience, and attention to detail, and by dedicating the time to do things correctly from the start, we often save time in the end.

When we make the effort to do something thoroughly, we feel accomplished, knowing we have given our best. This, in turn, boosts our reputation and reliability, both with ourselves and others. People recognize when someone takes the time to produce quality work, which helps build trust and respect. While perfectionism can be a hindrance in some cases, taking the time to do things with care and intentionality is a sign of discipline and personal growth that leads to more efficient and successful outcomes in the long run.

Challenge

One effective way to learn to take the time to do something right the first time is to practice mindfulness and focus on the task at hand. This means eliminating distractions and setting aside dedicated time for the task, allowing yourself to fully engage with it.

Before diving in, take a moment to plan and prioritize. Think about the steps needed to accomplish the task and the standard of quality you want to achieve. Break it down into smaller, manageable parts if necessary. By intentionally focusing on each step, you're less likely to rush through or overlook important details. Practicing patience and self-discipline in this way not only helps you do things right the first time but also builds a habit of mindful productivity that can carry over to all areas of life.

TEACHING

STORY

My twin sister is a wonderful nurse practitioner today. She and I had a blast taking an anatomy and physiology class together when we were both students at Brigham Young University. She insisted I tell you about the man who changed her life. If you're about my age, you might even know him!

Dr. Kent Van de Graff wasn't just an anatomy and physiology professor; he was an experience. Some professors walk into a lecture hall and immediately assert themselves as the smartest person in the room. Dr. Van de Graff? He walked in like he had just discovered something amazing and couldn't wait to teach us all about it! His passion for the subject was so contagious that even students who originally signed up for the class just to fulfill a requirement found themselves geeking out over muscle contractions or dissected cadavers. His lectures were a blend of comedy, intrigue, and a taste of lifelong learning.

Now, anatomy isn't exactly known as a laugh-out-loud subject. It involves a lot of memorization, a lot of Latin, and a lot of realizing just how many ways the human body can go horribly, horribly wrong. But Dr. Van de Graff had a gift; he made learning not just engaging but downright fun. He wore costumes, conducted wild experiments, and somehow managed to make phrases like "endoplasmic reticulum" sound like the punchline to a joke.

One of his favorite lines before an exam was "This test is going to be really hard, but you can do it! Let's study together so you can do well!" And somehow, hearing that from him made you believe it was true, even when you were on the verge of tears, desperately trying to remember all the cranial nerves at 2 a.m.

His enthusiasm was so legendary that on the last day of class, something miraculous happened. Without anyone planning it, all 400 students in the lecture hall spontaneously stood up and gave him a standing ovation. Think about that. College students, voluntarily standing. For a professor. Who constantly gave us hard exams.

Dr. Van de Graff did more than just teach. He shaped my twin sister's future. He often spoke about how nurses were the real heroes of hospitals, the ones who knew their patients far better than the doctors did. That stuck with her. His words, combined with his passion for the human body, inspired her to become a nurse. Both she and I have taught at nursing colleges over the years and have both tried to become the kind of teacher that Dr. Van de Graff was.

Quote

"The art of teaching is the art of assisting discovery." —Mark Van Doren (American poet, scholar, and professor at Columbia University)[105]

Scripture

"And as all have not faith, seek ye diligently and teach one another words of wisdom; yea, seek ye out of the best books words of wisdom; seek learning, even by study and also by faith." (Doctrine and Covenants 88:118)

Lesson Learned

A great teacher knows that their role is not just to impart knowledge but to inspire and empower students to think critically and believe in their own potential. A good teacher is not afraid to show vulnerability, sharing their own experiences and mistakes to make learning more relatable. They also listen to their students, understanding their individual needs and learning styles and adjusting their methods accordingly. A great teacher believes that every student can succeed and invests the time and effort to help them reach their full potential, offering guidance and encouragement along the way.

A good teacher doesn't just fill minds with knowledge but ignites a fire of curiosity, shaping not just what students know but who they become.

Beyond the classroom, being a good teacher involves fostering a lifelong love of learning in others. It's about creating an environment where students feel comfortable asking questions, making mistakes, and growing from their experiences. The best teachers are constantly learning themselves, always seeking to improve their own skills and stay up to date with new developments in education. Through leading by example, showing respect, and modeling a growth mindset, good teachers leave a lasting impact, shaping the minds and hearts of their students for years to come.

Challenge

If you're a teacher, whether professionally or simply in the Sunday School program at church, build relationships with your students—because a good teacher understands that relationships are at the core of effective teaching. When students feel valued and understood, they are more likely to engage and succeed.

If you're a parent, you *are* a teacher. Recognize that everyone learns at their own pace and may face unique challenges. Practice patience and show empathy when students struggle. Instead of showing frustration, offer encouragement and be ready to support them through difficulties.

Passion is contagious. When you show enthusiasm for the subject matter and for teaching, your students are more likely to feel motivated and engaged. Show them that learning can be exciting and rewarding.

Encourage students to think critically and ask questions. Provide opportunities for problem-solving and allow students to explore concepts in a creative and meaningful way. In other words, allow your students to do some of the teaching too! There is so much we can learn from each other!

Tenacity

Story

Many years ago, I hit the jackpot: an all-expenses-paid trip to Jamaica for my family. Yep, people actually do win prizes like that! I couldn't wait to share the news with my friends. When I told one of them, her face dropped, and she stuck out her bottom lip like a deflated balloon. She sighed dramatically and said, "Man, I never win anything like that!" Well, naturally, I was curious, so I asked her, "Do you ever enter any contests or sweepstakes?" She stared at me as though I had just asked her to do a handstand on a tightrope. After a long, awkward pause, she muttered, "Well . . . no . . ."

At that moment, I couldn't help but chuckle and gently said, "Well, it's kind of tough to win when you don't even play!" She blinked a few times, processing the simple truth bomb I had just dropped on her. The real truth is that I had entered *many* of those mail-in sweepstakes back in the day without winning, but I kept trying.

The same thing happened when my kids were seniors in high school. I worked with them to fill out tons of scholarship applications. They were rejected by many organizations, but they also won thousands of dollars from dozens of scholarship companies that *did* select them! Their friends would whine and say, "Awww man. I never win any scholarships!" When we asked them which ones they applied for, they would hang their heads and admit they hadn't submitted anything. It's funny how that works, eh?

Whether it's entering a sweepstakes, applying for a scholarship, or taking a chance at something that scares you, getting in the game is the first step to actually winning. The worst thing that could happen is that you get rejected. That's okay; you can survive that! The best thing that could happen is . . . well . . . prizes, money, a scholarship, a first-place trophy, or whatever it is you're going for. In other words, it doesn't hurt to *try*!

Quote

"You miss 100% of the shots you don't take." —Wayne Gretzky (Canadian professional ice hockey player and coach, often referred to as "The Great One")[106]

Scripture

"Wherefore, ye must press forward with a steadfastness in Christ, having a perfect brightness of hope, and a love of God and of all men. Wherefore, if ye shall press forward, feasting upon the word of Christ, and endure to the end, behold, thus saith the Father: Ye shall have eternal life." (2 Nephi 31:20)

Lesson Learned

Tenacity is the secret ingredient that turns dreams into reality. It's not enough to simply have goals; achieving them requires persistence, determination, and an unwavering commitment to keep going, even when the road gets tough. Life is full of obstacles, and setbacks are inevitable.

The difference between those who succeed and those who give up is often tenacity—the ability to bounce back from failure and continue moving forward. When we develop tenacity, we gain the resilience to face challenges head-on and remain focused on our objectives. It's not about how many times we fall but how many times we rise again with even more determination.

Challenge

Develop an "I can do this" mindset. You have to make an effort. You can sit on the sidelines and feel sad that you're not winning, but you'll feel better if you at least get in the game and try. As people approach the end of their lives, their regrets rarely center on mistakes they made but rather on the chances they never took, the dreams they left unpursued, and the words they left unsaid. They don't lament the risks that led to failure as much as the fears that kept them from trying in the first place. Missed opportunities for love, adventure, or reconciliation weigh heavier than any past misstep.

The common refrain from those on their deathbed is not "I wish I hadn't" but rather "I wish I had." In the end, it becomes painfully clear that life is not measured by the caution we exercised but by the courage we embraced.

Yeah, you'll probably lose sometimes, but at least you're out there trying! Don't live with regrets. Get out there and start participating in the world. Be tenacious.

THOUGHTS

STORY

There's a story about a family who was working in their yard on a Saturday morning. Everyone grumbled and complained about the hard work in the dirt until they noticed that the youngest girl in the family was laughing and having fun. Shocked that she wasn't wallowing in their shared misery, her brother asked, "Why don't you think this is the worst job ever? I hate it! I mean, I could be inside playing video games!"

She simply explained, "I just imagine that the weeds are flowers and then it's fun. It's like playing a game!" Her enthusiasm eventually rubbed off on the family. They were able to appreciate the fact that they were together, and they could actually enjoy their shared task with images of flower baskets instead of garbage bags.

I think Tony Robbins is amazing. Except for his potty mouth—if swear jars were a thing at his motivational seminars, we'd all be millionaires. But profanity aside, the man is brilliant. He has spent decades inspiring millions of people around the world to step up, take charge, and live a more empowered life. The guy knows what he's talking about.

One of his most famous quotes is "Whatever you hold in your mind on a consistent basis is exactly what you will experience in your life."[107] He's also known for saying "Where focus goes, energy flows."[108]

What Tony is saying is that our thoughts shape our reality. We become what we think about most. We build our lives based on the mental blueprints we create every single day. If you constantly dwell on how unfair life is, how miserable you are, and how everything seems to go wrong, guess what? That's exactly what you'll keep experiencing—because your brain will be on a never-ending scavenger hunt to find proof that life is, in fact, terrible.

But flip that around. Imagine waking up every morning and choosing gratitude. Instead of groaning about getting out of bed, you take a deep breath and think, "Wow, I get another day on this earth!" You immediately begin to focus on opportunities instead of obstacles. You start asking yourself, "How can I make someone's day better? How can I show up for my family, my friends, and my work in a way that makes a difference?"

Guess what happens then? You begin to experience joy. You start attracting positive people and incredible opportunities. Your relationships improve because you're focusing on appreciation instead of complaints.

Tony's philosophy is simple but profound: What you feed your mind, you create in your life. If you feed it negativity, you'll get negativity. But if you fuel it with purpose, gratitude, and action, you'll build a life that's not just successful but deeply fulfilling.

So yeah, Tony Robbins might drop more F-bombs than a stand-up comedian, but when it comes to understanding the power of the mind, he's a master. And if there's one thing to take away from his teachings, it's this: Be intentional about your thoughts because they're shaping your future, even when you're not paying attention.

Your thoughts are the architects of your reality—what you dwell on shapes your perspective, your choices, and, ultimately, the life you build.

Quote

"Whatever you hold in your mind on a consistent basis is exactly what you will experience in your life." —Tony Robbins (American author, entrepreneur, and life coach)[109]

Scripture

"Finally, brethren, whatsoever things are true, whatsoever things are honest, whatsoever things are just, whatsoever things are pure, whatsoever things are lovely, whatsoever things are of good report; if there be any virtue, and if there be any praise, think on these things." (Philippians 4:8)

Lesson Learned

Controlling our thoughts is one of the most powerful tools we have in shaping our lives. Our thoughts influence our feelings, which in turn guide our actions and ultimately determine our outcomes. If we allow negative or unproductive thoughts to dominate our minds, we may find ourselves trapped in cycles of doubt, fear, and anxiety.

However, when we focus on uplifting, positive, and empowering thoughts, we set ourselves on a path toward peace, growth, and success. In essence, the thoughts we entertain today lay the foundation for the person we become tomorrow. This is why it's so crucial to be intentional about what we think about and the narratives we create in our minds.

The scriptures teach us that our thoughts are not just random, fleeting things; they hold incredible power. When we make a habit of training our thoughts to focus on what's good, we not only improve our mental well-being but also strengthen our spiritual connection and pave the way for better outcomes in all areas of life.

Challenge

Experts will often encourage people to meditate, but for many people, their mind starts to wander and eventually begins to circle the drain in a spiral of negativity. If your mind works like that, consider listening to guided meditations, podcasts, or uplifting music that puts your head in a positive space.

Did you know that exercise can actually reduce negative thinking? It's true! When you exercise, your body releases endorphins, the feel-good chemicals that make you feel better about life. Being in nature can do the same thing.

Transformation

Story

My twin sister had a patient who taught her an important lesson in transformation.

Tim was a man who had known struggle, both physical and emotional. At sixty-two years old, he had already survived a five-time cardiac bypass. He weighed 385 pounds and his health was a ticking time bomb. Prediabetes, hypertension, hyperlipidemia, obstructive sleep apnea, morbid obesity, and depression were the daily companions of his life.

Even the smallest tasks had become monumental challenges. His wife had to help him put on and tie his shoes because bending down was impossible. Chairs with arms, airplane seats, and restaurant booths were no-go zones. Clothes shopping was a frustrating ordeal—Tim couldn't buy shirts off the rack and had to order special extra-large sizes that made him feel even more alienated. As his waistline was getting bigger, his world was shrinking, and so was his hope.

But one day, everything began to change. Encouraged by his doctor and family, Tim started on a medically supervised weight-loss program, which included a newly approved weight-loss medication, weekly weigh-ins, nutrition counseling, and exercise guidance. At first, he was skeptical. Could he really turn his life around after so many failed attempts? But he decided to try—one small step at a time.

At each doctor's visit, my sister would ask him a simple question: "What's your triumph this week, Tim?" At first, his answers were modest. "I stuck to my meal plan," he'd say, or "I didn't snack late at night." But as the weeks went on and the pounds began to come off, something extraordinary started happening.

One week, Tim walked into the clinic with a grin that couldn't be contained. "You're not going to believe this," he said, his voice brimming with excitement. "For the first time in years, I sat in a regular restaurant booth! My belly fits now!"

The following week, he was just as enthusiastic. "Guess what? I bought a shirt off the rack—an actual, normal-sized shirt! No more special orders. I can't remember the last time that happened."

Week after week, the victories kept coming. Ten pounds lighter month by month, he found himself able to bend down and tie his own shoes after stepping off the scale—a moment that brought tears to his eyes. Twenty pounds lighter, he noticed he could walk more at his job without feeling winded. He even started taking walks with his wife, something he hadn't done in decades.

But perhaps the most symbolic triumph came on a sunny day at the local lake. Tim, who had once been so ashamed of his body that he avoided public places, decided to go snorkeling. As he floated in the water, he felt weightless—not just physically but emotionally. For the first time in years, he wasn't tethered by his insecurities or his health. He was free.

Tim's journey wasn't just about losing weight; it was about reclaiming his life. With every pound he shed, he gained something far more valuable: independence, confidence, and a renewed sense of joy. He no longer lived in the shadow of his health conditions. He was living, truly living, for the first time in years.

When he reached his milestone goal, he reflected on his journey. "It wasn't just about the scale," he said. "It was about the small wins—fitting in a booth, tying my own shoes, walking without pain. Those are the things that brought me back to life."

Tim's story is a testament to the resilience of the human spirit and the power of small, consistent victories. It's a reminder that transformation isn't about perfection; it's about progress. And for Tim, progress meant getting his life back—one triumph at a time.

Quote

"The best way to predict the future is to create it." —Peter Drucker (Austrian-American management consultant and educator)[110]

Scripture

"Therefore if any man be in Christ, he is a new creature: old things are passed away; behold, all things are become new." (2 Corinthians 5:17)

Lesson Learned

Transformation is one of the most powerful and hopeful aspects of personal growth. We are not bound to remain the same person we were yesterday; instead, we are capable of changing, evolving, and improving ourselves every single day. This change starts with a decision—the decision to become better, to work on our weaknesses, and to cultivate strengths we didn't even know we had. The ability to transform our thoughts, habits, and actions is a gift we are given.

With effort, faith, and the right mindset, we can become new creatures, just as the scriptures teach, leaving behind old ways that no longer serve us and embracing a higher purpose. Every step toward self-improvement is a victory, no matter how small it seems.

Transformation doesn't happen overnight, and it usually requires patience, persistence, and a willingness to face challenges. It's easy to believe that we're stuck in our old ways, but the truth is, our capacity for change is endless. We may stumble along the way, but with each setback, we gain experience and the knowledge needed to rise again and try even harder.

The key is to never lose sight of the potential for growth within us and to continue striving toward the person we want to become. Change is a continual process, and by focusing on the small, daily improvements, we can achieve lasting transformation that not only enriches our own lives but also the lives of those around us.

Challenge

Set clear intentions and goals. What kind of transformation do you want? Who do you want to be? Here are a list of ideas that can aid you in your transformation:

- Expect challenges and make a plan for what you'll do when they come
- Cultivate a growth mindset
- Create new, positive habits
- Practice self-compassion and give yourself grace when you slip up
- Surround yourself with support
- Evaluate your progress and make adjustments when needed
- Nurture your mind, body, and spirit every day
- Get a priesthood blessing for added strength to change
- Pray for strength and power to change
- Reward yourself often for reaching milestones on your long-term path
- Define success clearly so you'll know when you've reached it
- Visualize your success
- Journal what's working and what's not

Turning Weakness into Strength

Story

This story is about another nursing student, Megan. My twin sister taught her at the nursing college where we both worked as professors.

For Megan, life before her illness felt like a distant memory. A young woman with dreams and endless potential, she had never imagined that her world could shift so drastically in a matter of days. What began as a minor infection spiraled into a life-threatening battle. Her body succumbed to septic shock, and she was rushed to the critical care unit, clinging to life by the thinnest of threads.

The days blurred together in a haze of machines, monitors, and whispered prayers. Powerful medications coursed through her veins, their purpose to save her life, though not without consequence. One drug, a vasopressor designed to maintain her fragile blood pressure, restricted blood flow to her extremities. It was a calculated risk, a choice between life and limb.

When Megan finally opened her eyes, weeks had passed. Her body was weak, her mind clouded, and the news of what she had lost hit her like a tidal wave. Four of her fingertips were gone. Her hands, once graceful and whole, now bore the scars of survival. She felt as though the very tools that connected her to the world had been taken away.

The grief was suffocating. For months, Megan mourned the person she used to be. Tasks she once took for granted—buttoning a shirt, holding a pen, brushing her hair—became monumental challenges. She wondered if she would ever find herself again.

And yet amid the darkness, a spark began to glow.

During her time in the hospital, Megan had been surrounded by nurses—people who not only cared for her physical needs but also lifted her spirit. They treated her not as a patient defined by her injuries but as a person with strength and potential. Their compassion and dedication planted a seed of hope in her heart.

One day, as Megan struggled to adjust to her new reality, a nurse sat beside her. "You've been through more than most people ever will," she said gently. "But you're still here. And that means you have a purpose."

The words lingered in Megan's mind. Slowly, she began to see her scars not as a mark of loss but as a testament to her strength. Her hands, though changed, still had power. She could feel, she could hold, she could heal.

With that realization, Megan made a decision that would redefine her life. She enrolled in nursing school. She wanted to be the same kind of light for others that her nurses had been for her—a beacon of hope for patients who felt lost in the shadows of illness and those who had struggled with a distorted body image.

Nursing wasn't easy. Megan had to adapt in ways few could imagine. She learned to use her partial fingers with remarkable ingenuity, proving to herself and others that her limitations would not define her. Her empathy and resilience became her greatest tools, allowing her to connect with patients on a profound level.

Years later, Megan stood in a hospital room—not as a patient but as a nurse. She looked at her hands, at the scars that once brought her so much pain, and felt nothing but gratitude. Those hands, imperfect yet capable, had helped her find her purpose.

Megan's journey taught her to see beauty in what remains rather than what is lost. She often shares her story with patients, reminding them that even in the face of unimaginable challenges, there is hope, there is strength, and there is a future.

Her fingertips were gone, but her touch was more powerful than ever.

Quote

"Kites rise highest against the wind, not with it." —Winston Churchill (British statesman, military leader, writer, and Prime Minister of the United Kingdom during World War II)[111]

Scripture

"And if men come unto me I will show unto them their weakness. I give unto men weakness that they may be humble; and my grace is sufficient for all men that humble themselves before me." (Ether 12:27)

Lesson Learned

Turning our weaknesses into strengths is an empowering process that begins with self-awareness and humility. The first step is to recognize and accept our weaknesses rather than ignoring or denying them. Everyone has areas where they struggle, whether it's a lack of confidence, poor time management, or emotional vulnerability. Instead of seeing these weaknesses as permanent flaws, we can view them as opportunities for growth.

Challenge

An important way to turn weaknesses into strengths is through education and skill-building. When we recognize an area of weakness, we can focus on gaining the knowledge or tools necessary to improve. Mentors, friends, and family members can help us see our blind spots and provide the perspective needed to overcome challenges. Their support can be a source of strength, reminding us that we don't have to be perfect to be successful.

These strategies—self-awareness, consistent practice, resilience, and seeking support—create a powerful path for turning weaknesses into strengths, leading to both personal and professional growth.

Have you seen a common pattern in all these chapters? To change and become better, you need to have an awareness of the problem, a clear intention of what you want to improve, a thought-out plan, and determination to make it happen in your life!

Virtuous Activities

Story

I absolutely love traveling around the world. Some trips are pure indulgence, where I'm just a tourist soaking in the sights and doing whatever my heart desires. Let's be honest, those trips are super fun. But several years ago, I went on a very different kind of adventure with my twin sister. She's a nurse practitioner with a doctorate in nursing education, and every year, she takes a group of nursing students to countries across the globe to teach cultural competence while providing vital medical care to underserved communities. Since I speak Spanish, I got to join them in Colombia, serving as their translator.

By the end of those two weeks, I was exhausted in ways I didn't even know were possible. We worked incredibly hard, walking through jungles and spending long hours delivering medical services to families in need. I was hot, tired, sunburned, and . . . incredibly happy. It was one of the most meaningful travel experiences I had ever had. I had the privilege of seeing the country where my twin sister served her full-time mission, but more importantly, I knew I was making a real difference in the lives of poor families who lived so far from medical clinics or hospitals that they weren't getting the care they desperately needed.

As members of The Church of Jesus Christ of Latter-day Saints, we're counseled to be engaged in virtuous activities and to do good in this world. There is a very different feeling when I travel to an exotic island just to soak in the sun versus when I join my sister on service-oriented trips like these. Our souls crave virtuous activities that feed our heart and mind.

Scrolling through TikTok or Instagram reels won't feed your soul; in fact, it might leave you even more hungry for real substance. Think about how you spend your free time. Is that the best you can do?

Quote

"Happiness does not consist in pastimes and amusements but in virtuous activities." —Aristotle (ancient Greek philosopher)[112]

Scripture

"If there is anything virtuous, lovely, or of good report or praiseworthy, we seek after these things." (Articles of Faith 1:13)

Lesson Learned

Focusing on virtuous activities is crucial for personal growth and spiritual development. When we choose to engage in acts of kindness, honesty, service, and integrity, we align ourselves with principles that uplift not only our own lives but also the lives of those around us. Virtue is a reflection of inner strength and purity, and when we make virtuous choices, we open ourselves up to greater peace, happiness, and fulfillment.

By nurturing our character and making virtuous decisions, we become better equipped to face challenges, lead with compassion, and contribute positively to our communities. Virtue also helps to cultivate a deep connection with our spiritual beliefs, drawing us closer to God and the higher purpose He has for us.

Focusing on virtuous activities allows us to become instruments for good, contributing to a more loving, just, and harmonious world. Fun activities that help build the kingdom of God are even better!

Challenge

Think about the way you entertain yourself. There's nothing wrong with relaxing because your mind and body both need time to decompress after a long day. But now think about ways you could engage in "virtuous" activities that feed your soul. Plan one of those things by putting it on your calendar and making it happen. Be adventurous. Be mindful of the way you're spending your time.

If you're ever bored or can't think of a "virtuous activity," consider some of these ideas:

- Volunteering at a shelter, food bank, or community organization
- Helping clean your ward building when it's your ward's turn
- Writing letters of encouragement for patients in a hospital
- Seeking wisdom through reading and learning
- Journaling about lessons learned and goals for self-improvement
- Fasting for someone
- Taking care of your home and surroundings
- Helping teach and mentor others in your field or community
- Exercising and taking care of your body
- Writing, painting, or playing music to uplift yourself and others
- Using talents to serve (e.g., baking for others, crafting gifts, or performing music at a nursing home)
- Learning a new skill that enriches your life and those around you

Womanhood

Story

Albertson's grocery store was the training ground for learning how to walk with poise and femininity. And you probably thought it was just for food! Daddy would show us three girls how to walk one foot at a time on the lines of the linoleum floor tiles in the grocery store, swaying our hips from side to side ever so gently. Once in a while, we'd even get lucky and be offered a dance to the background elevator music with the most handsome man in the frozen food section (my dad).

When he was a single dad and began dating, he would point out the classy qualities of the women he dated. He was very aware of the influence each one of them would have on us. He was right; there were only three that we knew of, and I remember each of their lovely qualities very clearly to this day.

When my twin sister and I were in that awkward middle-school age, he paid for modeling and etiquette lessons for us. The grand finale of the class was to select a cute outfit, strike a pose in a store's window for ten minutes, and then walk down a runway in front of applauding parents. As a surprise "graduation" present to us, he gifted us with the outfits we had chosen.

Entering womanhood was just as scary for me as it was for my father. Years later, I asked him how he knew to be so gentle with me and my sisters when it came to all that "girl stuff." He explained that he dated a happy, bubbly cheerleader in high school (he was the captain of the football team) and how her personality became quiet and withdrawn once a month. He knew that what women go through each month must be pretty important and difficult. His respect for women was impressive and comforting.

Quote

"A woman is the full circle. Within her is the power to create, nurture, and transform." —Diane Mariechild (American author, speaker, and teacher of personal growth)[113]

Scripture

"Who can find a virtuous woman? for her price is far above rubies." (Proverbs 31:10–11)

Lesson Learned

Teaching girls to become lovely women involves cultivating qualities that go beyond external appearance. It's about encouraging them to embrace their uniqueness, value their inner strength, and develop self-confidence. By nurturing emotional intelligence, empathy, and grace, we can equip the young women in our lives with the tools to build meaningful relationships and face life's challenges. Helping girls learn to appreciate their worth without relying on societal standards fosters a strong sense of self and inner strength.

It's essential to create a space where they can explore their own values and passions, understanding that true beauty lies in embracing who they are—mind, body, and spirit. With these foundations, they will not only become lovely women but also individuals who inspire and lead with compassion. The world is already filled with enough crass girls and women; let's help our sweet girls become women of virtue and grace.

Challenge

One of the key goals in helping girls mature into women is to guide them toward understanding and managing their emotions. By teaching them how to recognize their feelings, express them in healthy ways, and respond with empathy to others, we equip them with the emotional intelligence necessary for strong personal relationships and effective problem-solving.

Helping girls and women manage hormonal emotions involves a compassionate, informed, and proactive approach. First, it's important to acknowledge and normalize the emotional shifts that can come with hormonal changes—whether during puberty, menstruation, pregnancy, or menopause—and emphasize that these feelings are valid and not a sign of weakness. Education is key. Teaching about how hormones like estrogen and progesterone affect mood empowers women to recognize patterns and prepare for them.

Teach them that they don't have to be like men to be respected. Girls should know that their worth isn't defined by a boy's attention, and they should never feel pressured to give in to someone else's desires. Some boys and men may let their hormones lead their actions, saying things like "If you loved me, you would . . ." or using flattery to get what they want. But true love and respect never involve manipulation or guilt. A confident, wise girl learns to recognize red flags, set healthy boundaries, and surround herself with people who value her for who she is—not just what she can give. Don't trade your self-respect for temporary approval. You deserve to be treated with kindness, respect, and honor. Walk away from anything less.

If you have a daughter, wife, or living mother, give them flowers today and let them know how much you appreciate them. Being a woman isn't easy, especially in today's world.

Words

Story

When I was in Primary, I had a sweet teacher at church who always spoke kind words to the children. It was a pleasure to spend time with her each week in our class. She taught me the gospel and the words of Christ, but I'll never forget when she taught me how important my own words were.

One Sunday, she taught us about the Word of Wisdom and how to take good care of bodies. It all made logical sense to me, so I decided that day I would never partake of harmful substances like alcohol or tobacco.

But my Primary teacher didn't just talk. She encouraged us to make a commitment to ourselves, written in our own words. She passed out three-by-five note cards and invited us to write down our promise to ourselves to obey the Word of Wisdom. She taught us how to write with clear and specific words. Suddenly, the words of her lovely lesson had more impact on my little heart because I was using my own words. I still have that three-by-five card. I've never broken that promise to myself.

Words have power. After all, "in the beginning was the Word, and the Word was with God, and the Word was God" (John 1:1).

I have always been enamored by language. When my older sister came home from school one day, she was excited to teach me some words in Spanish that she had learned from her teacher. I was utterly captivated by the idea that entirely different sounds coming out of my mouth could express the exact same meaning in a completely new way. It felt like unlocking a secret code!

Words are not just sounds or letters on a page; they are the architects of thought, the builders of relationships, and the seeds of faith. The scriptures, history, and modern wisdom all point to the same truth—words matter. Whether spoken or written, let us choose words that heal, inspire, and uplift.

Quote

"Kind words can be short and easy to speak, but their echoes are truly endless." —Mother Teresa (Catholic nun, missionary, and humanitarian)[114]

Scripture

"Angels speak by the power of the Holy Ghost; wherefore, they speak the words of Christ. Wherefore, I said unto you, feast upon the words of Christ; for behold, the words of Christ will tell you all things what ye should do." (2 Nephi 32:3)

Lesson Learned

Words hold immense power. They have the ability to inspire, heal, build, and uplift, but they can also destroy, hurt, and tear down. Every word we speak has the potential to influence the thoughts, emotions, and actions of others. As Proverbs 18:21 reminds us, "Death and life are in the power of the tongue."

Our words can bring life to someone's spirit, offering encouragement and hope, or they can create divisions and cause pain. The impact of words extends far beyond a single conversation, as they have the potential to shape our relationships, self-esteem, and even the course of our lives.

The words we choose are also reflective of our inner thoughts and feelings. When we speak kindly, thoughtfully, and with love, we invite positivity and light into our lives and the lives of others. Our words *create.* On the other hand, when we speak in anger, frustration, or bitterness, we invite negativity and conflict.

The Book of Mormon teaches us to "feast upon the words of Christ" (2 Nephi 32:3) because His words bring peace, guidance, and comfort. Do you feast or just snack on the scriptures? Do you memorize and savor the words of Christ to feed your soul when you are in need of spiritual strength?

As we become more mindful of our words, choosing them with care and wisdom, we create an environment where love and understanding can flourish. It's a powerful reminder that what we say can either lift others up or weigh them down, so we must choose our words with intention and kindness.

Challenge

What kind of words come out of your mouth? What do you say to others? What do you say to yourself? Words have power.

Think of a positive word theme each day and challenge yourself to use a specific word each day in your conversations. It will be uplifting for others and entertaining for you! Here are some words you can try to work into conversations:

- Hope
- Lovely
- Wisdom
- Gratitude
- Excellence
- Kindness
- Christlike
- Inspiration
- Intention
- Faith
- Miracle
- Truth

Work

Story

Many years ago, I worked as an intern for a congressman in Washington, DC. I had great hopes of changing the world and thought of myself as the girl version of *Mr. Smith Goes to Washington* (a great movie you need to see sometime!). I was excited to serve my country in whatever small way I could. I really wanted to make a difference and prove that I was a deep-thinking, valuable contributor to our country.

Each week, a different intern was chosen as "Intern of the Week." I had no idea what that meant, but the title sounded very impressive, so I wanted to achieve that. Then the long-awaited day arrived. I was told that I had been chosen as the "Intern of the Week"! I was thrilled! It was explained that the first part of the assignment was to arrive an hour early, open up the office, prepare the congressman's office, go through the mail that had gathered overnight, and get the rest of the office ready for the day. I was so excited that I arrived two hours early! After I had finished the assigned tasks, I still had a half hour before anyone would even arrive in the office.

I noticed the office bathroom and kitchenette were pretty disgusting because no one in the office ever had time to clean them, so I decided to straighten things up and do some extra cleaning. When the congressman arrived and saw what I had done, he was completely amazed. He couldn't stop talking about how great the bathroom looked. You would have thought I had cured cancer or balanced the national budget by how much he praised me.

What surprised me was how doing such a simple thing, like cleaning the bathroom, made him trust and respect me so much that he invited me to represent him at big, fancy events from then on. My work ethic showed him I was capable of bigger things. By being willing to do a few things that no one else in the office was willing to do, I was invited to make a positive difference in other areas too.

Quote

"Genius is one percent inspiration and ninety-nine percent perspiration." —Thomas Edison (American inventor and businessman, best known for his invention of the light bulb)[115]

Scripture

"This we commanded you, that if any would not work, neither should he eat." (2 Thessalonians 3:10)

Lesson Learned

Being willing to work hard is an essential principle in building a successful and fulfilling life. It teaches perseverance, discipline, and responsibility. When we embrace hard work, we not only develop valuable skills but also gain a sense of pride and accomplishment in our efforts. It's easy to fall into the trap of expecting immediate rewards or results, but hard work teaches us patience.

Whether the tasks are big or small, putting in effort consistently is what sets people apart in their personal and professional lives. Every achievement, no matter how small, is a result of hard work, and recognizing this helps to build a strong sense of self-worth and satisfaction.

Equally important is the understanding that no job is beneath us. Many people may hesitate to take on certain roles or tasks because they believe those things are "too low" for their abilities or status. However, adopting a mindset that every job, no matter how simple or menial it may seem, holds value is a powerful way to approach life. It shows humility and a willingness to serve. Every task we do, whether it's cleaning a bathroom, helping a colleague, or offering assistance in a basic task, contributes to the larger picture of a community, family, or business running smoothly.

No task is too small to make a difference, and being willing to take on any job shows character and leadership. The value of humility is demonstrated when we put the team's goals above our own ego or preconceived notions of what's "worthy" of our time.

Working hard, regardless of the task's perceived importance, is a reflection of our commitment to living with purpose and integrity. It enables us to grow in character, find joy in the process, and ultimately contribute to a better world.

Challenge

If you have a paid job, think about what you could do that others around you aren't willing to do. Then do it! If you work from home, think about what extra thing you could do for your clients that would give them a "Wow!" user experience. Then do it!

If you have a calling at church, think of ways you could really step up your game and build the kingdom in that area. You heard me: Then do it!

You Can Do It!

Story

Three snow bunnies dressed in powder blue could often be seen following the skillful yellow and blue streak on skis every winter at Squaw Valley Ski Resort at Lake Tahoe. Down Dad would go, and slowly, 1 . . . 2 . . . 3 . . ., we would try to duplicate his every movement, always with encouraging words from the teacher below. He would yodel and yell, "Let's go down the slopes, you dopes!" More often than we would like to admit, we would end up on our backs, buried in a foot of snow and frustrated by our failure to match Dad's perfect techniques.

Feeling sorry for ourselves, we would sit there in the snow and cry, fully expecting Dad to have pity on us and kindly lift us to our feet. But Dad was kinder than we realized. He would stand next to us and instruct us on how to get up by ourselves, sometimes with a demonstration and always with a smile. He knew that if we always relied on him, we would never learn to do it for ourselves. If we cried in frustration, he'd laugh and say, "Don't be silly. You can do it!"

This theory would also extend to putting our snow boots on, carrying our own ski equipment, and, of course, all other aspects of our lives. We learned to love skiing. Now we dopes go down the slopes!

I absolutely love that he introduced us kids to snow skiing and loving outdoor sports. Breathing that fresh mountain air is even more important today in a world filled with indoor video games and screen time. Being physically fit was important to him, and the daily habit of exercise gifted him with ninety years of healthy living!

Quote

"Nothing worthwhile comes easily. Half effort does not produce half results. It produces no results. Work, continuous work and hard work, is the only way to accomplish results that last." —Hamilton Holt (American educator, editor, author, and politician)[116]

Scripture

"For we labor diligently to write, to persuade our children, and also our brethren, to believe in Christ, and to be reconciled to God; for we know that it is by grace that we are saved, after all we can do." (2 Nephi 25:23)

Lesson Learned

Being self-reliant means taking responsibility for your own life and decisions, trusting your abilities to overcome challenges and pursue your goals. Self-reliance encourages personal growth, as it requires individuals to be proactive in problem-solving, to be resilient in the face of setbacks, and to learn from their experiences. Instead of waiting for others to guide or provide for you, self-reliance empowers you to take the initiative and create opportunities for yourself, building confidence in your ability to navigate the world.

Self-reliance also fosters a sense of inner strength and mental fortitude. While collaboration and support from others are important, being self-reliant means knowing when to lean on your own inner resources. It teaches you to trust that you're capable of handling whatever comes your way, instilling in you a powerful sense of autonomy and self-assurance. Those are all such powerful lessons to teach your kids!

Challenge

If you have young kids or grandchildren, help them develop self-confidence and self-reliance by giving them choices. For example, when helping them get dressed for the day, ask them "Would you like to wear the white socks or green ones?" At snack time, invite them to choose between two different food choices. Making decisions and experiencing the natural consequences helps them feel independent and in control.

One challenge in developing self-reliance is overcoming self-doubt. It can be difficult to trust your own abilities, especially when facing unfamiliar situations or difficult decisions. Self-doubt often leads to seeking validation or help from others rather than relying on your own judgment. Overcoming this requires building confidence through small successes, learning from mistakes, and gradually taking on more responsibility. The key is to embrace failure as a learning experience, recognizing that making mistakes is part of the journey to becoming more self-reliant.

Another challenge is managing the fear of failure. The prospect of making the wrong decision or failing at a task can be paralyzing, leading individuals to avoid taking risks or trying new things. To develop self-reliance, it's important to reframe failure not as a negative outcome but as an essential step in growth. Tell your child (and yourself) that it's okay to make mistakes because that's how we learn and grow.

By adopting a growth mindset and viewing challenges as opportunities for learning, you can reduce the fear of failure and build resilience. This shift in perspective empowers you to face challenges with more courage and trust in your ability to navigate setbacks independently.

Conclusion

Life's most important lessons often come through simple, meaningful moments. In our fast-paced world, where we're constantly bombarded with distractions, it's easy to overlook the small yet profound lessons that can change our lives. These lessons are often wrapped up in everyday experiences, like a quiet conversation with a friend, a moment of reflection during a walk in nature, or even a challenge that seems insurmountable at first but later reveals a lesson that helps us grow. When we take a step back and allow ourselves the space to reflect, we begin to realize that life is full of subtle moments that hold the keys to the wisdom we need.

Looking back at my own life, I see countless examples of these simple, meaningful moments that have taught me more than any book or lecture ever could. For example, there was one time I was struggling with a decision, feeling overwhelmed by the pressures around me, and an unexpected encounter with a stranger who shared a kind word helped put everything into perspective. That moment didn't come with fanfare or celebration, but the impact it had on my heart was profound. I realized that sometimes the answers we seek aren't found in the grand, orchestrated events of life but in the everyday interactions and experiences that we often dismiss as unimportant at first.

As we reflect on our own lives, we can all identify similar moments that have shaped us. These lessons are often subtle, but they're powerful. It's important to take the time to recognize them and to appreciate the value they bring to our lives.

It's also important to remember that these lessons are not just for us. They're meant to be shared with others. When we take the time to reflect on the lessons we've learned, we can offer them to others as a source of encouragement and guidance. Sometimes the greatest gift we can give someone is simply sharing our own experience, reminding them that they're not alone in their struggles and that there's value in every moment, no matter how small it may seem.

This is why we're encouraged to be mindful of our interactions with others. We never know when a simple word or action might be exactly what someone else needs. A smile, a listening ear, or a piece of advice from our own lives can provide someone else with the perspective they need to move forward. Just as we have been shaped by the simple moments in our lives, so too can we shape the lives of others by sharing what we've learned. In doing so, we not only help them grow but also solidify the lessons in our own hearts, reinforcing the idea that life's most important teachings are often passed along through simple acts of kindness, love, and understanding.

I encourage you, as you continue on your journey, to look for these lessons in your own life.

May you continue to seek the lessons in your life, and may those lessons bring you closer to becoming the person you were always meant to be. Keep your heart open to the small, meaningful moments that have the power to transform you and help others along the way. As you share your wisdom with those around you, may you find that the lessons you pass on enrich your life just as much as they enrich the lives of others.

If you enjoyed this book, please leave a positive review on Amazon and/or Goodreads. Thank you!

Notes

1. "We Are Each of Us Angels," Goodreads, accessed Apr. 30, 2025, https://www.goodreads.com/quotes/383337-we-are-each-of-us-angels-with-only-one-wing.
2. *The 7 Habits of Highly Effective People* (Free Press, 2004), 71.
3. "The Atonement: Our Greatest Hope," *Ensign*, Nov. 2001, 18.
4. "Attitude is a Little Thing," BrainyQuote, accessed Apr. 24, 2025, https://www.brainyquote.com/quotes/winston_churchill_104164.
5. "Example Is Not the Main Thing," BrainyQuote, accessed Apr. 30, 2025, https://www.brainyquote.com/quotes/albert_schweitzer_112973.
6. *Discovering the Laws of Life* (Continuum Publishing, 1994), 288.
7. *As a Man Thinketh* (Dover Publications, 2008), 12.
8. *Broca's Brain: Reflections on the Romance of Science* (Random House, 1979), 14.
9. "Missionary Work: Sharing What Is in Your Heart," *Ensign* or *Liahona*, May 2019, 15.
10. Quotation found in John Bartlett, *Bartlett's Familiar Quotations* (Little, Brown and Company, 2002), 543.
11. *This Is My Story* (Harper & Brothers, 1937), 176.
12. *What I Know for Sure* (Flatiron Books, 2014), 156.
13. "Enjoy the Little Things," PassItOn, accessed Apr. 30, 2025, https://www.passiton.com/inspirational-quotes/6601-enjoy-the-little-things-in-life-for-one-day.
14. *Nothing Venture, Nothing Win* (Hodder & Stoughton, 1975), 123.
15. *An Ideal Husband* (Dover Publications, 2000), 23.
16. *The Five Major Pieces to the Life Puzzle* (Success Media, 1991), 47.
17. *Sermons for the New Life* (Charles Scribner, 1858), 196.
18. *Mother Teresa: In My Own Words*, comp. José Luis González-Balado (Gramercy Books, 1996), 92.
19. *Following the Equator: A Journey Around the World* (The American Publishing Company, 1897), 133.

20. *You Learn by Living: Eleven Keys for a More Fulfilling Life* (Harper & Brothers, 1960), 29.
21. *You Learn by Living,* 95.
22. *The Quotable Winston Churchill* (Running Press, 2013), 112.
23. "Light Shining Out of Darkness" (Hymn 68), in *Olney Hymns* (W. Oliver, 1779), 249.
24. "Launch Out," in *Hymns of the Christian Life* (Christian Alliance Publishing Co., 1891), no. 243, verse 3.
25. Quoted in *Oxford Essential Quotations*, ed. Susan Ratcliffe, 5th ed. (Oxford University Press, 2017), https://www.oxfordreference.com/display/10.1093/acref/9780191843730.001.0001/q-oro-ed5-00007046.
26. "A Person Who Won't Read," Goodreads, accessed Apr. 30, 2025, https://www.goodreads.com/quotes/891507-a-person-who-won-t-read-has-no-advantage-over-one.
27. "Unraveling the Complexities of Literacy Education," University at Buffalo, spring 2024, https://ed.buffalo.edu/magazine/issues/spring-2024/cover.html.
28. "A Word of Encouragement," Pass It On, accessed Apr. 30, 2025, https://www.passiton.com/inspirational-quotes/5531-a-word-of-encouragement-during-a-failure-is.
29. "Theodore Roosevelt Quotes," Theodore Roosevelt Center, accessed Apr. 30, 2025, https://www.theodorerooseveltcenter.org/Learn-About-TR/TR-Quotes?page=16.
30. "A Conversation With Florence Nightingale," American Association of Critical-Care Nurses, Apr. 24, 2019, https://www.aacn.org/nursing-excellence/nurse-stories/a-conversation-with-florence-nightingale.
31. *Long Walk to Freedom* (Little, Brown and Company, 1994), 617.
32. *Long Walk to Freedom*, 622.
33. "The Two Most Important Days," Goodreads, accessed Apr. 30, 2025, https://www.goodreads.com/quotes/505050-the-two-most-important-days-in-your-life-are-the.
34. Linda Kracht, "The Family That Eats Together, Stays Together," Catholic365, Aug. 16, 2021, https://www.catholic365.com/article/12805/the-family-that-eats-together-stays-together.html.
35. *The Note Book of Elbert Hubbard* (Wm. H. Wise & Co., 1927), 104.
36. *The Language of Letting Go: Daily Meditations on Codependency* (Hazelden Publishing, 1990), 313.
37. "Giving Thanks Can Make You Happier," Harvard Health, Aug. 14, 2021, https://www.health.harvard.edu/healthbeat/giving-thanks-can-make-you-happier.
38. Robert A Emmons and Michael E McCullough, "Counting Blessings Versus Burdens: An Experimental Investigation of Gratitude and Subjective Well-Being in Daily Life," *Journal of Personality and Social Psychology* 84, no. 2 (2003): 377–389, https://doi.org/10.1037/0022-3514.84.2.377.
39. "It Does Not Matter How Slowly," BrainyQuote, accessed Apr. 30, 2025, https://www.brainyquote.com/quotes/confucius_140908.

40. "Excellence Is a Habit," The Gentleman Philosopher, May 28, 2022, https://thegentlemanphilosopher.com/excellence-is-a-habit/.
41. Sam Horn, "Day Right Quote #3," SerenDestiny, Mar. 22, 2017, https://serendestiny.com/day-right-quote-3-most-people-are-about-as-happy-as-they-make-up-their-minds-to-be/.
42. "Success Is Not Final," Goodreads, accessed Apr. 30, 2025, https://www.goodreads.com/quotes/3270-success-is-not-final-failure-is-not-fatal-it-is.
43. "Hardships," Goodreads, accessed Apr. 30, 2025, https://www.goodreads.com/quotes/8188266-hardships-often-prepare-ordinary-people-for-an-extraordinary-destiny.
44. "Honesty Is the First Chapter in the Book of Wisdom (Quotation)," Monticello, accessed Apr. 30, 2025, https://www.monticello.org/research-education/thomas-jefferson-encyclopedia/honesty-first-chapter-book-wisdom/.
45. *Self-Help; With Illustrations of Character and Conduct* (John Murray, 1861), 397.
46. *The Purpose-Driven Life: What on Earth Am I Here For?* (Zondervan, 2003), 186.
47. *Religion, Spirituality and the Way of Life in the Himalayas* (Malcolm Teasdale, 2024), ix.
48. "Just Living Is Not Enough," BrainyQuote, accessed Apr. 30, 2025, https://www.brainyquote.com/quotes/hans_christian_andersen_103515.
49. Carlos H. Amado, "Service, A Divine Quality," *Ensign* or *Liahona*, May 2008, 36.
50. *Teachings of Presidents of the Church: Spencer W. Kimball* (2006), 82.
51. As quoted in Dave Stone, *Refining Your Style: Learning from Respected Communicators* (Group Pub Inc., 2004), 143.
52. "The Happiness of Life," Forbes Quotes, accessed Apr. 30, 2025, https://www.forbes.com/quotes/8505/.
53. "Joy and Spiritual Survival," *Ensign* or *Liahona*, Nov. 2016, 82.
54. *"The" Chinese Classics*, ed. James Legge (self-published, 1861), 34.
55. "No Act of Kindness," BrainyQuote, accessed Apr. 30, 2025, https://www.brainyquote.com/quotes/aesop_109734.
56. "Acts of Kindness and Happiness: A Randomized Controlled Trial", 2017 Nelson et al., published in Emotion.
57. "Nurse braids hair for patients on her days off | Humankind," posted Apr. 17, 2022, by USA Today, YouTube, https://www.youtube.com/watch?v=0ONvr1bqmOg.
58. Frank Lewis Dyer and Thomas Commerford Martin, *Edison: His Life and Inventions* (Harper & Brothers, 1910), 413.
59. "The Secret to Success," Goodreads, accessed May 1, 2025, https://www.goodreads.com/quotes/123948-the-secret-of-success-is-to-know-something-nobody-else.
60. "The Effect of Mirthful Laughter on Stress and Natural Killer Cell Activity", 2005, Berk et al., American Journal of Cardiology.

61. Marelisa, "How to Laugh More – 22 Ways to Bring More Laughter into Your Life," Daring to Live Fully, accessed May 1, 2025, https://daringtolivefully.com/how-to-laugh-more.
62. "Leadership Quotes," The University of Tennessee Chattanooga, accessed May 1, 2025, https://blog.utc.edu/mark-mendenhall/leadership-resources/leadership-quotes/.
63. "Happiness," Bartleby, accessed May 1, 2025, https://www.bartleby.com/lit-hub/hoyts-new-cyclopedia-of-practical-quotations-1922/happiness-6/.
64. Deborah E. Barnes and Kristine Yaffe, "The Projected Effect of Risk Factor Reduction on Alzheimer's Disease Prevalence," *The Lancet Neurology* 10, no. 9 (2011): 819–828, doi:10.1016/S1474-4422(11)70072-2.
65. "We Have Two Ears," BrainyQuote, accessed May 1, 2025, https://www.brainyquote.com/quotes/epictetus_106298.
66. "The Single Biggest Problem," BrainyQuote, accessed May 1, 2025, https://www.brainyquote.com/quotes/george_bernard_shaw_385438.
67. he Principles of Psychology, 1890, chapter 10 "The Consciousness of Self."
68. "To Love and Be Loved," BrainyQuote, accessed May 1, 2025, https://www.brainyquote.com/quotes/david_viscott_162271.
69. Nagesh Belludi, "Inspirational Quotations by Johann Wolfgang von Goethe (#647)," Aug. 28, 2016, https://www.rightattitudes.com/2016/08/28/johann-wolfgang-von-goethe/.
70. Parmis Parsamanesh and Mykhailo Vysochyn, "A Psychological Exploration of the Power of Our Mindset and Its Influence on Our Physiological Health," *Cureus* 16, no. 1 (2024): e54918, doi:10.7759/cureus.54918.
71. Quoted in William Fay and Linda Evans Shepherd, *Share Jesus Without Fear* (B&H Books, 1999), 22.
72. Maurie Backman, "It's Official: Most Americans Are currently in Debt," *Motley Fool*, Feb. 15, 2018, https://www.fool.com/retirement/2018/02/15/its-official-most-americans-are-currently-in-debt.aspx.
73. Sylvia, "Money Quotes, Sayings & Expressions," accessed May 1, 2025, https://mommyoverwork.com/money-quotes-expressions-sayings/.
74. Celia Fernandez, "10 Celebrities on the Importance of Setting Boundaries," Nov. 21, 2018, https://www.oprahdaily.com/life/relationships-love/g23323893/celebrity-setting-boundaries-quotes/.
75. "You've Got to Get Up," BrainyQuote, accessed May 1, 2025, https://www.brainyquote.com/quotes/george_horace_lorimer_130710.
76. "If You Have Built Castles," Goodreads, accessed May 1, 2025, https://www.goodreads.com/quotes/3234-if-you-have-built-castles-in-the-air-your-work.
77. "The Creation of a Thousand Forests," Goodreads, accessed May 1, 2025, https://www.brainyquote.com/quotes/ralph_waldo_emerson_151956.
78. Megan Rathz, "Go Home & Love Your Family," Dec. 4, 2024, https://readthereporter.com/go-home-love-your-family/.
79. *Henry VIII*, Act I, Scene 1, Line 131. First published in the First Folio, 1623.
80. "It Does Not Matter How Slowly You Go," BrainyQuote, accessed May 1, 2025, https://www.brainyquote.com/quotes/confucius_140908.

81. Helen Keller, *The Story of My Life* (Doubleday, Page & Company, 1902), chapter IV.
82. *Give Yourself the Gift of Encouragement Every Day* (ItsSoarTime, 2023), 36.
83. "Think Celestial!," *Liahona*, Nov. 2023, 117.
84. "Life Is Too Important," Goodreads, accessed May 1, 2025, https://www.goodreads.com/quotes/282056-life-is-too-important-to-be-taken-seriously.
85. Bible Dictionary, "Prayer."
86. "Nobody's Life," BrainyQuote, accessed May 1, 2025, https://www.brainyquote.com/quotes/elisabeth_hasselbeck_538326.
87. "Punctuality," BrainyQuote, accessed May 1, 2025, https://www.brainyquote.com/quotes/thomas_chandler_haliburto_140395.
88. "All Our Dreams," BrainyQuote, accessed May 1, 2025, https://www.brainyquote.com/quotes/walt_disney_163027.
89. Suresh Semwal Mohan, *Best Management Quotes* (Prabhat Prakashan, 2020), 100.
90. "Our Greatest Glory," BrainyQuote, accessed May 1, 2025, https://www.brainyquote.com/quotes/confucius_101164.
91. "Take Care of Your Body," BrainyQuote, accessed May 1, 2025, https://www.brainyquote.com/quotes/jim_rohn_147499.
92. Mari Kesselring, *How to Analyze the Works of Winston Churchill* (ABDO Publishing Company, 2013), 68.
93. "Taking Care of Myself," Goodreads, accessed May 1, 2025, https://www.goodreads.com/quotes/9180745-taking-care-of-myself-doesn-t-mean-me-first-it-means.
94. "Self Care is How You Take Your Power Back," Project Helping, Dec. 20, 2018, https://projecthelping.org/self-care-take-power-back/.
95. "46 Motivational Bios for Instagram to Fuel Your Determination," Pensador, accessed May 1, 2025, https://www.pensador.com/en/motivational_bios_for_instagram/.
96. "The Way You Treat Yourself," Goodreads, accessed May 1, 2025, https://www.goodreads.com/quotes/222325-the-way-you-treat-yourself-sets-the-standard-for-others.
97. "The Only Person," Goodreads, accessed May 1, 2025, https://www.goodreads.com/quotes/73656-the-only-person-you-are-destined-to-become-is-the.
98. Dan Bova, "9 Motivational Quotes from Serena Williams," Entrepreneur, Aug. 9, 2022, https://www.entrepreneur.com/living/9-serena-williams-quotes-on-motivation-and-success/278918.
99. "Slow Down and Enjoy Life," Goodreads, accessed May 1, 2025, https://www.goodreads.com/quotes/6955-slow-down-and-enjoy-life-it-s-not-only-the-scenery.
100. Richard Bränström, Pia Kvillemo, Yvonne Brandberg, and Judith Tedlie Moskowitz, "Self-Report Mindfulness as a Mediator of Psychological Well-Being in a Stress Reduction Intervention for Cancer Patients--a Randomized Study," *Ann Behav Med* 39, no. 2 (2010): 151–61, https://doi.org/10.1007/s12160-010-9168-6.

101. "I've Missed More Than 9,000 Shots," Forbes Quotes, accessed May 1, 2025, https://www.forbes.com/quotes/11194/.
102. "Happiness Does Not Come From Doing Easy Work," BrainyQuote, accessed May 1, 2025, https://www.brainyquote.com/quotes/theodore_isaac_rubin_126226.
103. "We Are Each of Us Angels," BrainyQuote, accessed May 1, 2025, https://www.brainyquote.com/quotes/luciano_de_crescenzo_389616.
104. "Whatever Is Worth Doing," BrainyQuote, accessed May 1, 2025, https://www.brainyquote.com/quotes/philip_stanhope_4th_earl_138620.
105. "The Art of Teaching," BrainyQuote, accessed May 1, 2025, https://www.brainyquote.com/quotes/mark_van_doren_108042.
106. "You Miss 100%," BrainyQuote, accessed May 1, 2025, https://www.brainyquote.com/quotes/wayne_gretzky_378694.
107. "Whatever You Hold In Your Mind," Goodreads, accessed May 1, 2025, https://www.goodreads.com/quotes/8561116-whatever-you-hold-in-your-mind-on-a-consistent-basis.
108. "Where Focus Goes, Energy Flows," Tony Robbins, accessed May 1, 2025, https://www.tonyrobbins.com/blog/where-focus-goes-energy-flows.
109. "Whatever You Hold In Your Mind."
110. Siladitya Ghosh, "The Best Way to Predict the Future is to Create It: A Guide to Proactive Management," Sept. 1, 2024, https://medium.com/@siladityaghosh/the-best-way-to-predict-the-future-is-to-create-it-a-guide-to-proactive-management-7e667f33175d.
111. "Kites Rise Highest Against The Wind," Daily Stoic, accessed May 1, 2025, https://dailystoic.com/kites-rise-highest-wind/.
112. "Happiness," AZ Quotes, accessed May 1, 2025, https://www.azquotes.com/quote/723118.
113. "Diane Mariechild Quotes," Goodreads, accessed May 1, 2025, https://www.goodreads.com/author/quotes/157038.Diane_Mariechild.
114. "Kind Words," Goodreads, accessed May 1, 2025, https://www.goodreads.com/quotes/18064-kind-words-can-be-short-and-easy-to-speak-but.
115. "Genius Is One Percent Inspiration and Ninety-Nine Percent Perspiration," Dictionary.com, accessed May 1, 2025, https://www.dictionary.com/browse/genius-is-one-percent-inspiration-and-ninety-nine-percent-perspiration.
116. Luka Bogavac, "149 Hard Work Quotes to Keep You Motivated," Plaky, Dec. 6, 2024, https://plaky.com/blog/hard-work-quotes/.

About the Author

Dr. Trina Boice grew up in California, went to college in Utah, raised her family in Georgia, and later moved to Las Vegas. In 2004, she was honored as the California Young Mother of the Year, an award that completely amuses her four sons. She's the author of thirty-five books, with another hitting store shelves soon! You can see them all on TrinaBoice.com. She's also a professional author coach at FromBook2Business.com.

Trina currently teaches online for Brigham Young University–Idaho. She's a film critic and writes movie reviews at MovieReviewMom.com and on her YouTube channel.

A popular speaker, Trina has gone on several speaking tours in China, Colombia, Mexico, and Puerto Rico. She loves to travel all over the world and now shares her travel tips and tricks with others at EmptyNestTravelHacker.com.

Dr. Trina earned her doctoral degree from Colorado Technical University in management with a concentration in higher education leadership. She also earned two master's degrees and two bachelor's degrees, where she competed on the speech and debate team and the ballroom dance team. She was president of the National Honor

Society Phi Eta Sigma and served as ASBYU Secretary of Student Community Services.

For a summer, Trina studied at the University of Salamanca in Spain and later returned there to serve in the Spain Madrid mission for one and a half years. She has a real estate license, a travel agent license, and a black belt in Tae Kwon Do.

Trina worked as a legislative assistant for a congressman in Washington, DC, and was given the "Points of Light" Award and the Presidential Volunteer Service Award for her domestic and international community service. She wrote a column called "The Boice Box" for a newspaper in Georgia, where she lived for fifteen years. She writes for several websites and is currently the Entertainment News Editor for BellaOnline.com.

You can take a variety of fun online courses written by Trina for personal enrichment or career development at LifelongLearningEducation.com. If you have an Amazon Echo device, you can hear Trina's daily podcast called "Daily Inspirational Quote Hosted By Trina." You can add it to your Flash Briefing or find it at https://amzn.to/2HoKVFL.

Trina was selected by KPBS in San Diego to be a political correspondent during an important presidential election. If she told you what she really did, she'd have to kill you.

Scan to visit

www.TrinaBoice.com

I, JUDAS

A NOVEL

Taylor Caldwell
and Jess Stearn

OPEN ROAD
INTEGRATED MEDIA
NEW YORK

This is a work of fiction. Names, characters, places, events, and incidents either are the product of the author's imagination or are used fictitiously. Any resemblance to actual persons, living or dead, businesses, companies, events, or locales is entirely coincidental.

Cover design by Connie Gabbert

ISBN: 978-1-5040-4779-1

This edition published in 2017 by Open Road Integrated Media, Inc.
180 Maiden Lane
New York, NY 10038
www.openroadmedia.com